HARLEM MOON
BROADWAY

D1319222

June 21, 2006

From : your
Friends & Coworkers
celebrating your
retirement !

Spoonbread and Strawberry Wine

Recipes and Reminiscences of a Family

Norma Jean and Carole Darden

Harlem Moon
BROADWAY BOOKS
NEW YORK

A paperback edition of this book was published by Main Street Books in 1994.

SPOONBREAD AND STRAWBERRY WINE. Copyright © 1978, 1994 by Norma Jean Darden and Carole Darden. All rights reserved. No part of this book may be reproduced or transmitted in any form or by any means, electronic or mechanical, including photocopying, recording, or by any storage and retrieval system, without written permission from the publisher. For information, address: Broadway Books, a division of Random House, Inc.

PRINTED IN THE UNITED STATES OF AMERICA

HARLEM MOON, BROADWAY BOOKS, and the HARLEM MOON logo, depicting a moon and a woman, are trademarks of Random House, Inc. The figure in the Harlem Moon logo is inspired by a graphic design by Aaron Douglas (1899–1979).

Visit our website at www.harlemmoon.com

First Harlem Moon trade paperback edition published 2003

Book design by Marysarah Quinn

The Library of Congress has cataloged the Main Street Books edition as follows:

Darden, Norma Jean.
Spoonbread and strawberry wine: recipes and reminiscences
of a family / by Norma Jean and Carole Darden. — 1st ed.
p.   cm.
"Main Street books."
Includes index.
1. Afro-American cookery.   2. Darden family.
3. Sampson family.   4. Afro-Americans—Social life and
customs.   I. Darden, Carole.   II. Title.
TX715.D222   1994
641.59′296073—dc20   93-34264
CIP

ISBN 0-385-47270-6

20   19   18   17   16   15   14   13   12

Dedicated to "Bud" and Mamie Jean

Acknowledgments

Maxine McKendry
who was there at the conception

Bernadine Morris
who shone the light

Jean Naggar and Marie Dutton Brown
who had confidence

Hattie, Jed, Scott, Diana, and Joshua
who pushed

Ed Lloyd, Carole's husband
for his encouragement

Peggy, Cordell, Jeanie, Louella, Barbara, and Lola
who typed

The host of cousins
who gave generously of their time,
recipes, and reminiscences

and

The many friends
who so cheerfully tested and partook

Contents

Acknowledgments   *vi*

A Note upon the 25th Anniversary Edition of Spoonbread and
   Strawberry Wine   *x*

Preface to the Second Edition   *xi*

Introduction   *xiii*

Papa Darden's Grace   *1*

Papa Darden   *3*
   WINES

Dianah Scarborough Darden   *18*
   CANNING AND PRESERVING

Uncle John   *39*
   ICE CREAM

Aunt Maude   *53*
   CANDY AND CONFECTIONS

Uncle J.B.   *66*
   MEAT AND POTATOES

Aunt Lillian   *74*
   BEAUTY FOODS

Uncles C.L., Arthur, Russell, and Charlie   81
   SEAFOOD

Aunt Norma   91
   PARTY POTPOURRI

Aunt Alice   106
   HEALTH AND PLANT FOODS

The Darden Sisters   115
Aunt Annie   115
   SWEET POTATOES

Aunt Lizzie   128
   BREAKFAST TIME

Aunt Artelia   138
   ASSORTED BREADS

"Bud"—Walter T. Darden   148
   FOURTH-OF-JULY PICNIC,
   WEEKEND CONCOCTIONS, AND
   OLD-TIME FAVORITES

The Sampsons   169
Granddad Sampson   170
   HONEY FOODS

Grandmother Corine Johnson Sampson   179
   CHRISTMAS AND "DAIRY" DISHES

The Sampson Brothers   188
Clyde   188
   IN THE WILD

William 199
POT ROAST AND BREAD PUDDING

Glen 203
FRUITCAKES

Asa 208
CHICKEN IN THE POT AND
DEVIL'S FOOD CAKE

Mamie Jean Sampson Darden 213
SURPRISES AND SHERBETS,
SOUPS AND BASICS

Holiday Time with the Winner Sisters 245
DINNER MENU FOR 12

New Year's Day Dinner at Our House 259
DINNER MENU FOR 10,
PLUS COMPANY PIES

Funerals 271
CAKES, FRUIT PIES, AND ROLLS

On the Road 289
RECIPES FROM FRIENDS AND
NEIGHBORS

Glossary of Cooking Terms 325
Equivalents 327
Weights and Measures 328
Index 329

Contents

A Note upon the 25th Anniversary Edition of Spoonbread and Strawberry Wine

It is incredible to us that twenty-five years have passed since this book was first published and that it's been in print continuously. We are indebted to an active core of readers who have passed this book along to family and friends, and in turn have kept this book alive and in print for this long passage of time. To our loyal readers, we welcome you as the extended family you have become and give you our heartfelt gratitude. Thank you, thank you, thank you.

NORMA JEAN AND CAROLE
2003

Preface to the Second Edition

In rereading *Spoonbread and Strawberry Wine* for this reissue after so many years, we felt once more a sense of having been blessed by the opportunity to entrust our family's history to paper.

We also became acutely aware of two things: First, we had forgotten some of the details and were grateful for having the book as a way to reacquaint ourselves with and renew our knowledge of family lore. Second, the rereading made us aware that we still had unanswered questions but that, sadly, with the exception of Aunt Ruth, Uncle Asa, and his wife, Gertrude, all of the family members upon whose stories we relied to write this book have now passed on.

The lessons we learned from this are everyone's lessons: Oral history is fragile and should be made concrete by all methods available (tapes, photos, videos), with a sense of urgency. One never knows what life will bring or when there will be no one left to answer the questions that provide such valuable windows into ourselves.

Everyone has some form of a *Spoonbread and Strawberry Wine* that deserves documentation and organization. The easiest place to begin is to create a family tree. This used to be done as a matter of course through the recording of deaths and births in the family Bible. Our family tree led us to a central family theme—cooking—which then became the key to our family history. For each family the key is different, and we hope that reading this book will inspire you to find your own.

So, preserve those recipes, learn the best care for photographs, include the history of each family member in your photograph albums. When there is no family, create one, through those who influenced your life, through the history of your chosen career or avocation. When the history is negative, see it as a positive—worth documenting as testimony to inner strength and instincts toward survival. Collect artifacts that represent the work history and quality of life of those who went before you. Aunt Norma's biscuit cutter, Aunt Maude's crocheted afghan, our father's old medicine bottles (representing a medical practice of over sixty years) all evoke powerful and loving memories. If you are not fortunate enough to have inherited the artifact that most represents a loved one for you, perhaps you can find a replica that symbolizes the memory of that life.

It's important to see yourself as a history maker and history preserver. Keep journals, not only of joyous occasions but of the difficult times as well—a record of how you coped and how a problem was solved. Encourage your children to keep diaries and photo journals as practice for the time when the responsibility of preserving a heritage will be theirs, and as a way to develop a love for that history.

Particularly for African Americans who despair at the loss of so much of our history through the "peculiar institution" of slavery, the task of restoring that history is an imperative in which we all should participate.

. . .

The recipes contained in this book span a culinary time frame that began before the turn of the twentieth century. The nineties' emphasis on healthy, low-fat, nonprocessed foods is certainly one we applaud and live by, and many of the recipes in this book fall within those guidelines. But through the 1950s, recipes contained ingredients such as bacon fat and salt pork, with some calling for marshmallows, Jell-O, cream of mushroom soup, and garlic powder, ingredients we rarely use now. You may wish to substitute turkey for pork, or use a healthful oil to replace bacon fat or butter. Certainly, fresh garlic is preferable to garlic powder. Nonetheless, we purposely did not change the original recipes, opting for authenticity and a clear reflection of how our family ate through the years.

Introduction

We are two sisters who love to cook, especially together. During a small party we were giving, the conversation drifted into talk of ethnic heritages. We mentioned that we were definitely homegrown, since our grandfather, Papa Darden, had been a slave and a great-grandmother whom we know nothing about had been a Cherokee Indian. A guest offhandedly remarked that we must have a lot of old-time recipes. It seemed a strange statement at the time, for we had never viewed our genealogy in precisely that way. However, someplace deep down in our imaginations a chord had been struck.

Yes! We were indeed the heirs to many old and wonderful recipes, but had never thought to collect them. Growing up around the large families of our mother and father who were scattered throughout the South, Midwest, and West had exposed us to some spectacular dishes that for the most part we had taken for granted and could not reproduce.

At the same time, we realized that we had many relatives whom we knew very little about. Our father had been the youngest child in a family so spread in age that many had died before we were born, and our mother had been separated from her well-dispersed family by distance. A chat with our Aunt Maude, now in her nineties, hastened our desire to jot down some of the family stories and recipes before time had erased them. So we decided to make a pilgrimage back to the old spots of our childhood.

As children, we had always been intrigued by the women in our family as they moved about in their kitchens, often preparing meals for large numbers of people. Each one worked in a distinct rhythm, and from the essence of who they were came unique culinary expressions. They rarely measured or even tasted their food but were guided, we guessed, by its aroma and appearance, and perhaps by some magical instincts unknown to us.

We felt it was time to capture that elusive magic, strengthen family ties, and learn more about our ancestors' history and tradition. So we initiated correspondence with a myriad of long-lost relatives and friends, and decided to hit the road for Petersburg, Virginia; Wilson, North Carolina; Opelika, Alabama; Delaware, Ohio; and points in between.

It had been a while since we had been united with our relatives for any occasion other than weddings or funerals. Memories of longer stays flooded our minds: catching June bugs and making mud pies under Aunt Lizzie's peach tree; watching Cousin Artelia making dandelion wine; and listening to our Uncle William's ham radio set. And how evenings with Aunt Norma would find us in freshly ironed dresses and polished white Mary Jane shoes, walking down the mainly dirt roads of Wilson, calling on the neighbors or sitting in the *balcony* of the local movie house (yes, those were the separate and unequal days), followed by a trip to old man Shade's drugstore (with its slow-turning ceiling fan) for pineapple ice. Other evenings in Wilson would find us sitting on Uncle C.L.'s front-porch swing, smelling his cigar as he, the local mortician, would relate (forgive us) how many "bodies" he had versus his competitor up the road.

In our recent travels we encouraged people to talk about the times of their youth—their hopes, dreams, highs, lows, and, of course, thoughts on food. To our delight, many had collections of old photographs that gave a greater sense of reality to their reminiscences. We scouted out old-timers who had known departed family members and combed through their memory banks. Our composite picture of the ambitious, high-spirited Darden family from North Carolina was in total contrast to the more sober, religious, Ohio-based Sampsons, our mother's family. But both revealed seriousness of purpose and flashes of humor. Unfortunately, we could not trace our family roots past our grandparents, and this was frustrating; but such was the effect of slavery and its resulting destruction of family ties.

Nonetheless, our journey was immensely successful for us, and after returning to New York City, we amazed ourselves with the short time it took us to acquire such skills as wine making, canning and preserving, bread making, and even preparing homemade cosmetics—all parts of our family's repertoire. Some of our recipes were a bit sketchy, so we cooked a lot (and ate a lot), creating miracles and catastrophes in order to pinpoint measurements for you.

We have divided this book into two main sections, the Dardens and the Sampsons, and each chapter includes a photograph, a personal anecdotal sketch, and the recipes that relative was most fond of or noted for, such as Uncle Asa's favorite meal—chicken-in-the-pot and devil's food cake—Uncle John's ice-cream making, and Aunt Maude's candies and confections. We have many family members, so we have provided two family trees for clarification. There are also four miscellaneous chapters: "Holiday Time with the Winner Sisters" and "New Year's Day Dinner at Our House," which include complete menus and recipes for those celebrations; "Funerals," which suggests an assortment of cakes and pies to take to a bereaved family; and "On the Road," which contains recipes received from friends during our travels.

So, you see, this book is the reflection of our pilgrimage "home," which revealed to us not only good food but the origins, early struggles, and life-styles of our family. Our mother used to tell us that good food inspires good thoughts, good talk, and an atmosphere of happiness and sharing. It was in such an atmosphere that this book grew, and it is therefore a testimonial to those who lovingly fed us and at the same time gave us a better sense of ourselves by sharing themselves.

NORMA JEAN AND CAROLE DARDEN
August 1978

The Dardens

Charles Henry Darden   Dianah Scarborough

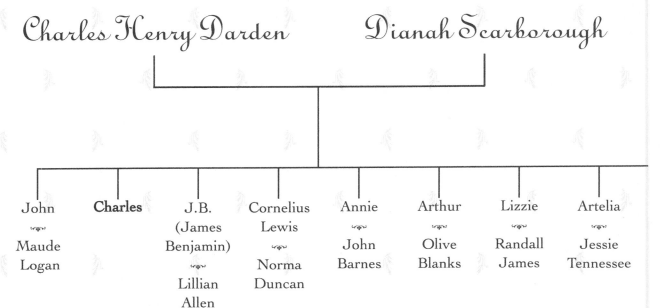

John	**Charles**	J.B. (James Benjamin)	Cornelius Lewis	Annie	Arthur	Lizzie	Artelia
Maude Logan		Lillian Allen	Norma Duncan	John Barnes	Olive Blanks	Randall James	Jessie Tennessee

The Sampsons

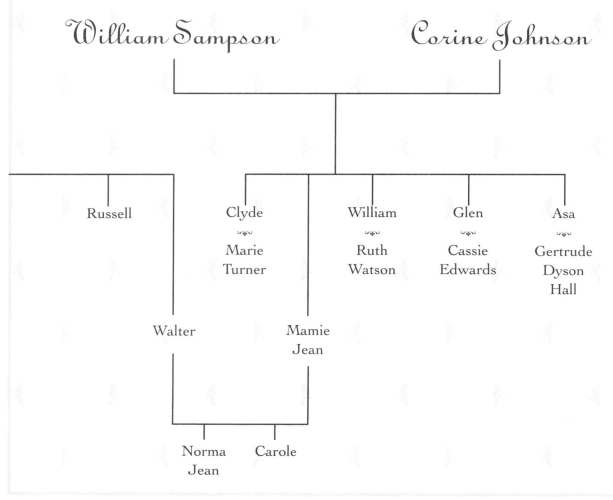

William Sampson   Corine Johnson

Russell

Clyde
Marie
Turner

William
Ruth
Watson

Glen
Cassie
Edwards

Asa
Gertrude
Dyson
Hall

Walter

Mamie
Jean

Norma
Jean

Carole

Papa Darden's Grace

Heavenly Father,
From the abundance of Your streams, fields and earth
You have seen fit to bless our table,
And we are grateful.
We pray for Your constant guidance in all things

and

Let us never forget
To give thanks for the way You have
Blessed the hands of the cook.
Amen.

Papa Darden

Gentle, wise, ingenious—these are the adjectives most used to describe him by those who knew him. Family legend has it that in 1868, at the age of fourteen, Charles Henry Darden walked into Wilson, North Carolina. He had no money, no relatives, no friends there, and no one knew where he had come from—he wouldn't say. Somehow, somewhere in his mysterious fourteen years, he had gained considerable skill as a blacksmith and could make and repair wheels. These abilities allowed him to eke out a small living and to put together the long wooden toolbox that was to become his trademark as he traveled door to door repairing broken locks and sharpening knives. In a short time he established a good reputation and at seventeen was able to open a small repair shop at the end of the main street in Wilson.

Charles Darden's future in his new town was shaped by a chance encounter. While attending a church social, he met and fell desperately in love with the perky and haughty young lady who was serving the lemonade. She was Dianah Scarborough, a fourteen-year-old seamstress and daughter of a freeborn couple who owned a small confectionery store in Wilson. Charles was shy, but not too shy to propose after a few breathless meetings. However, the Scarboroughs were firm in their refusal. After all, Charles was new to town, a stranger of untested character, and Dianah had many suitors. With the added pressure of love denied, Charles literally hammered his way out of this dilemma. Working with wood, glass, and iron, he produced washing boards, ax handles, troughs for animals; shoed horses; and made and repaired wagons and carriages. His business quickly prospered. Within a year after their first meeting, the Scarboroughs were sufficiently impressed by Charles's diligence and his quiet persistence in wooing their daughter to reverse their previous stand and welcome the marriage.

The first of thirteen children (ten lived), a son, John, was born when Dianah was sixteen, and the rest followed in rapid succession. As the family grew, so did the business. Because of his skill as a carpenter, Charles was asked to make coffins. As requests multiplied, he realized the need for a funeral establishment and became the first black undertaker in the State of North Carolina. But wagons, wheels, and coffins did not content such an enterprising soul.

Ever mindful of the needs of his expanding family, as well as those of the community, he began growing vegetables and fruits in volume and opened a little store to sell his produce. His hot roasted peanuts, melons, and soda water were popular items, but the thing that brought the customers in was Charles Darden's own homemade wines. Wine making was his hobby. He used whatever fruits were in season and was especially known for his grape, dried peach, and watermelon wines. People seemed to enjoy his company and gathered at the store for wine and discussion.

By the middle 1870s, politics was the subject most discussed by folks who came into the store. There were three black senators and nineteen black members of the House in the North Carolina legislature during those post–Civil War days, and all black folks took an optimistic interest in voting. Charles Henry was a forceful, sometimes humorous speaker, who never used profanity and never smoked or drank—even his own wines. His opinions were valued and sought after, and it was known that he harbored political aspirations. Wilson was a small, slow-paced, rather quiet tobacco town with about 4,000 citizens, 40 percent of whom were black, so the climate looked encouraging for black political progress. But by 1875, Reconstruction had given way to terrorism. In Wilson as well as throughout the rest of the South, the Ku Klux Klan had spread its sheets. Voting was over. First by intimidation and finally by law, blacks were banned from the ballot box. Political power as a tool for black advancement had failed, so Charles Henry Darden focused his energies on his business, the education of his family, and the leadership of his community. He was convinced that economic self-reliance now held the key to the survival of the black community.

Papa Darden would have been about nine when the Emancipation Proclamation was signed, but he did not talk about being a slave. Never did he tell his family about a single day in his life before the day he came to town as his own man. He merely set an example. Always self-contained, even in tense times he radiated optimism and confidence. He became head of the trustee board of his church, which he attended twice on Sundays and one day during the week, and led his family in an orderly life. As his children grew, they were put to work, before and after school, in the repair shop, the funeral parlor, store, or garden.

The evening hours were sometimes spent playing ball, sewing, having a candy pull, or brushing up a musical talent. But most often, the children were asked to recite their homework. The one thing Charles Darden most desired for his children was the thing he himself had been denied—a formal education. He was naturally swift with mathematics and somehow had learned to read and to write in a clear hand, but all in all, he only had the equivalent of a fourth-grade education.

Wilson did not have a high school for black youngsters, so

Papa Darden visits son
Walter T.'s first office in
Newark, New Jersey

all ten Darden children had to be sent some distance away to larger towns at the age of thirteen. Papa Darden was seldom known to travel, yet he attended the graduations, from elementary to graduate school, of every one of his children. Without a doubt, he must have been the proudest "papa" in the group, for in his lifetime, against many odds, he saw three sons become physicians, two become lawyers, and two become morticians, while two of his daughters became teachers and one a nurse.

It was a fitting tribute that when Wilson built a high school for black students, it was named Charles H. Darden High for the inspiration his life had given the community.

Papa Darden died before we were born, and we truly regret that we never knew him.

GRANDDADDY AND WINE

Our father, "Bud," remembers that Papa Darden experimented a great deal before perfecting his concoctions and placing them on the "local market" in his store at 10 cents a water glass. As our father tells it, one glass would make the buyer stay and talk. Talking usually led to a second glass. But he never knew anyone to go past three without needing assistance home. Granddaddy made his wines in quantity and served them from a spigoted barrel. Bud also claims that the pan placed on the ground to catch the spigot drippings used to fill with so many flies too drunk to wobble away that it depleted the fly population for a five-mile radius.

The recipes to follow are a near approximation of Granddaddy's original recipes, based upon our father's memories and our own experiments. We have limited our quantities to approximately two gallons, since most people do not have room in their homes for spigoted barrels.

Equipment for Wine Making

1. *Stone crocks or plastic pails able to hold 3 to 5 gallons.* Aesthetically, we prefer crocks. However, plastic pails are more convenient for making large quantities, since stone crocks are extremely heavy to handle and sometimes crack.

2. A clean cloth to cover the crock or pail to prevent bug visits. A tea towel will do.

3. *A long wooden spoon for stirring.* Metal is taboo because it seriously affects the flavor of the wine.

4. *A large cooking vessel*—able to hold 5 to 10 quarts (for dried fruit wine).

5. *A straining bag made of cheesecloth*—for squeezing the juice from the fruit base. These are obtainable in wine-making equipment stores, but you can easily make one yourself. It should be about 15 inches long and 8 inches wide. Muslin can also be used.

6. A very large bowl in which to strain the wine.

7. *Gallon jugs with screw-on fermentation locks.* We prefer glass rather than pottery jugs. First, you can watch the wine at

work, which is really good fun. Second, you can determine when fermentation has ceased by the lack of activity (small air bubbles rising to the top), and, third, you can see if the wine is clear enough for final bottling. The fermentation locks allow the air bubbles caused by fermentation to escape without letting any air in. If these are not obtainable, loosely placed corks can be used.

8. *Clear plastic or rubber tubing, about 4 feet long for siphoning.* This can be bought at stores specializing in wine-making equipment, or at pet shops, where it is sold for draining fish tanks.

9. *A large plastic funnel.*

10. *Wine bottles with corks or screw-on tops.*

11. *An assortment of small bottles and jars* — for storage of excess wine.

12. *Wine rack* — to store your prized vintages.

STEPS AND TIPS ON HOW TO MAKE WINE

Wine making requires patience and a willingness to experiment. Try our method and use it to create your own.

There are four main steps in wine making. The first step is to mix the fruit and liquid in a crock or pail and put it in a warm place (60° to 75°) to ferment. At this stage the mixture will bubble, hiss, and give off an extremely strong odor until it turns to wine.

After the wine has quieted, the second step is to extract the liquid from the fruit pulp by straining it through a funnel lined with cheesecloth into gallon jugs. The jugs are then topped with fermentation locks filled with water or with corks loosely placed, so that the air given off during the fermentation process can escape. Extra wine is stored in smaller jars, but try not to leave more than a two-inch air space at the top of any vessel for better brewing action. During this stage a quieter, slower fermentation occurs. Now the wine should be allowed to rest undisturbed for at least a month or until it clears.

As the wine clears, a layer of sediment settles at the bottom of the jug, so the third step in wine making is siphoning the wine off the sediment with a plastic tube and into a second jug. This process is called "racking." It is very important to siphon rather than pour because too much contact with the air can turn good wine into bad vinegar. The extra wine stored in small bottles can be used to replenish the loss in volume that results from discarding the layer of sediment. The wine now rests again. Some wines require two rackings, but if after two to four months no sediment has formed, fermentation (bubbling) has ceased, and the wine is perfectly clear, a second racking will not be needed and the wine is ready for bottling.

The fourth step is the final bottling and corking. The clear wine should be siphoned from the jug into wine bottles, leaving about an inch of air space at the top, and corked tightly. Lay the bottles on their sides (preferably in a wine rack) to keep the corks moist and to prevent them from shrinking and popping out. The wine should then be stored in a cool, dark place where it can be aged for a period of six months to two years or longer.

Be sure to keep a thorough written record of the entire process. This should include the kind of wine and the dates of the four steps. In this way you can keep an accurate account of fermentation, clearing, and aging times of different wines as you strive to find which is the most pleasing to your taste.

It should be noted that some wines are drinkable after the second step, but, like most good things, they mellow with age.

Strawberry Wine

Our favorite.

7 pounds strawberries, fresh picked
    (store-bought simply do not provide
    the flavor)
2 gallons boiling water

Juice of 1 lemon
5 pounds sugar

Mash strawberries in a crock. Add boiling water and lemon juice, and stir vigorously. Cover with a cloth and let stand for 1 week, stirring once every day. Strain through a cheesecloth bag into a large bowl and discard fruit. Return liquid to a clean crock. Stir in sugar, cover with a cloth, and let stand for 1 more week, stirring once every day. Transfer through a funnel to gallon jugs. Top with fermentation locks or cork loosely. Rack (see page 9) after about 3 months. Bottle when fermentation has ceased and wine is clear. Age for 1 year.

YIELD: APPROXIMATELY 2½ GALLONS.

Dandelion Wine

9 cups dandelion petals (discard stems
    and pods)
1 lemon, unpeeled, seeded and sliced
    thin
1 orange, unpeeled, seeded and sliced
    thin

1 gallon boiling water
3 pounds sugar
1 pound light raisins
1 package wine yeast (see Note), or one
    ¼-ounce package active
    dry yeast

Pick the dandelions on a hot, dry day, when petals are fully open and fairly bug free. Wash them well to remove any hidden insects. Pluck petals, measure, and place them in a crock, adding the lemon and orange slices. Pour the boiling water over them and stir well. Cover with a tea towel and let stand for 10 days. Strain off liquid through a cheesecloth bag into a large bowl and discard petals and fruit slices. Return liquid to a clean crock. Stir in sugar and raisins, then the yeast. Cover and leave undisturbed for 3 days. Strain into gallon jugs topped with fermentation locks or loose corks. Rack (see page 9) after 3 months. Bottle when fermentation has ceased and wine is clear. Age for 6 months to 1 year.

YIELD: APPROXIMATELY 1½ GALLONS.

NOTE: *Wine yeast is obtainable in stores specializing in wine making.*

Dried Peach (or Apricot) Wine

Very sweet.

3 pounds dried peaches (or apricots)
1½ gallons cold water
4½ pounds sugar

1 package wine yeast (see Note), or one
¼-ounce package active dry yeast

Soak peaches in cold water overnight. Place peaches and water in a large cooking vessel. Bring to a boil and simmer for about 5 minutes. Let mixture cool to the point where it can be handled easily. Then strain it through a cheesecloth bag into a crock, using your hands or any other method you can think of to press out as much liquid as possible. Stir in sugar. When mixture cools to room temperature, sprinkle yeast on top and cover. After 12 hours, stir yeast into the mixture. Let stand for 1 week, stirring daily. Transfer to gallon jugs, place fermentation locks or corks on the jugs, and allow wine to continue fermentation undisturbed. Rack (see page 9) after 3 months. Bottle when wine has cleared and fermentation has ceased. Age for 9 months to a year.

YIELD: APPROXIMATELY 2 GALLONS.

NOTE: *Wine yeast is obtainable in stores specializing in wine making.*

This is a delicious, rather sweet wine that can be used in many ways other than sipping it straight. We have tried the following:

1. Mixed with a fresh fruit compote

2. Mixed with champagne as a punch

3. Served on the rocks, straight or with soda water, and garnished with a sprig of mint

4. As a substitute for rum when making cakes, such as baba cake (page 316)

5. As a substitute for brandy in brandying fresh peaches

Another feature is the dried peach pulp that remains after the liquid has been strained off the original mixture. It has innumerable uses. Sweeten to taste, and try it in the following ways: as a pie, tart, or crepe filling; in pancake or flapjack batter; in a ham, sparerib, or pork roast glaze; in breads and muffins.

Blackberry Wine

A few years ago we made the discovery that our backyard had been blessed by the winds or the birds with rambling wild blackberry bushes.

That first summer the yield was only 2 pounds of small but delicious berries. We contacted the mother of Hester White, a dear friend, who was kind enough to pick 4 more pounds of a larger variety that grows near her home in Virginia. She sent them to us and we made blackberry wine.

6 pounds blackberries, washed   *5 pounds sugar*

2 gallons boiling water

Place berries in a large crock. Pour the boiling water over them. Stir, cover, and let stand for 10 days. Strain through a cheesecloth bag into a large bowl. Return to a clean crock. Add sugar, stirring vigorously. Cover and leave for another week, stirring daily for the first 3 days. Transfer to jugs and top with fermentation locks or cork loosely. Rack (see page 9) after about 3 months. Bottle after fermentation has ceased and the wine has cleared. Age for 6 months.

YIELD: APPROXIMATELY 2½ GALLONS.

Rice and Raisin Wine

1 pound dark raisins

2 pounds raw rice

2½ pounds sugar

1 orange, unpeeled, seeded and sliced

1 gallon warm water

One ¼-ounce package active dry yeast

Place all ingredients in a crock. Stir well, cover, and set in a warm place. Stir daily for the first week and every other day for the second week. Then let stand undisturbed for 2 weeks. After 1 month, strain through a cheesecloth bag into a gallon jug. Top with fermentation locks or cork loosely. Rack (see page 9) after 3 months. Sediment produced from rice frequently takes quite a while to settle, so the wine may have to be racked again. Have patience and bottle only when crystal clear. Age for at least 1 year, preferably 2.

YIELD: APPROXIMATELY 1 GALLON.

Watermelon Wine

1 large watermelon

6 pounds sugar (4 pounds to each measured gallon of watermelon juice)

One and a half ¼-ounce packages active dry yeast

Cut watermelon into several pieces. Remove all red meat from rind (see Note). Place red fruit in a cheesecloth bag and squeeze out juice. Add sugar. Place sweetened juice and yeast in a crock. Stir vigorously. Cover and ferment 2 weeks, stirring daily the first week, not at all the second. After 2 weeks, strain through a cheese-cloth bag into gallon jugs topped with fermentation locks or cork loosely. Rack (see page 9) after about 3 months. Watermelon wine seems to spoil more easily than other wines, so make certain your equipment is as sterile as possible. When wine is completely clear, bottle. Age for 1 year.

YIELD: APPROXIMATELY 1½ GALLONS.

NOTE: *The rind can be reserved for Watermelon Rind Pickles (page 28).*

Grape Wine

Every year Papa Darden donated this wine to his church for sacra-mental ceremonies, and we are sure that afterward the pastor looked out on smiling parishioners in his congregation.

1½ gallons grapes (we use wine or jelly grapes)

1½ gallons water

6 pounds sugar, or as needed

Wash, stem, and place undamaged grapes in a crock. Mash them a bit with a wooden spoon, taking care not to crush open the seeds. Bring the water to a boil, cool to lukewarm, and pour over grapes. Let mixture stand for 10 days, stirring daily for the first 3. At the end of 10 days, discard grapes, which will be floating on the top, and strain remaining liquid through a cheesecloth bag into a large bowl or pan. Measure and pour the liquid back into a clean crock, adding a pound of sugar for each quart of juice (1½ gallons of grapes yield approximately 6 quarts of juice). Let liquid stand for 1 week, then siphon into jugs. Top with fermentation locks or cork loosely. Bottle after the wine has cleared and fermentation has ceased. Age for 6 months.

YIELD: APPROXIMATELY 1½ GALLONS.

Old-fashioned Persimmon Beer

Brother Sheridan, a longtime Wilson resident, told us how the old folks used to brew this one. No one that we know makes this anymore, but it was once considered an old-time treat. You may not wish to make it either, but it's a recipe worth recording nonetheless.

Pine straw (2–3 bunches of needles from a pine tree)

Wild persimmons —enough to fill a 2-gallon crock with a spigot (about 4 dozen)

1 cup sugar

Place pine straw at the bottom of the crock. Fill crock with whole persimmons, leaving a 3-inch air space at the top. Sprinkle with sugar. Add warm water to cover. Seal. Let stand for 1 week. Strain off free-flowing liquid through spigot and drink.

Plum Lightning Wine

For those who want instant gratification, here's a quickie. This wine can be aged but has an exceptionally good flavor when new.

8 pounds red or purple plums

7 pounds sugar

1½ gallons lukewarm water

Two ¼-ounce packages active dry yeast

Place whole, unpitted plums in a crock. Sprinkle with 5 pounds of the sugar. Add water and yeast. Stir vigorously, cover, and let stand for 4 weeks. Carefully remove plums and any mold that may have formed. Then strain the liquid into a large bowl. Return liquid to a clean crock and add remaining 2 pounds of sugar. Stir daily for 3 days. On the fourth day the wine is ready for a sip. In 2 weeks it's ready for serving or bottling.

YIELD: APPROXIMATELY 2 GALLONS.

Papa Darden's last picture
before retiring

Dianah Scarborough Darden

The personal legacy our grandmother Dianah Scarborough left behind is one of passionate pride and determination. Her erect carriage, penetrating gaze, and strong sense of self made an indelible impression on all who met her. In contrast to the easy warmth of Papa Darden and the diplomatic way he approached the public, she could appear stern and aloof and was decidedly outspoken. Yet she was a fiercely loving person, and no sacrifice was too great for her to make for family or a friend. Her greatest joy came from church and family, and for both she labored tirelessly and fervently.

Our father tells of an evening when he, then a preschooler, had missed the children's matinee of a traveling show in Wilson because he had a cold. Only adults were allowed in the nighttime performance. Unfazed by that news, and knowing how much he wanted to see the show, Mama Darden bundled him up and took him to the theater, where she demanded two tickets. When the man in the box office protested, she narrowed her eyes and, with sparks flying, swept past the startled ticket taker and into two seats where her electrically defiant attitude kept them undisturbed for the duration of the show.

A woman with little time for nonsense, Dianah set serious standards for her family and herself. She was adamant, as was Papa Darden, that her children have a trade that would give them some control over their destinies and also offer a service to the community. She was not one to merely accept second-class citizenship and instilled in each child what was then called "race pride," insisting that they hold their heads high and assert their equality before God and among men.

She was a seamstress by trade, and professional pride kept her particularly interested in the immaculate appearance of her many offspring. After all, they were walking advertisements for her business. The ladies of Wilson—black and white—were well acquainted with her testy temperament, yet they continued to come to her because she could always be relied upon to deck them out in the latest dress and millinery styles, often embellished with her own lace and special touches. She taught her three daughters dressmaking, needlepoint, and other homemaking skills—notably baking, canning, pickling, and preserving—in which she excelled and expected excellence.

Once, when a traveling photographer came to Wilson, Mama Darden, anxious to record her family and work for posterity, hired him to make a family portrait. For three days straight, she and the older daughters, Annie and Lizzie, sewed until everyone had a new Sunday outfit. The photographer arrived at the appointed time, set up his equipment, and began shouting instructions from under the black cloth, moving the family back and forth from pose to pose. For two hours on that hot summer day he tested the patience of the family, dressed up in stiff collars, satin, and taffeta. In the end, he collected a partial payment and promised to return in three days. Three weeks went by and the man never returned. Papa Darden tried in vain to get Dianah to forget the phony photographer, but she continued to steam for months. And everyone knew that the black cloth, the picture machine, and the man himself would be torn to shreds if Mama Darden ever set sight on him again.

Although she was a churchgoer all her life, one incident sparked a lasting religious experience for Mama Darden and resulted in calming her extremely tempestuous nature. Once when her oldest daughter Annie failed to carry out her sewing instructions, Dianah's notorious temper flared, and she threw an iron at the wall. But Annie made an unexpected turn and was struck and knocked unconscious. When Annie could not be revived, Dianah, beside herself with grief, dispatched her son John to find a doctor. Dianah prayed and prayed—vowing to change her ways if Annie recovered. John returned from an hour's run without having found a doctor to see about poor Annie. After what seemed like an eternity Annie opened her eyes. Dianah, true to her commitment, emanated a sense of calm—unless unduly provoked—for the rest of her life.

There are still those in Wilson who tell us that Dianah worked herself into the grave. But, perfectionist that she was, she could not be stopped. Toward the end of her life, when she was feeling poorly and had taken to her bed, she told a visiting neighbor that her life had been fulfilled and blessed by her many children. Dianah died in the arms of her youngest son, Bud, our father, who was then nine years old. Her last words to him were: "When God sent me you, He must have wrapped up a little piece of Himself." And that was how she felt about them all.

MAMA DARDEN'S CANNING AND PRESERVING

They say that Dianah Darden would attack all that had to be done with the energy of a whirlwind. And there were so many things to be done for a family the size of hers—curing the meat in the smokehouse, making the soap, boiling the clothes for laundry, and baking. But canning and preserving were the things that gave her the most satisfaction. She felt that the whole process just seemed to pull her into the rhythm of the universe. She'd plant her seeds in the spring, pick and prepare the vegetables and fruits from the earth in summer and fall, and serve them in the winter.

We thank Mrs. Elizabeth Sheridan of Wilson, North Carolina, and our cousin, Thelma Byers, whose mother, Annie, watched Mama Darden and was able to pass along many delicious recipes. All of the following pickles, relishes, and preserves may be refrigerated and eaten at once, but we have included processing times for those who want to put a little something up for the wintertime.

Mama Darden with older sons J.B., Charlie, and John

Equipment for Canning and Preserving

1. *Jars:* Self-sealing Mason jars may be purchased at most hardware and grocery stores. They are recognizable by their flat lids and separate screw-on bands.

2. *Water-Bath Canner:* A large pot with a tight-fitting lid and a rack or wire basket inside that prevents jars from touching the bottom or sides. It can be bought in hardware stores or you can improvise by using a big pot with a cake rack placed inside. Be

sure, though, that the pot has a tight lid. It must be large enough so that the jars do not touch the sides or bottom or each other, to prevent cracking, and it must be deep enough for water to come 2 inches above the jars, allowing 2 inches more for boiling space.

3. Large kettles capable of holding 6 to 8 quarts (do not use copper, iron, or brass).

4. Slotted spoons for removing food from kettles.

5. Food mill or blender for pureeing and grinding.

6. Ladle, funnel, or dipper for filling jars.

7. Tongs for lifting jars in and out of water-bath canner.

8. Jelly jars.

9. Paraffin for sealing jellies.

SEALING

To create a vacuum seal and to keep food in Mason jars airtight and bacteria free, filled jars must be processed (boiled) in a water-bath canner, then cooled. Heat melts the sealing compound on the flat lids, and as the hot contents of the jars cool, the lids contract and seal so that no air can enter the jars. A musical ping can be heard as this occurs.

CANNING

Always select choice, firm, ripe produce for canning and be sure to wash it well, cutting out and discarding any damaged spots. Wash jars and tops in hot soapy water and rinse well in hot water before using. Jars that are to be processed do not need to be sterilized, but it is best to sterilize jelly and jam glasses by boiling them for 15 minutes. There are two standard methods for preparing food for processing: cold and hot pack.

Cold Pack: Raw fruits or vegetables are placed in clean jars and hot water or syrup is poured over the contents, leaving a ½-inch air space at the top. The flat lids and bands are then screwed on and the jars placed in the water-bath canner or a large pot filled with enough hot water to cover the jars by 2 inches. The pot is then covered and the jars processed (boiled) for the time indicated in the recipe.

Hot Pack: Fruits or vegetables that have been cooked in water or syrup are packed while still boiling hot in heated clean jars (they may be heated either by rinsing in very hot water or by leaving in the oven at 250° for at least 15 minutes). When filled, the tops are screwed in place and the jars processed for the time indicated in recipe.

Easy Canned Fruit— Cold Pack

3 pounds fresh peaches, peeled and sliced

2 tablespoons light honey per quart jar (see Note)

Boiling water

Dash of ground cinnamon (optional)

Pack peach slices in 2 heated pint jars or 1 quart jar. Put full table-spoons of honey on top of fruit and add boiling water, leaving a ½-inch space at the top. Add a dash of cinnamon if a slightly spicy flavor is desired. Screw on lids and place in warm water in a water-bath canner. Make sure jars are completely covered with water, cover canner, and bring to a boil. Processing time is counted from the time the water boils. Allow 25 minutes for pints; 30 minutes for quarts. Then remove jars. Cool away from drafts, on racks or tow-els. As jars cool, the lids will seal.

NOTE: *You can cover the fruit with a syrup composed of ½ cup sugar and 2 cups water if you wish. We prefer honey, though.*

Easy Canned Fruit— Hot Pack

½ cup mild honey or sugar

2 cups water

3 pounds fresh peaches, pears, etc., peeled and sliced

Cinnamon stick (optional)

Make a syrup by combining honey or sugar with the water. More or less sugar or honey may be added according to your taste. Add fruit and simmer until boiling hot and tender, then place in heated jars (1 quart jar or 2 pint jars), leaving ½-inch space at the top. Be sure that no spilled fruit lingers on rims, as that will interfere with the sealing process. Screw on lids, place in hot water in the water-bath canner, adding more water to cover if necessary. Cover pot, bring to a boil, and process pints for 20 minutes and quarts for 25 minutes from the time water boils. Remove from canner and cool to seal. Some people feel the hot pack gives better flavor, and others prefer the cold pack for truer color. Try both methods to find out which suits you better.

Extra Canning Tips and Steps

1. If air pockets form in jars after filling them, run a knife along the side of jar to dispel them.

2. If water should boil down below the height of jars during processing, have boiling water handy to replenish it.

3. Screwing bands may be used over and over, but the flat self-sealing lids only once.

4. Always remove bands and check lids 12 hours after canning to make sure lids are sealed tight and cannot be removed without prying. (Refrigerate and eat food if not properly sealed, or else completely reprocess.)

5. Label each jar with contents and date of canning.

6. Store jars in a cool, fairly dry place. Properly stored food will keep its color and flavor for at least 2 years.

7. If you wish 10 quarts of canned fruit, start out with half a bushel of fresh fruit.

Very Spicy Pickled Peaches

5 pounds fresh peaches

2½ cups cider or white vinegar

4 cups dark brown sugar

2 cups white sugar

½ cup water

2 tablespoons pickling spice

2 bay leaves

Blanch peaches for easy removal of skin by dipping them in boiling water for 1 minute, then dipping them in cold water. After peeling, halve peaches and remove pits. In a large saucepan combine vinegar, sugars, and water. Boil for a few minutes, until a thin syrup forms. Add peaches. Continue boiling until peaches are tender. Immediately spoon peaches into 2 quart jars, pouring over them the syrup in which they have been cooked, leaving a ½-inch space at the top. Sprinkle 1 tablespoon (use 1½ teaspoons for more subtle flavor) of pickling spice on top of each jar. Slide 1 bay leaf toward the side of each jar. To seal, process for 15 minutes. (Excess syrup can be used for basting pork or beef roasts or for pickling other fruits such as plums.)

YIELD: 2 QUARTS.

Bread and Butter Pickles

5 large cucumbers, unpeeled, sliced in
    rings

3 large onions, sliced

¼ cup salt

1 cup cider or white vinegar

1 cup water

¾ cup sugar

¼ teaspoon turmeric

½ teaspoon celery seed

½ teaspoon mustard seed

½ teaspoon ground ginger

½ teaspoon dillweed or seeds

Combine cucumbers with onions. Add salt and let stand for 2 hours, then rinse in cold water and drain. In a saucepan add remaining ingredients together and heat to boiling point. Add cucumbers and onions. Simmer for about 5 minutes or until cucumbers are greenish and somewhat translucent. Pack while hot into heated jars. To seal, process pints for 5 minutes, quarts for 10 minutes.

YIELD: 2 QUARTS.

Dianah Scarborough Darden

Sour Pickles

8 small pickling cucumbers, 3–5 inches long

¼ cup salt

1 quart water, plus 3 cups

1 cup cider or white vinegar

1 teaspoon mustard seed

Place cucumbers in brine composed of salt and 1 quart water. After 2 days, drain cucumbers and place in a saucepan with vinegar and 3 cups water. Bring to a low boil and simmer for 5 minutes, then pack pickles in a hot quart jar, sprinkle with mustard seed, and cover with the hot vinegar and water mixture. To seal, process quart for 10 minutes.

YIELD: 1 QUART.

Watermelon Rind Pickles

1 pound watermelon rind

1 quart water

¾ teaspoon slaked lime (also called calcium hydroxide, can be purchased at drugstores) or ½ cup salt

½ tablespoon mace

1 stick cinnamon

½ tablespoon whole cloves

½ tablespoon ground allspice

¾ teaspoon ground ginger

2 cups sugar

1½ cups cider or white vinegar

With a sharp knife, cut the thick rind of a melon into 1- to 2-inch squares. Remove outside green skin and any remaining fruit. Soak rind for 3 hours in quart of water with slaked lime, which will make the pickles crisp. (Soak rind in ½ cup salt and the water for 6 hours if slaked lime is unobtainable.) Then drain and rinse well in cold water. Cover with ice water and let stand for about an hour. Then cook in water to cover until tender (10 minutes). Combine spices, sugar, and vinegar in a kettle and bring to a rapid boil, then simmer for 10 minutes. Add rind and enough water to cover if needed. Boil very gently—almost at a simmer—until the melon cubes are transparent and tender. This should take about 10 minutes more. Turn into 2 hot pint jars. To seal, process for 5 minutes.

YIELD: 2 PINTS.

Pickled Peppers

About 1 dozen hot red and green chili
    peppers

2 teaspoons sugar

1 cup cider or white vinegar

Fill a pint jar with whole hot red and green peppers. Add vinegar and sugar. Screw on top and let stand for 2 weeks. Use as a hot sauce seasoning. Excellent on fried fish, pigs' feet, or anything else that needs spicing up.

YIELD: 1 PINT.

Dianah Scarborough Darden

Beet Relish— A Quick Condiment

3 cups peeled, chopped cooked beets

⅔ cup sugar

½ cup cider or white vinegar

¼ cup prepared horseradish

¼ teaspoon salt

¼ teaspoon celery seed

Mix all ingredients. Chill for several hours to blend flavors before serving.

YIELD: ABOUT 1 QUART.

Home-Canned Tomatoes

3 pounds firm, ripe tomatoes

1 teaspoon salt per quart or to taste

Pinch of sugar per quart jar

Blanch, core, and peel tomatoes. Stuff whole or quartered tomatoes into a hot 1 quart jar, leaving a ½-inch space at the top. Don't add water—simply allow their own juices to cover them. To the jar add salt and a pinch of sugar. Boil in a water-bath canner for 45 minutes. (If using pint jars, boil for 35 minutes.) Then cool to seal. Use in soups, stews, and sauces to greatly enhance flavor. (1 bushel of tomatoes yields about 18 quarts.)

YIELD: 1 QUART.

Green or Red Tomato Chowchow

3 cups cider vinegar

3 pints white corn syrup

1 dozen green or red tomatoes, unpeeled

6 medium onions

3 green bell peppers

1 head green cabbage

6 stalks celery (discard tops)

3 cucumbers (peeling optional)

1½ teaspoons salt

Place vinegar and corn syrup in a large saucepan. Bring to a boil, add vegetables, which have previously been chopped, diced, or sliced according to one's own artistic sense. Add salt. Bring to a second boil. Lower heat and simmer slowly for 1 hour, stirring occasionally. Fill 3 quart or 6 pint jars, leaving ¼-inch space. To seal, process pints for 10 minutes and quarts for 15 minutes. (When making red tomato chowchow, add 1 teaspoon ground cayenne pepper to the recipe above.)

YIELD: 3 QUARTS.

Brandied Peaches

2 pounds small clingstone peaches

1 pound sugar

Brandy as needed

Place whole, unpeeled peaches in a large saucepan. Add water to cover and simmer (do not boil) until peaches are tender but still fairly firm. Take out peaches and remove skins. In each of 2 quart jars arrange 1 or 2 peaches and cover with sugar (about ⅛–¼ cup). Add more peaches and more sugar. Continue alternating peaches and sugar until the jars are filled. Then pour in enough brandy to cover peaches completely and screw lids on tightly. Store in a dark place for 2 months before serving. For a less pungent peach, add ¼ cup brandy to Easy Canned Fruit—Hot Pack (see page 25) before processing in boiling water bath.

YIELD: 2 QUARTS.

Peach Preserves

3½ cups sugar

2 cups water

2 pounds fresh peaches, pitted, peeled,
    and quartered

Juice of ½ lemon

In a saucepan boil sugar and water until sugar is dissolved. Add peaches and cook over moderate heat for 8 to 10 minutes or until syrup is clear and slightly thickened, and peaches are tender. Cover and let stand overnight. Remove fruit from syrup and place fruit in hot self-sealing pint jars. Boil remaining syrup with lemon juice, stirring frequently, until syrup reaches the consistency of molasses or honey. Pour over peaches and top with self-sealing lids. To seal, process in simmering, not boiling, water for 20 minutes.

YIELD: 2 PINTS.

Cherry, Orange, and Peach Preserves

4 pounds peaches, pitted, peeled, and sliced

2 pounds sugar

1 orange, peeled, minced, and rind cut in thin slivers

¼ pound blanched slivered almonds

Small bottle of Maraschino cherries, cut in thin rings, including juice

Combine all ingredients in a saucepan. Slowly simmer, stirring frequently, for about 45 minutes or until thick (the consistency of honey). Pour into small jelly jars. To seal, process pint and half-pint jars for 10 minutes in simmering water. This makes a very nice Christmas present, and you can substitute nectarines for peaches.

YIELD: 4 PINTS OR 8 HALF PINTS.

Dianah Scarborough Darden

Fig Preserves

4 pounds ripe but firm figs, unpeeled

3½ pounds sugar

1 teaspoon ground cinnamon

2 dozen whole cloves

1 teaspoon ground nutmeg

2 lemons, chopped fine

Wash figs. Leave a short section of stem on, so as to preserve juices. Let stand in the sugar for 24 hours, or until figs make their own juice. Then put in a saucepan to simmer (no water added). Add spices and chopped lemon. Simmer slowly, uncovered, for 2 to 2½ hours, stirring occasionally. Pour into jars while hot. To seal, process half pints or pints in simmering water for 20 minutes.

YIELD: 4 PINTS OR 8 HALF PINTS.

Plum Butter

3 pounds damson plums, halved
and pitted

2½–3 cups honey, depending upon
desired sweetness

Juice and grated rind of ½ lemon

Place plums in a large saucepan. Add a small amount of water, just enough to prevent burning. Cover and cook over medium heat until soft (10 to 15 minutes). Allow softened fruit to cool slightly. Then puree in a blender or press through a sieve or food mill. Return to saucepan. Add honey, lemon juice, and grated lemon rind. Cook, uncovered, over very low heat for 2 to 2½ hours, until dark and thick. Pour immediately into heated jars. To seal, process pints or half pints for 10 minutes, quarts for 15 minutes.

YIELD: APPROXIMATELY 2½ PINTS OR 5 HALF PINTS.

Peach-Raisin Conserve

12 peaches

2 cups seedless raisins

4½ oranges, unpeeled

Sugar as needed

1 cup chopped walnuts

Dip the peaches in boiling water for 1 minute, then dip in cold water to better remove the skins. Halve, remove pits, and slice peaches. Put raisins through a food grinder or chop fine. Wash and thinly slice the oranges, then quarter the slices, removing seeds. Combine these ingredients and measure by the cupful. For each cup add an equal amount of sugar. Simmer together very slowly until thick (about 30 minutes), stirring frequently. Add nuts and cook 5 minutes more. Pour into hot pint jars. To seal, process for 10 minutes.

YIELD: 4 PINTS.

Three-Fruit Marmalade

1 grapefruit

1 orange

1 lemon

Sugar as needed

Grate about a quarter of the rind of each fruit. Then slice each fruit in half (including remaining rinds). Remove and discard seeds and white fibrous centers. Slice half of each fruit as thinly as possible through the rind and pulp. Peel the rind off the remaining halves and cut in thin, narrow strips; chop the fruit pulp. Place all fruit and rind in a bowl; cover with cold water and let stand overnight. The next day, boil rapidly for a half hour in the same water. Cover and again let stand overnight. Measure fruit and its liquid, and for each cupful add 1 cup sugar. Return to stove and boil rapidly for about 45 minutes, stirring often. Toward the end of cooking time, test frequently, until marmalade jells, by dropping a small amount on a cold dish. Runniness indicates that marmalade needs to cook a little longer. Place in half-pint jars. To seal, process in simmering water for 10 minutes.

YIELD: ABOUT 2 PINTS OR 4 HALF PINTS.

Strawberry Jam

1 pound strawberries

1 pound confectioners' sugar

Paraffin for sealing

Slice a quarter of the berries; coarsely mash the rest. Place berries in a heavy saucepan. Add sugar. Simmer at first, stirring frequently to prevent sticking. When sugar has melted, boil slowly for about 20 minutes. Pour into sterilized jelly glasses. There are many options for putting up jams and jellies. Ours rarely make it through the month, so we rarely process, but if you would like to seal them, process pints and half pints for 10 minutes in simmering water. We do sometimes use paraffin for short-term sealing. To do so, melt the paraffin in the top of a double boiler, and pour a ⅛-inch layer of the liquid wax on top of the hot preserves, tipping the jar in a circular motion to make sure the edges are tightly sealed. Prick any bubbles with a pin and let the wax solidify. Leftover paraffin can be stored and reused at a later date. The nice thing about using paraffin to seal jams and jellies is that you can use any attractive glass as a container. Also, a bit of bright cloth and ribbon on the top makes it an attractive gift.

YIELD: 1½ PINTS.

Dianah Scarborough Darden

Mrs. Sheridan's Scuppernong Jelly

This is a delicious grape indigenous to North Carolina and thereabouts. So if you don't live there and don't know anyone there who could send you some, you may be out of luck. However, Concord grapes may be substituted.

5 pounds red scuppernongs   *Sugar as needed*

Wash grapes well. Place them in a large saucepan and cook over medium heat for 10 to 15 minutes or until the skins burst (do not add water). Strain through a cheesecloth bag and squeeze out all of the juice. To every 2 cups juice add 1 cup sugar. (For Concord grapes, use ¾ cup sugar for each cup juice.) Boil the mixture for about 25 minutes, stirring frequently. Mixture is ready when it drips heavily from a spoon. Pour immediately into hot sterile jelly jars and seal with paraffin (see previous recipe).

YIELD: APPROXIMATELY EIGHT 6-OUNCE JELLY JARS,
DEPENDING UPON JUICINESS OF GRAPES.

Uncle John

Uncle John was the oldest son of Charles and Dianah Darden. The dreams and hopes of the family centered on him, and he proved worthy of their confidence. From the beginning, John was a carbon copy of his father. Even in his youth, he was disarmingly self-assured and knew how to survive and to protect others. But from the age of ten, when he was unable to find medical assistance for his unconscious sister Annie, John had one driving goal, and that was to become a doctor.

At the age of thirteen, he was sent by Papa Darden to high school in Salisbury, North Carolina. Lean years followed as he worked his way through Livingstone College, medical school, and an internship in Long Island, New York. His was a long, hard struggle, but when he made it, he established a pattern the younger children would follow. Summer jobs, mainly on the railroad and ships, took John all over the country. But he always found his way back to Wilson to share what he had seen and learned of the world, and to encourage his brothers and sisters in their pursuits. By the time he was ready to put out his shingle in 1903, Wilson already had black medical service, so John went deeper south, settling in Opelika, Alabama, where, as the only black doctor in a thirty-mile radius, he was greeted with an eighteen-hour workday.

His overloaded practice in that remote little town almost caused him to lose his fiancée, Maude Jean Logan, who questioned his long absences from her. But Uncle John's persuasive letter, which we found in Aunt Maude's Bible, saved the wedding day:

Sat. Noon

My own darling Jean:

Here on the very verge of our approaching happiness comes the saddest news pen could write. . . . Sweetheart Jean, the condition of half dozen patients demands that I keep constant watch over them for at least three days. Had thought to see you at the cost of their lives; but you would care so much less for me then. . . . Won't you sympathize with me just a little, the responsibilities on this end and realize that no man under the canopy of heaven could love you more. . . .

Soon after, John, making calls with his new wife in his horse and buggy, became a familiar sight on the narrow dirt roads around the Opelika countryside.

Emulating his father's diversified business tactics, John opened a drugstore on Avenue A, the main street of town. His brother J.B. had just earned his degree in pharmacy from Howard University, so he was recruited as a partner. The two brothers dispensed prescriptions, cosmetics, ice cream, and a lot of good cheer, and the store became a meeting place for the community. Local residents tell us that their Sundays were not complete without a stroll to the drugstore for a chat and a scoop of John's homemade ice cream. After the death of their mother, baby brother Bud, our father, joined the group and, at the age of nine, became the ace soda fountain man, specializing in a tutti-frutti sundae. Eventually Opelika proved to be too quiet for J.B., so, with John's blessings, he returned to medical school in livelier Nashville, Tennessee, leaving the oldest and the youngest brothers together. John was like a second father to Bud, who nicknamed him Toad because of his protruding abdomen.

According to Bud, John was a natural leader of men and was considered the guardian of minority rights. People brought him their sorrows, their joys, and news of gross community injustices. Long outraged at the lack of public medical facilities for black people, he established a private hospital. It was a simple one-story wooden building, but many complicated operations were performed there and many lives saved. Like most country doctors, he had his thumb glued to the pulse of the community and became the town chronicler. He knew who had been born, who had died, and who had moved in or out. (Because of his two additional jobs as the Lee County Jail doctor and a conscription doctor, he even knew who was incarcerated or who was inducted into the Army.) Thus, he had firsthand knowledge of the jailing of people for minor infractions of the law, of assaults on defenseless females, and of the countless other indignities perpetuated on blacks. During his time, the air was indeed permeated with clouds of sudden and irrational violence.

Once Dr. John's quick presence of mind was able to avert the lynching of a black stranger. Bud remembers that he and John were in the drugstore when they heard a commotion coming from the street and upstairs, where John's brother-in-law, a dentist, had an office. Dr. John Clark came down to tell them that a stranger seeking refuge from a lynching mob had run into his office quite out of the blue. With no questions asked, John left and returned in a flash with a few fearless and daring black citizens and the white Republican postmaster (a federal appointee in those days when Republicans were considered liberals). The mob had gathered momentum and was threatening to storm the building. But the postmaster, whom John knew to be sympathetic to the plight of blacks, had arrived heavily armed, and he kept the mob distracted while John and his friends spirited the man out of town. The man's crime? A visitor from Chicago unfamiliar with local customs, he had almost lost his life for taking a seat in an empty white restaurant while waiting for directions to another town.

Afterward, some local residents conducted a campaign of harassment against John and Maude, who remained cautious, cool, and armed until the fervor died down. We asked Aunt Maude if John had ever considered leaving town. She answered that in the darkest days in the backwoods of Alabama, he had

Leonard Medical College, now Shaw University, Class of 1901 (John W. Darden— top row, fourth from right)

never wavered in his determination to remain in the community he loved and to aid others.

She also told us that the balance and harmony so sorely missing in John's hostile environment were supplied by his love of music, of religion, of gardening, and, surprisingly, of fashion. A meticulous dresser, he had developed an appreciation for good fabric and fit from his mother, the seamstress. He was a steward in his church, raised livestock and pigeons, and kept a beautiful flower and vegetable garden, as had his father. However, the talent that set him apart was his melodious baritone voice, and it is said that he could be heard singing a mile away.

In a life that had so many parallels to Papa Darden's, it is interesting to note that after John's death the local black high school was named for him in appreciation for the many things that he had done for the citizens of Opelika.

UNCLE JOHN'S ICE CREAM

Aunt Maude said that Uncle John got a big kick out of making ice cream. She could see him in her mind's eye in the pre-drugstore days—sleeves rolled up, spreading old newspapers, and chipping up a block of ice; packing the ice into the tub of his machine along with coarse salt; churning and whistling, churning and whistling until it was time to lick the dasher. Our father still remembers making the homemade ice cream for the Sunday crowd in his drugstore days. Vanilla and chocolate were the two regular flavors, but every week a special flavor was added from a recipe invented or given by friends.

Once you have tasted John's homemade ice cream, you will become an addict. If you want the true feeling of the old days, buy a hand-crank ice-cream maker. It is wonderful to do things from scratch! However, if taste alone is what you're after, the electric models give you almost the same flavor with half the work.

Spice Ice Cream

1 quart milk	2 tablespoons vanilla extract
Two 2-inch sticks of cinnamon	½ teaspoon ground cinnamon
1½ cups sugar	½ teaspoon grated nutmeg
1 teaspoon salt	¼ teaspoon ground cloves
1 quart heavy cream	

Place milk and cinnamon sticks in a large saucepan. Heat almost to boiling, then dissolve sugar and salt in the milk. Let cool. Add remaining ingredients. Chill for approximately 2 hours. Remove the cinnamon sticks. Freeze in an ice-cream maker according to manufacturer's directions.

YIELD: ABOUT 3 QUARTS.

Fig Ice Cream

2 cups milk	1 pint heavy cream
6 eggs, separated	½ teaspoon vanilla extract
1 cup sugar	1 quart peeled and mashed figs

Heat milk almost to a boil in a medium-size saucepan. Beat egg yolks and sugar in a bowl. Stirring constantly, slowly pour half the hot milk over sugar and yolks. When well blended, return entire mixture to saucepan. Cook over medium heat, stirring constantly, about 5 minutes or until mixture is thick enough to coat a spoon. Cool, then chill for 2 hours. Stir in cream. Beat egg whites until stiff and fold into mixture. Add vanilla and figs. Stir well. Freeze in an ice-cream maker according to manufacturer's directions.

YIELD: ABOUT 2 QUARTS.

Strawberry Ice Cream

3 cups light cream

3 cups heavy cream

2 cups sugar

½ teaspoon salt

2 teaspoons vanilla extract

3 cups fresh strawberries (or raspberries), hulled

Combine light and heavy creams in a bowl. Stir in sugar and salt until dissolved. Add vanilla. Crush strawberries and put through a sieve, or puree in a blender. Add to cream mixture. Pour into ice-cream maker and freeze according to manufacturer's directions.

YIELD: 2 QUARTS.

Banana Ice Cream

7 cups milk

12 egg yolks

2 teaspoons salt

3 cups sugar

2 tablespoons vanilla extract

6 large ripe bananas

1 quart heavy cream

In a large saucepan, heat milk, bringing it almost to a boil. In a large bowl, beat egg yolks until light. Add salt. Stirring constantly, slowly pour about half the milk over the eggs. When well blended, return entire mixture to the saucepan. Add sugar and cook over medium heat, stirring continuously for 6 to 8 minutes, until mixture is thick enough to coat a spoon. Pour into a large bowl and add vanilla. Cool, then chill in the refrigerator for 2 hours. Mash the bananas thoroughly with a fork. When the mixture is well chilled, stir in the heavy cream and mashed bananas. Freeze in an ice-cream maker according to manufacturer's directions.

YIELD: 2½ QUARTS.

Pineapple Ice Cream

8 egg yolks

1 cup sugar

¼ teaspoon salt

1 quart milk

½ cup pineapple juice (from drained
    crushed pineapple)

1 tablespoon vanilla extract

1 pint heavy cream, stiffly whipped

3 cups drained crushed pineapple

Beat egg yolks until light and foamy. Add ½ cup sugar and the salt. Gradually stir in milk. Pour into a large saucepan. Simmer, stirring constantly, until thick and smooth. Remove from heat and cool. Add remaining sugar, the pineapple juice, and vanilla. Freeze according to your ice-cream maker manufacturer's directions. When mixture begins to form a mush, add whipped cream and pineapple. Continue freezing until solid.

YIELD: ABOUT 2 QUARTS.

Rum Raisin Ice Cream

1½ cups seedless raisins

¾ cup dark rum

8 egg yolks

1½ cups sugar

1 teaspoon salt

1 quart milk

1 quart heavy cream

2 teaspoons vanilla extract

Uncle John

Chop raisins and soak them in the rum overnight. Beat egg yolks until light and fluffy. Blend in sugar and salt. Scald milk in a large saucepan, bringing it almost to a boil. Pour half the milk into the yolk mixture, stirring constantly. Return this mixture to the saucepan and simmer, stirring, about 5 minutes or until the custard is thick enough to coat a spoon. Remove from the heat and let cool. Stir in the heavy cream and vanilla, and chill for 2 hours. Freeze according to ice-cream maker manufacturer's directions. When mixture becomes mushy, add rum and raisins. Finish freezing.

YIELD: ABOUT 2 QUARTS.

Tutti-Frutti Ice Cream

The most popular ice cream at Uncle John's drugstore.

3 cups light cream

3 cups heavy cream

¾ cup sugar

½ teaspoon salt

2 teaspoons vanilla extract

½ cup strawberry sundae topping

½ cup pineapple sundae topping

½ cup chopped Maraschino cherries

1 cup pecan or walnut sundae topping, drained

Combine light and heavy creams, and stir in sugar and salt until dissolved. Add vanilla. Freeze according to ice-cream maker manufacturer's directions. When ice cream begins to form a mush, add fruit toppings, cherries, and nuts. Finish freezing.

YIELD: 2 QUARTS.

Uncle John in his drugstore

Old-fashioned Fresh Peach Ice Cream

Uncle John got this recipe from his brother-in-law, John Barnes, who made this ice cream every Sunday.

1 quart half-and-half

4 or 5 eggs, depending on size, well beaten

2 tablespoons cornstarch

¼ teaspoon salt

2 cups sugar

10–12 ripe freestone peaches, pitted, peeled, and mashed

1 pint heavy cream

2 tablespoons vanilla extract

In a large saucepan, blend half-and-half and eggs. Combine cornstarch, salt, and sugar and gradually add to the half-and-half mixture. Cook over low heat, stirring constantly to prevent scorching. Custard is done when it drips heavily from a spoon. Do not overcook! However, if it does curdle, this in no way impairs the quality or taste when custard is frozen. Cool and chill for approximately 2 hours. Stir in mashed peaches, heavy cream, and vanilla. Pour into ice-cream maker and freeze according to manufacturer's directions. When hardened, remove dasher and lick same with tongue. Pack ice cream with ice and salt or place in refrigerator freezer until ready to serve.

YIELD: 2½ QUARTS.

Blueberry Ice Cream

6 cups fresh ripe blueberries, rinsed
and stemmed

2 cups sugar

½ teaspoon salt

3 cups heavy cream

3 cups light cream

2 teaspoons vanilla extract

Mash blueberries with a fork. Add 1 cup of sugar. Cook over medium heat, stirring constantly, until berries are soft (about 5 minutes). Let cool. Dissolve remaining sugar and the salt in the creams. Add vanilla and berries. Freeze according to ice-cream maker directions.

YIELD: 2 QUARTS.

Caramel Ice Cream

8 egg yolks
1 quart milk
1 cup dark brown sugar, packed

¼ teaspoon salt
1 tablespoon vanilla extract
1 pint heavy cream

Beat egg yolks well and place in a large saucepan over low heat. Add milk gradually, cooking slowly and stirring constantly. When custard is thick and smooth, remove from heat. In a smaller saucepan, heat brown sugar, stirring until melted. Stir this into custard mixture, along with salt and vanilla. Cool, then chill for 2 hours. Freeze, according to your ice-cream maker directions, until mushy. Whip heavy cream. Open ice-cream maker and add whipped cream. Finish freezing.

YIELD: ABOUT 1½–2 QUARTS.

Peanut Butter Ice Cream

This is a recipe Uncle John acquired from his neighbor at Tuskegee, George Washington Carver, who invented over a hundred uses for the peanut.

2 cups milk

3 egg yolks

½ teaspoon salt

1¼ cups brown sugar

2 cups cooked prune pulp

½ cup blanched and ground peanuts (or peanut butter)

1 teaspoon vanilla extract

1 quart heavy cream

Heat milk almost to a boil in a medium-size saucepan. Beat egg yolks until light. Add salt. Stirring constantly, slowly pour half the milk over the beaten egg yolks. When well blended, return entire mixture to the saucepan. Add sugar, prune pulp, and ground peanuts. Continue stirring over medium heat until mixture thickens. Cool, then chill for 2 hours. Add vanilla and cream. Freeze in an ice-cream maker according to manufacturer's directions. Enjoy a new taste sensation. The peanuts are high in protein, and the prunes are a good source of iron.

YIELD: ABOUT 2 QUARTS.

Fruitcake Ice Cream

A festive holiday treat.

3 cups light cream

3 cups heavy cream

1½ cups sugar

½ teaspoon salt

2 teaspoons vanilla extract

1 cup diced candied citron

1 cup chopped candied cherries

1 cup diced candied pineapple

½ cup chopped nut meats

⅓ cup dark rum

Combine light and heavy creams. Stir in sugar and salt until dissolved. Add vanilla. Freeze according to ice-cream maker manufacturer's directions. When ice cream begins to form a mush, add fruits, nut meats, and rum. Finish freezing.

YIELD: 2 QUARTS.

Lemon Ice

Juice of 4 or 5 lemons

2 cups sugar

1 quart water

8 egg whites, stiffly beaten

Blend lemon juice, sugar, and water. Freeze according to ice-cream maker manufacturer's directions until a mush begins to form. Add beaten egg whites and finish freezing.

YIELD: ABOUT 2 QUARTS.

Aunt Maude

Aunt Maude was married in 1905, and it was the greatest event in her life. She has been madly in love for seventy years. Even twenty-five years of widowhood have not dimmed her ardor for Uncle John. She remembers the details of their courtship and marriage as though they happened yesterday, and we never tire of hearing their story. She was the belle of the ball in her hometown, Montgomery, Alabama—a stylish dresser and a jazzy dancer with many beaux and no intentions of settling down. On Sundays she played the piano for the Methodist Church, and it was in church that she met John. The choir from his church had been invited to give a concert at hers. John was the soloist and she was called on to accompany him. Well! At the first note of their musical interlude, her ears perked up, and by the end of the song she was completely entranced. And so it was with his melodious voice that the country doctor, most famous for his rendering of "Oh Promise Me," was able to entice Maude to abandon "city" life for the small community of Opelika, Alabama.

It was a decision she never regretted, because life in Opelika was far from dull for her. She made house calls with Uncle John in their horse and buggy, helped with bookkeeping at the drugstore, taught Sunday school, and gave piano lessons. Tuskegee Institute was not too far away, and she and Uncle John were able to cultivate a friendship with Booker T. Washington, the founder of the school, and they also knew George Washington Carver, the agricultural scientist most acclaimed for his discovery of more than a hundred uses for the peanut. Some of the great cultural events of the times took place in Tuskegee. Celebrated concert singers Black Patti, Roland Hayes, and Todd Duncan; the famous trial lawyer Clarence Darrow; the actor Will Rogers are just a few of the many famous people John and Maude heard lecture or saw perform at Tuskegee. Once a year John would leave his busy practice to take her to visit their relatives and to see some of the spots he had been introduced to in his railroad days. They visited Los Angeles, where John's brother Charlie lived, and San Francisco, where her older sister Ida still lives. But Atlantic City, Boston, and Atlanta were their favorite haunts. Wherever they visited, Maude always kept an eye peeled for potential brides and grooms.

Maude Jean Logan Darden loves romance. She is a great believer in the power and joy of love and can relate the details of every tragic or wildly successful love story in her town for the last five generations. Not surprisingly, she has played matchmaker to countless couples. Two of her matches in the family were her sister Fannie to Dr. John Clark, the local dentist; and John's brother C.L. to Norma Duncan, a young woman from Maude's hometown. The latter two were married under the grape arbor in Maude's flower garden.

"It has been a good life, a rich life," she mused recently. "No woman ever had a more perfect husband. John was every inch a man and a gentleman. He was handsome, well dressed, so thoughtful—he knew exactly how to put things. For example, when I first came to Opelika, I had no intention of joining the church because you had to give up dancing and card playing, which I loved to do.

But one day John said that the organist had left and would I mind sharing my talent with the congregation. It was just how he put it. Before I knew it, I was not only providing the music, but teaching Bible class as well. Can't say that I didn't miss my cards and dancing, but I enjoyed pleasing my John and the pupils even more. Ideal companion that he was, he knew that it was truly what I needed, for I had just lost the only child we were to conceive.

"While waiting in our horse and buggy for John to minister to a sick patient, our horse bolted and threw me to the ground. I was pregnant at the time and was not to conceive again. So you see, teaching Sunday school for over sixty years has given me hundreds of children who are now dispersed all over the world."

Aunt Maude says, "Getting old doesn't mean giving up." Every day ninety-four-year-old Aunt Maude puts on her makeup and her pearl choker and earrings. She comes downstairs to greet the day, confident that it will be a good one. "Every day I relive the beautiful moments John and I shared, and I am never lonely."

We wish she could live forever. Aunt Maude, with her sweet sense of romance, is an avid candymaker, and here are some of her tried-and-true recipes for making confections.

The Logan family (from left to right: Maude Jean; her father, the local barber; Fannie; Mother; Ida Mae)

SWEETS FROM THE SWEET

Every Valentine's Day we would receive an enormous treat from Aunt Maude: two big shoe boxes, one filled with pecans from the tree in her backyard, and the other with candy—her divinity fudge and pecan brittle. Later we would see the avid candymaker at work in her own kitchen. In the center of the room was a large table covered with yellow oilcloth, and there she assembled her ingredients and applied great concentration to the job at hand. She used pecans in many of her confections because they were plentiful, and she tested the stages of her candymaking by that time-honored method of dropping a bit of syrup into a teacup filled with cold water until the syrup hardens. However, for the novice candymaker we recommend a candy thermometer.

Easy Peanut Brittle

A quickie.

3 cups sugar   *2 cups regular or Spanish peanuts*

Stir sugar slowly in a large frying pan over low heat. When melted to the color of clear caramel, add nuts. Pour onto a generously buttered cookie sheet. When cold, break up into small, bite-size pieces.

YIELD: 2 DOZEN SMALL PIECES.

Divinity Fudge

2½ cups sugar

½ cup light corn syrup

½ cup water

2 egg whites, stiffly beaten

1½ cups finely chopped pecans

½ teaspoon vanilla extract

Mix sugar, syrup, and water. Boil until a few drops placed in a cup of cold water form a *soft* ball when rolled between thumb and second finger (235° on a candy thermometer). Then pour half the boiling mixture over the stiffly beaten egg whites and stir. Return remaining half of mixture to the heat and boil until a few drops placed in a cup of cold water form a *hard* ball (260° on a candy thermometer). Combine with egg white mixture. Working fast, add nuts and vanilla, and drop by rounded teaspoons on a buttered cookie sheet. Let fudge set at room temperature. When cool, store in an airtight container.

YIELD: ABOUT 1 POUND.

Pecan Brittle

1½ cups pecan halves or pieces

¼ teaspoon salt

1 cup sugar

½ cup light corn syrup

½ cup water

1½ tablespoons butter

Sprinkle nuts with salt and warm them in a low oven. Mix the sugar, corn syrup, and water and heat slowly, stirring until sugar is dissolved. Continue cooking over moderate heat. The mixture is ready when a small amount dropped in a cup of cold water becomes brittle (260° on a candy thermometer). Remove from heat and stir in butter and warm nuts. Pour immediately onto a buttered cookie sheet. As soon as the brittle is cool enough to handle, cut into squares, and wrap in wax paper. Or wait until completely cooled and break into irregular pieces.

YIELD: ABOUT 1 POUND.

Molasses Taffy

Aunt Maude tells us that candy pullings provided high drama for many a family on a cold evening. Two people would butter their fingers and pull the ends of the candy as far as it would go without breaking, then double it over and pull again. This was repeated until the candy lightened in color and started to harden. At that point they would twist it, roll it, or braid it into long strips. Just before it was completely hard and the participants exhausted, they would cut it with scissors or break it into bite-size pieces and enjoy the fruits of their labor.

2 cups brown sugar	¾ cup water
1 tablespoon white vinegar	1 tablespoon butter
1 cup molasses	½ teaspoon baking soda

Boil first 4 ingredients together until a drop placed in a cup of cold water forms a hard ball (260° on a candy thermometer). Remove from heat and stir in butter and baking soda. When mixture stops foaming, pour into a buttered cake pan until cool enough to handle. Don't let it get too cool or it will be hard to pull.

At least two people should butter their hands liberally and pull the taffy as far as it will go, doubling it over and pulling it out again. Repeat this motion until the taffy begins to lighten in color and pulling becomes difficult. Form into desired shape (braids, twists, etc.) and break into bite-size pieces.

YIELD: OVER A POUND.

Caramel Kisses

1 cup sugar

¾ cup dark corn syrup

¼ cup butter

1 cup light cream

1 teaspoon vanilla extract

Slowly cook first 4 ingredients together until 250° is reached on a candy thermometer, or until a firm ball can be formed when a drop is placed in a cup of cold water. Remove from heat and add vanilla. Pour into a buttered 9-inch-square pan. When mixture cools, cut into small squares. Wrap individually in wax paper.

YIELD: ABOUT 36 KISSES.

Chocolate-Covered Candy

CREAM FILLING:

2 cups sugar

1 cup heavy cream

1 tablespoon light corn syrup

⅛ teaspoon salt

Shredded coconut

2–3 drops of peppermint, lemon, or
orange extract

Candied fruit

Chopped almonds or pecans

Place sugar, cream, corn syrup, and salt in a saucepan and cook over low heat until dissolved. Then boil until candy thermometer reaches 238° or mixture forms a soft ball when a few drops are placed in a cup of cold water. Now pour mixture onto a greased large platter and allow mixture to cool. When barely warm, begin to knead with your fingers or a spatula for 5 to 10 minutes. The texture will then become creamy, smooth, and doughlike. The filling can be chocolate-coated immediately, but its taste is improved by ripening. To "ripen," roll it into a ball and store in a covered glass jar in the refrigerator for 2 to 4 days prior to dipping. When ready to coat (see below), divide candy into 6 sections. Give each section a different flavoring by adding coconut to one, 2 to 3 drops of peppermint, lemon, or orange extract to others. One section may be left plain. Food coloring may be added for variety as well. Form each section into balls, squares, ovals, or patties and place on wax paper. Candied fruit and nuts may be pressed into the centers. Now prepare chocolate to coat them.

CHOCOLATE COATING:

2 (8-ounce) packages semisweet
coating chocolate

To cover the cream filling, weather is all-important. Pick a cool, sunny day, not a rainy, humid one, so that the candy can dry. Begin by slowly melting the chocolate in the top of a double boiler over boiling water. When 75°–80° is registered on the candy thermometer, it's time to dip. Using a long fork or your fingers, dip each cream filling into the chocolate. Make sure candy is completely coated. Then return each piece to the wax paper to dry. Coconut, candied fruit, or nuts can be used for decoration on top if you wish. If any chocolate is left after all the patties have been dipped, pour it into a small pan, sprinkle any leftover ingredients on top, cool, and cut in squares. These candies make an attractive gift or a charming afterdinner surprise.

YIELD: ABOUT 1 POUND.

NOTE: *Chocolate made specifically for coating candy hardens faster than regular chocolate, and can be found in specialty stores.*

Shoe Leather Balls

¾ pound dried apricots

¼ pound dried peaches

Superfine granulated sugar

Aunt Maude's recipe for shoe leather candy called for putting the dried fruits through a food grinder, coating a board with fine sugar, placing the fruit on top, rolling the fruit ⅛ inch thick with a rolling pin, and cutting it into 1-inch strips. To accomplish this, you must have *very, very* dry dried fruit. We discovered this the hard way, and if you should end up, as we did, with fruit too moist and too sugary to be rolled, don't despair. Simply form the fruit into small balls with your fingers and top each ball with a nut, cherry, or a sprinkle of coconut. Either way, it produces tasty candy. Store your shoe leather or shoe leather balls in the refrigerator.

YIELD: 1 POUND.

Candied Violet or Rose Petals

Candied violets and roses are such sweet and romantic confections—Aunt Maude used them as candies and as decorations for cakes and desserts.

30 violet and/or baby rose petals
1 egg white, beaten

1 cup superfine or sifted granulated sugar

Separate petals, rinse, and gently dry them. Dip petals into beaten egg white, then into sugar, coating them evenly. Dry in the refrigerator, then store in a covered container until ready for use.

One of the many marriages arranged by Aunt Maude, the matchmaker—her sister Fannie Logan's wedding to Dr. Clark.

Gingerbread

Dr. John Clark, Aunt Maude's brother-in-law, invented his own gingerbread, which she loved to bake.

2 eggs	½ teaspoon ground cloves
¾ cup sugar	½ teaspoon grated nutmeg
¾ cup molasses	½ teaspoon baking soda
¾ cup melted butter	½ teaspoon salt
2 teaspoons baking powder	2½ cups sifted all-purpose flour
2 teaspoons ground ginger	1 cup boiling water
1½ teaspoons ground cinnamon	Whipped cream

Preheat oven to 350°. Beat eggs well and blend in sugar, molasses, and melted butter. Add all other dry ingredients to sifted flour and sift together. Alternately add flour and boiling water to egg batter and beat well until smooth and lump-free. Pour batter into a well-greased 9-inch-square pan and bake for 30 to 40 minutes. Cut into squares and serve warm, with whipped cream.

YIELD: 9 SERVINGS.

VARIATION: PEACH GINGERBREAD UPSIDE-DOWN CAKE

Melt 3 tablespoons butter with 4 tablespoons brown sugar in the 9-inch-square pan. Then add 2 sliced fresh peaches or enough canned peaches to cover bottom of the pan. Pour gingerbread batter over peaches and bake as indicated above. Invert pan to serve upside down with peaches on top. Cut in squares and serve with a generous dollop of whipped cream on each portion.

Pecan Pie

3 eggs

½ cup dark brown sugar

1 cup dark corn syrup

½ teaspoon salt

1 teaspoon vanilla extract

¼ cup softened butter

1 cup pecan pieces, plus ½ cup pecan halves, for garnish

One 9-inch unbaked pie shell (see page 238), kept refrigerated until ready for use

Preheat oven to 375°. Beat eggs in a medium-size bowl. Add brown sugar, corn syrup, salt, and vanilla. Blend well. Stir in butter and broken pecans. Pour into pie shell. If you like, make a design when placing the pecan halves on top. Bake for 45 to 50 minutes or until the center is firm.

YIELD: ABOUT 8 SERVINGS.

Meringue Cups

These were the perfect containers for Uncle John's ice creams. He liked them filled with peach ice cream, fresh strawberries, and whipped cream on top.

2 egg whites	*⅔ cup sugar*
⅛ teaspoon cream of tartar	*⅔ cup finely chopped pecans*

Preheat oven to 325°. Beat egg whites with cream of tartar until foaming. Add sugar little by little, continuing to beat until mixture is stiff and glossy. Stir in pecans. Spread by spoonfuls on the bottoms and sides of extremely well-buttered muffin cups or custard cups, or form into little mounds on a buttered cookie sheet. Bake for 25 to 30 minutes until cups are light golden brown. Cool for 5 minutes. To remove, carefully loosen around the edges with a sharp knife. Let cool completely before filling. These can be stored in the refrigerator for several weeks if not used immediately.

YIELD: 1 DOZEN CUPS.

Aunt Maude

Uncle J.B.

Every family has its "sport." In ours, it was Uncle J.B.—James Benjamin, a hard worker and a hard player. He started his professional life as a druggist, but, encouraged by his older brother John, he went back to Meharry Medical School in Nashville, Tennessee, meeting his tuition there by teaching pharmacy. Both a man's man and a lady's man in his youth, he was naturally gregarious, a great mixer, and a captivating storyteller. Somehow he managed to juggle teaching, studying, and partying with minimum effort and maximum results; he was an excellent teacher, a superb student, and a much-chased bachelor.

While in school, he was invited by a classmate to visit Petersburg, Virginia. He liked the town so much that he decided to settle there after marrying his Nashville sweetheart, Lillian Allen. As a doctor in a small town, he was dedicated to his work, put in unusually long hours, and brightened the lives of his patients, but he always found time to play cards and go to the races, and his luck was sensational! Money never seemed important to him, yet he attracted it from many directions. Once, he thought one of his elderly patients couldn't afford to pay for his services, so he refused to accept any money from her. When this seemingly destitute senior citizen passed on, she willed him a considerable sum!

He appreciated a good joke (especially the racy kind), a good cigar, a drink or two, and keeping up with sports. When there was a major boxing bout or ball game, he was either glued to his radio or there in person if he possibly could be. He saw Jack Johnson fight, and loved to tell about being in New York when Joe Louis knocked out Max Schmeling, the German champion. During that fight, fans like J.B. were almost prostrate with prayer for Joe, and all of Harlem turned out with soaring spirits and pride to celebrate the Brown Bomber's victory. There was dancing at Small's Paradise, the Hotel Theresa, the Savoy Ballroom, and in the streets. Our Uncle J.B. never would have missed that kind of excitement — not for all the gold in Fort Knox.

Thoughts of J.B. conjure up images of big shiny cars, polished two-toned shoes, straw hats tipped to the side, and the continual party that always seemed to be going on around him. He loved people, action, and a good time, and when he stepped into a room, it all showed.

As if this were not enough, he was also a good cook and preferred to eat his "dinner" first thing in the morning. Uncle J.B. was a meat-and-potatoes man.

Beef Stew

4 tablespoons butter

3 pounds lean beef cubes

2 medium onions, chopped

1 clove garlic, chopped fine

3 cups water

2 bay leaves

Pinch of dried thyme

1½ tablespoons salt

2–3 dashes of pepper

5 good-size white potatoes, peeled and halved

6 carrots, cut in thirds

10–12 small white boiling onions

3 stalks celery, cut into thirds

2 medium ripe tomatoes, sliced into eighths

1 cup dry red wine

2 tablespoons flour

¼ cup cold water

Melt butter in a large Dutch oven. Add beef cubes and brown fairly rapidly. Remove beef cubes, lower heat, and add onions and garlic. Sauté until onions are limp. Return beef cubes and add 3 cups water, bay leaves, thyme, salt, and pepper. Simmer, covered, for 1½ hours. Then add potatoes, vegetables, and wine. Cook for 1 hour more. Mix flour with the cold water in a lidded jar and shake vigorously. Add to the stew to thicken gravy to desired consistency.

YIELD: 6 SERVINGS.

Beef and Lima Bean Stew

4 tablespoons vegetable oil

2½ pounds lean beef cubes

1 clove garlic, minced

1 large onion, diced

¼ teaspoon dried thyme

Salt and pepper to taste

One 12-ounce can beer

2 cups fresh raw baby lima beans, or 1 package frozen

Place oil in a Dutch oven. Add beef cubes and brown. Add garlic, onion, and seasonings. Sauté for 5 minutes more. Add beer, cover, and simmer for 2 hours, or until meat is just about tender. Add water if necessary, but only small amounts at a time, since a fairly concentrated essence is desired. After the 2 hours, add lima beans and continue cooking another half hour. Serve over steaming hot rice.

YIELD: 4 SERVINGS.

Lemon-Roasted Leg of Lamb

One 3-pound leg of lamb

½ cup white vinegar

½ cup water

Juice of 1 lemon

Rind of ½ lemon, chopped

1½ teaspoons dried mustard

1 teaspoon salt

¼ teaspoon pepper

Uncle J.B.

Preheat oven to 300°. Prepare lamb by making small inch-deep incisions, spaced 1 inch apart. In a small saucepan place remaining ingredients. Bring to a boil and pour over lamb. Bake for 1½ hours, basting frequently. When serving, slice thin and spoon pan juices over meat.

YIELD: 4 SERVINGS.

Smithfield Ham

Uncle J.B. used to mail us these hams from Virginia.

One 10-pound Smithfield ham
½ cup white vinegar
1 cup brown sugar
1 cup apple cider
2 bay leaves

Whole cloves
1 large can sliced pineapple, juice reserved
Maraschino cherries

Using a vessel large enough for the ham to float freely, cover ham with water and soak for 2 hours. Pour off water and scrub ham with a stiff brush under running water. Cover again with cold water and soak for 18 to 24 hours, changing the water periodically. Drain off water, rinse off any residue from the vessel, and cover with clean water. Then add vinegar, ½ cup of brown sugar, cider, and bay leaves, and bring to a boil (it may be necessary to use 2 burners). Lower heat and cook slowly, uncovered, just barely simmering, for 4 to 4½ hours (25 to 30 minutes per pound). Remove ham from liquid and cool.

Preheat oven to 375°. Slice skin off ham, leaving a thin layer of fat. Place ham fat side up in a shallow roasting pan. Spread with remaining brown sugar, which has been moistened with enough of the reserved pineapple juice to make a paste. Stud with whole cloves. Lay pineapple slices on top, with a cherry in the center of each. Bake for about 30 minutes or until brown. This is a deliciously salty ham which should be sliced thin and served as a second meat. It is a particularly good complement to a turkey dinner. Use leftovers for sandwiches, as breakfast meat, or as a seasoning for vegetables.

J. B. Darden

Roast Pork

One 4-pound pork roast, loin or center cut

2 cloves garlic, minced

Salt and pepper to taste

4 bay leaves

½ cup white vinegar

½ teaspoon dried thyme

Preheat oven to 325°. Pierce the roast in several places with a two-pronged fork. Force some minced garlic into each hole, again with the aid of the fork. Sprinkle liberally with salt and pepper. Place the bay leaves in the bottom of a roasting pan. Place the roast on top, fat side up. Combine vinegar and thyme, and pour evenly over the roast. Place in oven, allowing 35 minutes baking time per pound. Baste occasionally.

YIELD: 5 TO 6 SERVINGS.

Uncle J.B.

Hot Potato Salad

4 medium white potatoes, peeled and
    diced

⅓ cup vegetable oil

¼ cup apple cider vinegar

½ teaspoon salt

¼ teaspoon pepper

½ teaspoon paprika

¼ teaspoon dry mustard

¼ teaspoon dried savory

¼ cup chopped fresh parsley, for garnish

Place potatoes in a saucepan and cover with salted water. Cook until tender, then drain off water. Mix oil, vinegar, and seasonings together and pour over potatoes. Sprinkle with parsley and serve hot.

YIELD: 4 SERVINGS.

White Potato and Cheese Casserole

8 medium potatoes, peeled

½ cup milk

½ pint heavy cream

2 eggs, lightly beaten

1½ cups grated Swiss or Cheddar cheese

Salt and pepper to taste

Preheat oven to 450°. Boil potatoes in salted water until tender. Drain and mash with a potato masher until lump-free, adding milk as you do so. Stir in cream, eggs, and cheese, reserving some of the cheese to sprinkle on top. Season with salt and pepper. Place in an ungreased casserole dish and bake for 15 minutes or until golden brown.

YIELD: 6 SERVINGS.

Hashed Brown Potatoes

4 cups peeled, cubed raw white potatoes

Salt and pepper to taste

6 tablespoons bacon fat or vegetable oil

1 medium onion, halved and sliced thin

2 teaspoons dried oregano

Worcestershire sauce

Sprinkle potatoes with salt and pepper. Melt bacon fat, or heat vegetable oil, in a heavy skillet. Add potato cubes, turning until well coated. Cook for 10 minutes over medium heat. Add onion, oregano, liberal squirts of Worcestershire sauce, and more salt and pepper if desired. Cook for 20 to 25 minutes more, or until the potatoes are crusty brown and tender. Stir frequently. Add more bacon fat or vegetable oil if potatoes stick while cooking.

YIELD: 4 TO 6 SERVINGS.

Uncle J.B.

Aunt Lillian

If you think it's impossible to be a superstar at eighty-plus, you haven't met Aunt Lillian. A fireball of energy, she is always on the go, and at a pace that would stagger many a twenty-year-old. As the only survivor of her family of thirteen Allens, she jets from her home in Petersburg, Virginia, to Los Angeles, Cleveland, New York City, and Nashville to visit a host of grandnieces, nephews, and assorted friends. Wherever she goes, her fast and witty conversation makes her a welcome and valued guest.

Aunt Lillian possesses an uncanny gift for presenting people in the best possible light and inspiring them to reach elusive goals — "quitters never win; winners never quit" is her motto. We have never known her to utter a disparaging word about anyone — unless, of course, that person fully deserved it. Like her late husband, J.B., she has a passion for cards and humorous anecdotes, and effortlessly takes center stage in any group.

She lives so intensely in the present that it's hard to get her to reminisce. "I never dwell on the past, I'm too busy moving into the future," she will say with a smile. "But let's see. Papa was a headwaiter at the old Tulane Hotel in Nashville, and that was thought to be a good job for a black man in those days. It was a time when your people seemed to do so much for you with so very little." Aunt Lil loathes cooking and admits it. "Sorry, dearie, I can't even remember how to cook." However, a trip to her "icebox" reveals the secret of her flawless complexion: fresh fruits, vegetables, and homemade cold cream. She credits her sister Nell with introducing her to cosmetics. "I used to think what a vain old sister Nell is, but when she died at ninety, her skin was clear and beautiful." One of Nell's secrets, cerated (wax-based) violet vanishing cream, doesn't seem to be on the market anymore, but you can make it yourself if you follow Lil's formula.

Here are a few of Aunt Lil's beauty ideas. And she is truly a woman who knows how to keep her "Y & B"—Youth and Beauty!

BEAUTY FOODS

The garden is a woman's best source of cosmetic treasures. Aunt Lil says to eat plenty of fresh vegetables and fruits and to use them externally, too.

Cucumber: Cucumbers are renowned for their beautifying abilities, so rub a slice over your face and neck. It will soften and smooth skin by refining pores.

Watermelon: Watermelon rind has many of the same properties as cucumbers and is equally useful for beautifying skin. Rub the inside of the rind on face and neck. It is really refreshing on a hot summer day.

Tomato: Tomato juice is great for oily skin! Try swishing a slice of raw tomato over your face from time to time. It's so good for oily and pimply skin.

Potato: Peel and grate a little white potato and place it under the eyes. Good for relieving swollen bags and dark circles if you've been crying or are just tired.

Eggs: Egg whites, beaten and applied to the face, work as a tightening mask to draw up wrinkles. Skin can use external sources of protein from the yolk too, as time marches on. Smear on either white or yolk and rinse off with water after fifteen minutes.

Peaches, Cream, and Honey: Aunt Lil takes this one literally. Whip up a little heavy cream (¼ cup), mash in ½ peach, and mix with 1 tablespoon honey. Apply to face and leave on for 15 minutes. Enjoy licking your lips!

Lemon: To whiten nails, plunge them into the white part of a lemon rind for a minute or two. Also, to get an additional gloss on nails, buff with an old-fashioned buffer.

Buttermilk: Drink it and use it as a mask. It aids the digestive system and acts as a cleanser and astringent for the face.

Lillian Allen Darden displaying her flawless complexion

Violet Vanishing Cream

Aunt Lil gave us the recipe for sister Nell's own violet vanishing cream.

2 tablespoons white beeswax

2 tablespoons lanolin

9 tablespoons mineral oil

½ teaspoon borax (sodium borate)

3 tablespoons rose water, warmed

¼ teaspoon essence of violet oil

Place beeswax, lanolin, and mineral oil in the top of an enamel or glass double boiler. Heat until thoroughly melted. Dissolve borax in warmed rose water and add this to beeswax mixture. Remove from heat. Stir vigorously with a wooden spoon while mixture cools and thickens. Then add essence of violet. Continue beating until well blended. Jar and store in the refrigerator.

NOTE: *Aunt Lil's husband, J.B., was a pharmacist, and it wasn't hard for her to obtain these supplies, but they're much more difficult to find now.*

Homemade Perfume

Here is a simple way to make any essence. Steep a cupful of petals (violets, roses, honeysuckle, lilacs) or the skin of 1 orange or 2 limes in 1 cup safflower oil for a day or so. Then strain off and reserve the oil. Discard the petals or skins and replace with fresh ones every other day for at least 10 days or longer (about 5 times). When the scent is strong, discard the petals, measure the oil, and mix with an equal amount of ethanol rubbing alcohol. Keep tightly capped. Shake once or twice daily for 2 weeks. Now spoon off the alcohol (an eyedropper is useful for this). The remaining drops are your own precious essence oils. We have had the best luck with honeysuckle perfume, but without the fixatives used in commercial perfumes, the scent does not last long once applied. Still, it's fun to make and you can mix your own essences with regular colognes to produce unique and exotic fragrances.

Sachet

Distinctive fragrance is a part of Aunt Lil's aura. When you think of her neat white house with its sky-blue trim and rows of pink petunias leading up the walk, the first thing that floods the mind is its sweet smell. Old homes always seem to smell best. Aunt Lil uses sachet to refresh her rooms.

1 quart assorted flower petals and buds
½ tablespoon salt
1 cinnamon stick
6 cloves
Dash of grated nutmeg
Dash of ground mace

Dash of ground allspice
Drop of essence of lemon oil
Drop of essence of violet oil
1 tablespoon orrisroot,* chips or powder (optional)

Dry the flower petals and buds (rose, lilac, honeysuckle, lily of the valley, violets, whatever smells good or adds color) in the hot sun or in a 250° oven on a cookie sheet until they are crisp (about 15 minutes in the oven). Then place them in a jar that has a tight lid, alternating layers of petals and buds with a sprinkling of salt, spices, and essences so that everything is well distributed. (Orrisroot helps fix the scent but is not essential.) Every day for a week, shake the jar to toss the petals and spices to mingle the scents. Keep the jar closed for 2 weeks. The opened jar will scent a room. Some of the contents, crushed and tied in scraps of cloth, can be used as a drawer sachet and will fill a linen or clothes closet with a delightful aroma.

*Orrisroot comes from several varieties of European iris and is often used in perfumery.

BODY TIPS

Dry Hands: Before going to bed, rub your hands vigorously with lanolin, and put on a pair of gloves to retain heat and protect the bed linen. You may look odd, but your hands will soften.

Feet: If you have rough feet, Aunt Lil recommends rubbing them with a pumice stone, then applying castor oil.

The Allen family—little Lil (right corner), Sister Nell (behind Mother Allen)

Lines and Wrinkles:

Anti-wrinkle Cream for Under the Eyes

1½ tablespoons lanolin

2 tablespoons cocoa butter

2 teaspoons honey

Melt the above in a small enamel or glass pot. Apply a little bit while still warm. Cool and jar the rest. Pat gently onto the skin. Remove excess with a soft tissue after 10 minutes.

Hair: For dry scalp, warm ½ cup olive oil. Part hair in small sections and apply with cotton balls. Leave on overnight, wrapping the head in a scarf to protect the pillowcase. Shampoo in the morning.

Teeth: When we asked Aunt Lil what people did about dental care in her youth, she told us that they brushed with salt and the charcoal from fireplaces. Baking soda was used for mouthwash as well as for deodorant in the pre-aerosol era.

Aunt Lillian

Face:

Lemon Nourishing Cream

1 egg yolk

½ cup olive oil

1 tablespoon fresh lemon juice

3 drops of essence of lemon oil

Beat egg yolk with an electric beater at high speed until light and lemony. Add a few drops of olive oil at a time, beating vigorously until mixture becomes thick and creamy. Stir in lemon juice, then essence of lemon or a few drops of your favorite perfume. Blend well, jar, and keep this super-rich cream refrigerated. Massage into the skin as a night cream.

Two parting beauty secrets we received from Aunt Lil on our last visit:

"Peace of mind is radiated in one's countenance, and it's not so easy to come by in times of trouble unless you work at it every day. I begin and end my day by reading *The Daily Word* [a religious pamphlet with inspirational thoughts for each day]. And once a week I take a special, long, leisurely, floral-scented bath, preferably by candlelight.

"During my bath I sort out the weeds of the last week and sow the seeds for the coming one. In life you just have to keep moving — stepping higher all the time."

Lillian A. Darden, Fisk
University music student

Uncles C.L., Arthur, Russell, and Charlie

To each of his children, Papa Darden seemed to have transmitted some of his many talents. This was clearly in evidence in C.L. (Camillus Lewis), the only son who elected to remain home and help in the family business. Mechanical things fascinated C.L., and he inherited his father's ability to repair anything. At age eight, he could take a clock apart and reassemble it. Even if he had never seen the "contraption" before, if he knew what it was supposed to do, it was a matter of minutes before he had it better than new. This mechanical talent brought him so much revenue as a teen-ager that C.L. refused to leave Wilson and attend high school, though he encouraged the others to pursue their educations and financially assisted them.

By 1914, motorcycles, phonographs, and records had been introduced to the world. Many people thought these inventions were passing fads, so C.L. managed to acquire the only franchises in Wilson County to sell RCA Victor phonographs and records and Harley-Davidson motorcycles. He would travel deep into rural areas where records had never been heard, playing Bessie Smith and

Uncle C.L.

Bert Williams, or Caruso, as the occasion warranted. Black or white, anyone in or around Wilson who wanted a motorcycle or record player had to buy it from C.L. Eventually, new dealers flooded the market, so after Papa Darden retired, C.L. abandoned his mechanical interests, attended Mortuary Science School, and took over the funeral business with his younger brother, Arthur.

Opposite in every way to outgoing and outspoken C.L., Arthur, in early life, was a quiet, introspective soul who loved books and music. He derived great pleasure from playing the tuba with a local band and singing deep baritone in church and with a street-corner quartet. Although he had shown promise as a medical student, his studies were interrupted by World War I. Contrary to Papa Darden's strong conviction that blacks should avoid the military, Arthur was caught in the vortex of war hysteria and felt that participation in the armed forces would break down the doors of racial prejudice at home. He cut quite a splendid figure in his officer's uniform as he marched off, determined "to make the world safe for democracy." His letters home were at first filled with the excitement of Paris and foreign shores, but his enthusiasm quickly soured as the reality of the torment and anguish of war set in. While overseas, he was the victim of a nerve gas attack and returned to Wilson a bitter and disabled man, utterly disillusioned by the bigotry he had experienced and by the cruelty and horror of war. Despite an enormous struggle to regain his strength and resume his position as a wheelwright with Papa Darden, his health was shattered and he never fully recuperated. Even so, Arthur was able to finish Eckles Mortuary School, marry, and have a son. However, as the years passed, the debilitating effects of the gassing increased, sapping his energy and spirit and causing the failure of his marriage and ability to work. For the rest of his life, Arthur would resent the fact that he had fought and suffered for what he termed "the barest trickle of democracy."

Therefore, C.L. became the dominant force in the funeral parlor. He took his profession seriously and had a passion for ritual and routine, which ideally suited him to it. Ironically, one of the first funerals under his and Arthur's direction was that of their younger brother, Russell, who died during his last year at Howard University Law School. Russell had gone to New York City to look for adventure during the Christmas vacation. While there, he caught pneumonia and died at Harlem Hospital before any of the family could reach him. Russell had been a daring, fun-loving, robust, athletic young man known for his prowess on the football field. Our father remembers that the last time he saw Russell play football was at Livingston College. The score was Livingston 3, Biddle 3. The ball was snapped and thrown to Russell. He was running hard. The opposition tried for a tackle but missed and tore off the seat of his pants instead. Oblivious to the cheers and laughter of the crowd, Russell kept running and won the game for Biddle 9–3, with his rear end showing. He had an aggressive spirit and was the pride and joy of his family. His death left an unfillable void in the family circle.

Charles, the second oldest son, who had left home many years before, returned for the funeral and delivered a heartfelt eulogy. Russell had been his favorite brother, and both had looked forward to a partnership in legal and political careers, plus the development of the resort for black vacationers that Charlie had started to build

Russell Darden's last photo before his untimely death

Arthur Darden during World War I

on Lake Elsinore near Los Angeles. After Russell's funeral, Charles corresponded, but he returned to the East only once. For this reason he remains somewhat of an enigma. What is known about him, however, is that he was a dapper, lifelong bachelor who was renowned for his elocution; that he eventually became a presiding judge; and that he was frugal and had what was then considered "peculiar dietary habits" in that he was a confirmed vegetarian and a teetotaler, even running for office on the prohibition ticket.

Of all these uncles, C.L. was the only one we really knew. He was a man who courted the regard and respect of colleagues by taking on many community responsibilities, yet enjoyed fussing about his overloaded duties. That was just his way. Not a day went by that he didn't confer with his cronies. We would see them sitting on straw-backed chairs in front of the funeral home or on his front porch, smoking cigars while discussing sports, world politics, and the local news. Every issue—from what color to paint the church vestibule to bail money or employment for someone in need—claimed Uncle C.L.'s equal attention and bluster. Once he took a stand on an issue, he was not easily budged, and during his long years in Wilson he stood in the thick of many controversies, large and small.

One of the first town crises that Uncle C.L. helped resolve and told us about was the slap-that-started-a-school incident. In 1918 a "colored" schoolteacher was slapped in the face by the white superintendent of schools for alleged insubordination. Eight teachers decided to strike, and the community backed them by boycotting the public school. Uncle C.L., along with other community leaders, organized an effort to collect money from churches, lodges, and interested people to create an independent school. A building was bought and, despite a climate of fear and uncertainty about whether the school would be allowed to exist, three hundred children were enrolled by parents who willingly paid tuition. At the end of the school year the students presented a play (directed by Georgia Burke, later a Broadway actress) that attracted so many town well-wishers that a vacant warehouse had to be rented for the performance. This became an annual event for all Wilson, and the community-run school became a model for black educators of the day during the ten years it lasted. Uncle C.L. was duly proud of the part he played in the school's long success.

How our uncle enjoyed all the activities and accolades that his little town offered! He was a member of the Masons, the Elks, the Odd Fellows, the Civic Club, the Knights of Pythias Lodge, and was the chairman of the church trustees as well. Every town needs its solid citizen and, one thing is for sure, C.L. personified that role.

No, Uncle C.L. could not cook. As far as we know, none of these uncles did much in the cooking department. It is said that Russell had a hearty appetite, Arthur ate like a bird, and Charlie was a devotee of health foods who never ate meat; but none of their favorite recipes survives. We do know, however, that Uncle C.L. loved good food, and his special delight was the excellent seafood that was prepared by his wife, Norma—and sometimes caught by C.L. himself.

Russell Darden—front row, second from left, in his class at Biddle (now Johnson C. Smith) in Charlotte, North Carolina

Uncles C.L., Arthur, Russell, and Charlie

Baked Stuffed Shad

STUFFING:

1 large green bell pepper, seeded and chopped

2 medium onions, diced

1 cup diced celery

2 small cloves garlic, minced

¼ cup bacon fat or butter

6 slices buttered toast, coarsely crumbled

An equal quantity of leftover corn bread, coarsely crumbled

½ cup hot water

2 eggs, beaten

Salt and pepper to taste

SHAD:

One 5-pound shad, split for stuffing, head and tail intact

Salt

3 slices bacon

Bachelor Uncle Charles and Hollywood throng

For the stuffing: Sauté vegetables and garlic in bacon fat until limp. Combine toast and corn bread crumbs. Pour hot water over them. Add the sautéed vegetables and the beaten eggs. Mix well. Season to taste. Mixture should be fairly dry. For the fish: Preheat oven to 400°. Clean shad. Make 3 shallow slits across the top side. Sprinkle salt in stuffing cavity and the slits. Stuff cavity and close it with a skewer. Place fish in a shallow baking pan. Top with bacon for basting purposes. Bake for approximately 45 minutes. Remove bacon about 15 minutes before end of baking time.

YIELD: 4 GENEROUS SERVINGS.

Sautéed Shad Roe

2 fairly large sacs of shad roe

2 cups boiling water

Salt and pepper to taste

2 tablespoons butter

3 eggs, beaten

Place roe in a sieve. Pour boiling water over the roe and remove as much of the skin or sac as possible. Season with salt and pepper. Melt butter in a skillet. When bubbly but not brown, add roe, stirring constantly to prevent lumping and sticking. Roe is done when no longer red in color. Texture should be grainy. Add the beaten eggs to this and stir as in scrambling. Cook until eggs are done. Serve hot for breakfast with grits and bacon.

YIELD: 4 SERVINGS.

Oyster Stew

From Ed Lloyd, a fellow fisherman.

½ cup diced celery

3 cups milk

1 cup light cream

1½ teaspoons salt

½ teaspoon pepper

½ teaspoon paprika

2 tablespoons butter

1 pint oysters, shucked

In a small saucepan cook the celery in a little boiling water until celery is tender. Combine milk, cream, and seasonings in the top of a double boiler. Heat thoroughly, taking care not to allow mixture to boil. Add celery, butter, and oysters and their liquid. Cook for about 5 minutes or until the oysters curl around the edges.

YIELD: 4 TO 6 SERVINGS.

Uncles C.L., Arthur, Russell, and Charlie

Oyster Casserole

A specialty of Wilson's star caterer—Georgia Dupree.

*1 quart oysters, shucked, liquid
   reserved*
Milk, as needed
½ cup butter
2 cups saltine cracker crumbs

Salt and pepper to taste
1 cup grated sharp Cheddar cheese
Paprika

Preheat oven to 350°. To the oyster liquid, add enough milk to make 2 cups. Melt butter and add to crumbs. In a casserole place a layer of crumbs, then a layer of oysters. Season with salt and pepper, then sprinkle with cheese. Continue alternating, ending with a layer of crumbs. Pour reserved liquid over the top. Sprinkle with paprika. Bake for 20 to 30 minutes.

YIELD: 6 TO 8 SERVINGS.

Uncle C.L. (center front) arranged for Booker T. Washington (second row center) and Dr. John Kenney (fifth from left) of Tuskegee, Alabama, to address businessmen of Wilson.

Fried Oysters

1 quart oysters

Salt to taste

2 eggs, beaten

¾ cup saltine cracker crumbs

¼ cup yellow cornmeal

Vegetable shortening, for frying

Drain oysters in a sieve. Lay them out on paper towels and sprinkle with salt. Dip several oysters at a time into the beaten eggs. Mix cracker crumbs and cornmeal on wax paper. Roll oysters in this mixture and then drop into deep hot fat (450°), frying only 1 layer at a time until golden brown. Drain on paper towels. Serve immediately. Excellent for breakfast with grits, eggs, and bacon.

YIELD: 4 TO 6 SERVINGS.

Fried Salt Fish

Salt herring, mullet, or mackerel (fish that has been soaked in brine), allow 1 fish per person

Yellow cornmeal

Vegetable shortening, for frying

Have fish prepared at fish market (head, tail, and fins removed and fish split). Cover fish with cold water and soak for 2 hours. Drain, add fresh water, and soak overnight. In the morning, pat off excess water with paper towels. On the skin side, make 2 or 3 shallow slits. Coat entire fish with cornmeal. Fry in hot fat until golden brown. Serve hot for breakfast with grits and eggs.

Uncles C.L., Arthur, Russell, and Charlie

Potluck Gumbo

1 large slice (¼ pound) precooked ham, diced

1 pound raw shrimp, shelled to tail and deveined

1½ cups chicken giblets, parboiled and diced

1 pound fresh okra, cut into ¼-inch rounds

1 medium onion, diced

1 green bell pepper, seeded and diced

2 cloves garlic, minced

½ cup chopped parsley

½ cup scallion tops, sliced thin

Pepper to taste

5 cups water

2 crabs, cooked, meat removed from shells; or 4 ounces frozen crab meat

Salt to taste

1 tablespoon gumbo filé (see Note)

Sauté ham in its own border of fat, adding oil if ham fat is scant. Trim off any unrendered fat and set ham aside. Sauté shrimp in same pan until pink. Remove and set aside. Then sauté chicken giblets. Add okra, onion, green pepper, garlic, parsley, scallion tops, and pepper. Add the water. Simmer for 1 hour. Add ham cubes, shrimp, and crab meat. Continue cooking for another 15 minutes. During the last 5 minutes of cooking, add salt to taste, then gumbo filé. Serve over hot rice.

YIELD: 6 TO 8 SERVINGS.

NOTE: *Gumbo filé is powdered sassafras leaf. It was originally made by the Choctaw Indians and is most easily obtained in Louisiana, but it can be bought in most shops specializing in seasonings.*

Uncle John and Charlie visiting C.L. in Wilson

Aunt Norma

Norma Duncan Darden began life in Montgomery, Alabama, at the turn of the twentieth century as the middle child and only girl in the family. On a recent trip to her home, we browsed through her many photographs as she told us who was who and how and when they had entered her life. "My father ('Papa' to us), as the last male Duncan, inherited the ancestral home and rental houses, and owned a number of business places in the downtown part of the city. He was also a bondsman. Papa was known for his choice horses, as that was the era of the horse and buggy and sporty 'runabouts.' We could always tell when he was nearing home by Flora-Dora's (the horse that I remember) gait and sound on the brick-paved street. My father was considered the sport of his family. He was a betting man who loved to travel: Flora-Dora was named for a popular musical Papa saw on Broadway, and Mid-Way, our pug dog, was his gift to us from the exposition he attended in Atlanta. Mardi Gras time found him in Mobile or New Orleans while we anxiously awaited his return. It seems like yesterday when Aunt Arizona and her friends returned from the world's fair in St. Louis in their lovely frocks—long, sweeping taffeta skirts, leg-o'-mutton sleeves (the Gibson Girl look)—bringing confetti, dolls, and play-things for Henry, Richard, and me. What merriment! The paving blocks in front of our house were blue and white octagon shapes, so we played hopscotch without drawing the customary patterns. In back there was a stable with a loft and a playing area. On the other side was the chicken house, from the top of which my brothers and friends launched scooters and raced them down to the trolley-car tracks on our street. Behind all was a garden and fruit trees."

Against this idyllic childhood, tragedy struck. First, Aunt Norma's paternal grandmother, Ellen, died. Then, when Norma was seven, her mother, Evangeline, also died. The household was taken over by her Aunt Arizona, a young grade-school teacher and friend of our Aunt Maude. But two years later, Aunt Arizona contracted pneumonia and also died.

"My earliest memory of my mother was going to Sunday school and church with her—that she was tall, gentle, and beautifully dressed—and the pretty pinafores she made for me. She had at-tended Fisk University, and one of her best friends became Mrs. Booker T. Washington, who later escorted me in her car to my wed-ding. I still have the shocking pink ostrich fan, my wedding gift from her. The other memory of my mother still vivid is a ride in the train coach with her and my brother Henry to Savannah, Georgia. We traveled with a huge trunk of clothes, as it was the custom in those days when visiting faraway family members to spend a few weeks or even a couple of months. We were traveling to visit her uncle, R.R. Wright, then president of Georgia State College. As a ten-year-old, Wright had electrified General O.O. Howard of the Union Army [who later founded Howard University] and his party during their inspection of the Atlanta schools after the signing of the Emancipation Proclamation. At the end of his address, the gen-eral had asked the little black children who had assembled around the abandoned freight car that served as their school, 'What mes-sage shall I take to the people in the North?' Wright's stirring reply from one so young—'Tell them, sir, that we are rising!'—was immortalized in a poem by John Greenleaf Whittier. It was with the Wright family that I'm told I started kindergarten, although I don't remember."

After the death of all the women in her immediate family, Aunt Norma and her older brother were sent to Tallahassee, Florida, to live with her mother's brother, Major Henry Howard, a mathematics professor, commandant of a military unit, and bandleader at Florida A. & M. College. They spent two school terms there. Then her father, fearing that he could not raise a daughter alone, begged the faculty at Talladega College in Alabama to admit her as a special student. At twelve, she became the youngest boarder to enter, and for the next eight years, from eighth grade through college, Talladega was her second home.

Having spent most of her young life in black educational institutions, Aunt Norma tells us that many of them were started by Northern missionaries after the Civil War and were originally intended to meet the needs of both black and white Southerners, becoming segregated only after laws were passed enforcing separation of the races. She fondly remembers the dedication of the integrated faculty at Talladega.

Shortly before graduation, the news reached Aunt Norma of Mary McLeod Bethune's monumental struggle to expand the school she had started in 1904 with five students in a single room. Aunt Norma proudly joined the faculty as an English teacher there, twelve years after its inception. For a while, Mrs. Bethune encouraged what appeared to be a budding romance between Norma and her only son, Bert Bethune. However, our own Aunt Maude stepped into the picture, initiating correspondence between Norma and Uncle C.L., her husband's brother, and, after two years of letter writing, arranged a meeting of the two "pen pals" at her home in Opelika, Alabama. C.L., who had fallen in love with Aunt Norma's gracious personality and stately beauty via the mails and a photograph, proved to be an ardent suitor, courting her with flowers, candy, and watermelon. In 1922 he married her in John and Maude's flower garden under the grape arbor and took her to Wilson, North Carolina.

On first arrival the newlyweds lived with Papa Darden, but C.L., not wanting to move far from his father or the business, purchased a vacant lot across the street, and Aunt Norma designed her own floor plans for their "dream house." Her brother-in-law, John Barnes, built it. In similar fashion, she designed and supervised the renovation of the Darden Memorial Funeral Home. So, from the earliest days of her arrival in Wilson, Aunt Norma's innate sense of style and taste won extravagant and deserved praise. Accustomed to life in an academic setting, she filled her time with the cultural and social activities of the town and became "the hostess with the mostest." With over fifty years in her "dream house," she continues to give luster to the title "homemaker." We ought to know. A portion of nearly every summer of our childhood was spent in her home, and fresh are our memories of dusting the furniture, setting the table, putting the flowers out, and serving refreshments to the ladies from the Book and Garden Club; the Church Missionary Society; her sorority, the AKAs; the Links; the Mary Bethune Civic Club; and the Merry Matrons' Bridge Club, to name a few . . . and not to mention the gentlemen from Uncle C.L.'s groups. With so many meetings, activities, and visits from friends and relatives throughout the years, Aunt Norma has collected a large repertoire of delicious dishes and party potpourri. And here are a few of her unique entertaining ideas.

Once, when we were very young, Aunt Norma gave a breakfast come-exactly-as-you-were-when-invited party. One guest came in a bathrobe and curlers. Sensing the mood of abandonment at play here, we went upstairs and returned completely nude. What possessed us we will never know. Should you want to give a breakfast come-as-you-are party, your guests will love Aunt Norma's baked grits and brains.

Arizona Duncan, Aunt
Norma's aunt

Baked Grits

3 cups cooked grits

2 tablespoons melted butter

2 eggs, beaten

1½ cups evaporated milk

1¾ cups grated Cheddar cheese

Paprika to taste

Cayenne pepper to taste (usually no more than 1 or 2 dashes)

Preheat oven to 400°. Mash grits until smooth, if they are leftovers. Add melted butter, eggs, and evaporated milk. Then add 1½ cups grated cheese, reserving ¼ cup for the topping. Combine thoroughly. Add paprika and cayenne. Pour mixture into a buttered casserole. Bake for 25 to 30 minutes or until brown. Sprinkle with remaining grated cheese and more paprika. Return to oven and cook a few minutes more, until topping has melted.

YIELD: ABOUT 6 SERVINGS.

Scrambled Brains

1 pound pork brains

3–4 tablespoons butter or bacon fat

Salt and pepper to taste

4 eggs, beaten

Place brains in a sieve. Pour boiling water over them and remove as much of the covering membrane as possible. Melt butter or bacon fat in a skillet. When bubbling, add brains, stirring constantly to break them up and to prevent sticking and lumping. Season with salt and pepper. When nicely browned, stir in beaten eggs with a fork

Aunt Norma

as in scrambling. Cook until eggs are done. Serve hot for breakfast with Baked Grits and bacon.

YIELD: 4 TO 6 SERVINGS.

One year, one of Aunt Norma's clubs gave a hobo party to raise scholarship funds. Everyone came dressed as vagabonds, and the menu was baked beans, hot dogs, coleslaw, corn bread, and coffee.

Aunt Norma showing her flair for fashion.

Aunt Norma, top right, English teacher at Mrs. Bethune's college in Daytona Beach, Florida. Mrs. Bethune is left of center. Aunt Ruby Cornwell of Charleston, South Carolina, in center.

Spoonbread and Strawberry Wine

Baked Beans

1 pound navy beans, soaked overnight
1 medium onion, diced
2½ cups Stewed Tomatoes (see page 262)

1½ cups brown sugar, loosely packed
¼ pound salt pork, streaked with lean

Drain beans, place in a saucepan, cover with fresh water, and par-boil with onions until beans are tender but still firm, about 1 hour. Drain, reserving liquid. Add stewed tomatoes and sugar to beans. Put in a covered, ungreased casserole or bean pot. Slice salt pork ⅓-inch thick and place in strips over beans. Bake in a preheated 325° oven for 4 hours, turning salt pork over occasionally. As moisture evaporates, add enough reserved liquid to the pot to cover beans and prevent them from drying out. Then uncover and raise the oven temperature to 375° to brown the salt pork on both sides. If necessary, add more liquid. Cook for at least another hour, or longer, depending upon the texture of the beans.

YIELD: 6 TO 8 SERVINGS.

Another year, the Merry Matrons gave a gypsy party complete with a fortune-teller who read palms and cards. Red, purple, and green was the color scheme, so Aunt Norma contributed her Magnificent Stuffed Eggplant.

Magnificent Stuffed Eggplant

Aunt Norma, in the tradition of true Southern cooks, serves her stuffed eggplant as one of at least two accompanying vegetables in a meal. But we have found that it makes an exceptional meal by itself. Hot muffins with peach preserves make a delicious accompaniment to this dish. The recipe is fairly simple but time-consuming because of all the chopping, slicing, and dicing. For this reason, it is best prepared in quantity, with 2 large eggplants as a minimum.

2 large eggplants, halved lengthwise

2 medium onions, diced

3 medium green bell peppers, seeded and diced

3–4 tablespoons bacon fat or vegetable oil

8 ripe tomatoes, peeled and chunked

Salt and pepper to taste

8 ounces Cheddar cheese, grated (keep a fistful in reserve)

½–¾ cup bread crumbs

Preheat oven to 425°. Carefully scoop out the eggplant from the skin, taking care not to puncture what should be a thin shell, less than ¼-inch thick. Place the eggplant pieces in salted boiling water to cover and cook until very tender. Meanwhile, sauté the onions and peppers in the bacon fat or oil until onions are translucent. Then add tomatoes, salt, and pepper. Simmer for 10 to 15 minutes. When eggplant is done, drain well and return to saucepan. Add cheese, stirring to facilitate melting. Add enough bread crumbs so that the mixture is somewhat dry and very cheesy. Add the simmering tomato mixture to this, using a slotted spoon. Then add as much of the remaining juice as necessary to make a moist but not watery mixture. If too moist, add more bread crumbs. Fill eggplant shells.

Bake for 45 minutes to 1 hour. Toward the end of baking time, top generously with more grated cheese, and bake long enough for the cheese to melt.

YIELD: 4 SERVINGS.

Recently, Aunt Norma gave a "round-the-world" party with guests requested to come in the apparel of whatever country they chose and to prepare a stunt! A prize was given for the best display of talent, and an international buffet was served. She has also used this theme for a "historical character" party where guests presented a few facts about heroines of bygone eras. Good for a buffet or dinner anytime is her version of beef goulash.

Beef Goulash

3 pounds beef stew meat, cut into small cubes

¼ cup butter or vegetable oil

2 large onions, chopped

1 clove garlic, chopped

1 heaping tablespoon paprika

1½ teaspoons salt

1 cup beef stock

3 tablespoons dry white wine

2 tablespoons flour

3 tablespoons water

1 cup sour cream

Black olives, for garnish

Chopped parsley, for garnish

Brown beef cubes in butter or oil in a Dutch oven. Remove meat and brown onions and garlic. Return meat, add paprika and salt, and stir. Add stock and wine. Bring to a boil, then reduce heat and simmer slowly, covered, for about 2 hours or until tender. Blend flour in 3 tablespoons water, add to pot, and cook for 10 minutes more. Remove from heat and gently stir in sour cream. Garnish with black olives and parsley. Wonderful over noodles, mashed potatoes, or rice.

YIELD: 6 TO 8 SERVINGS.

We remember an Aunt Norma party where everything was yellow, from the plates and flowers to the tablecloth. She served her Chicken Purlo over yellow rice, with yellow summer squash, yellow string beans, and banana punch. For dessert there was Pineapple Ice Cream (page 46) served in miniature yellow flowerpots, with real daisies standing in each pot, and lemon cookies.

Chicken Purlo (Pilau)

3 medium stalks celery, diced

1 large onion, diced

1 medium green bell pepper, seeded and chopped

2 small cloves garlic, minced

3 tablespoons bacon fat or butter

One 4-pound stewing hen, cut into serving pieces

7¼ cups water

½ teaspoon poultry seasoning

½ teaspoon marjoram

Salt and pepper to taste

4 cups chicken broth, from boiling chicken

Pinch of saffron

2 cups raw rice

2 tablespoons flour

3 eggs, hard-cooked, coarsely chopped

In a large kettle, sauté vegetables and garlic in bacon fat or butter until tender. Add chicken pieces and 7 cups of water. Add seasonings and salt and pepper. Bring to a boil, cover, and simmer slowly until chicken is fork tender, about 1½ hours. When done, remove 4 cups of chicken broth and, in a separate pot, bring this to a boil. Add salt to taste, the saffron and raw rice. Cook, covered, until the rice is tender and the liquid is absorbed, 25 to 30 minutes. Remove chicken from its pot and thicken remaining broth with a mixture of the flour and remaining ¼ cup of water. Boil to reduce until desired thickness is reached. Adjust the seasonings and return the chicken to the pot. Heat thoroughly before serving. Chicken should be served nested in piping-hot rice, with coarsely chopped hard-cooked eggs on top and the gravy passed in a separate dish.

YIELD: 6 SERVINGS.

Southern Fried Corn

6 ears corn, shucked

3 tablespoons bacon fat or butter

2 tablespoons flour

1 tablespoon sugar

1 cup water

Salt and pepper to taste

Wash and remove silk from corn. After cutting the kernels in half with a sharp knife, cut kernels off. (This is called cream-style cutting.) Scrape juice out of corn cob into the corn. Pour bacon fat into a frying pan and heat. Add corn. Stir in flour, sugar, and water. Simmer at medium heat until kernels are tender. Then raise heat. Stir at intervals, letting mixture brown slightly on the bottom. Scrape brown off bottom and mix well into rest of corn. Add salt and pepper and, if necessary, add a little hot water. Mixture should be moist.

YIELD: 4 SERVINGS.

Aunt Norma

Aunt Norma's Banana Fruit Punch

6 oranges

8 lemons

1 scant cup sugar

6 cloves

1 cinnamon stick

2 trays of ice (see Note)

1 liter bottle ginger ale

28 ounces water

1 peach, sliced

Handful of blueberries

2 firm bananas, sliced

Squeeze juice from citrus fruits and pour into punch bowl. Add sugar and spices. Stir. Add ice. Pour in ginger ale. Dilute with equal amount of water. Garnish with sliced peach and blueberries. Top with sliced bananas.

YIELD: 12 SERVINGS.

NOTE: *For adding a decorative touch to tall glasses of lemonade or iced tea, Aunt Norma freezes Maraschino cherries, mandarin orange sections, strawberries, raspberries, or fresh mint sprigs in ice cubes.*

Automobiles were fairly novel machines when Aunt Norma arrived in Wilson, and one of the first parties she remembers was an auto-tour party. For these, many young people would get together and drive from house to house, having a different course, from appetizer to dessert, at each home. Aunt Norma was noted for a wide assortment of desserts, and the last stop was always at her house.

These little cupcakes are very dainty if baked in miniature muffin tins, but they can also be made in regular-size tins.

Pineapple Upside-Down Cupcakes

TOPPING:

¼ cup butter

7 tablespoons dark brown sugar

½ cup drained crushed pineapple, juice reserved

6 Maraschino cherries, cut into thin slices

CAKE BATTER:

¼ cup butter

¼ cup granulated sugar

1 egg, separated

1 cup sifted cake flour

1½ teaspoons baking powder

¼ teaspoon salt

½ cup pineapple juice, reserved from crushed pineapple

½ teaspoon vanilla extract

Preheat oven to 350°. To make topping: Melt butter in a saucepan and add brown sugar. Cook over low flame until well blended, then stir in crushed pineapple. Pour about a teaspoon of this topping into the bottom of each greased miniature muffin cup and add a sliver of a red cherry (see Note). To prepare batter: Cream butter, add sugar, and beat until fluffy. Beat egg yolk and add. Sift flour, baking powder, and salt together; add alternately with the pineapple juice. Stir in vanilla. Beat egg white until stiff and fold into batter. Pour batter over topping, filling each cup two thirds full, and bake for 25 minutes, or until cupcakes pull away from sides of pan and turn golden on top. Cool, then turn cupcakes carefully onto a cake plate, pineapple side up.

YIELD: 2 DOZEN MINIATURE OR 1 DOZEN REGULAR CUPCAKES.

NOTE: *The topping can be poured into a 9-inch skillet, using 5 pineapple rings instead of the crushed pineapple.*

Aunt Norma

Pecan Tartlets with Cream Cheese Pastry

FILLING:

1 egg, well beaten

¾ cup light brown sugar

¾ cup chopped pecan meats

1 teaspoon vanilla extract

Pinch of salt

PASTRY:

½ cup butter

3 ounces cream cheese, softened

1 cup flour, sifted

Preheat oven to 325°. For the pastry: Cream butter and cream cheese together. Mix in flour and refrigerate for easy handling. For the filling: Mix all ingredients together, blending well. Then shape chilled pastry dough into 1-inch balls. Place in tartlet tins (see Note) 2½ inches in diameter, press over bottoms and sides. Spoon filling into shells. Bake for 25 minutes or until risen in the center.

YIELD: ABOUT 18 TARTLETS.

NOTE: *Miniature muffin tins may be used if you cannot find tartlet tins. Five-and-ten-cent stores have tin-foil ones that will do in a pinch.*

Eggnog Pie

1 envelope (1 tablespoon) unflavored
    gelatin

½ cup sugar

1⅓ cups milk

3 eggs, separated

2 tablespoons dark rum

½ cup heavy cream

One 9-inch graham cracker pie shell
    (see page 269)

In a medium-size saucepan combine gelatin, ¼ cup of sugar, milk, and lightly beaten egg yolks. Cook over medium heat, stirring until mixture comes to a boil. Remove from heat. Chill for 15 to 20 minutes, stirring occasionally until mixture begins to thicken. Beat egg whites into soft peaks. Gradually add remaining ¼ cup of sugar and beat until thick and glossy. Add rum to chilled egg yolk mixture. Whip and fold in cream. Last, fold in egg whites. Pour into pie shell and chill for 3 to 4 hours.

YIELD: ABOUT 8 SERVINGS.

Aunt Norma with
her nieces —us

Aunt Norma

Aunt Alice

Alice Foster is our adopted aunt. Actually, she was Aunt Norma's roommate in college. The two were inseparable, so we grew up feeling she was part of the family.

Aunt Alice was a "divorced woman" at a time when that label carried a hint of mystery and intrigue. She left her native Birmingham (although the accent never left her) in the late forties and went to New York to seek her fortune and a better education for her daughters, Vicky and Leah. For many years she taught home economics in the public school system and ran an alteration shop evenings and Saturdays. After her girls began careers of their own, she decided to see a bit of the world, packed her bags, and toured Europe and Africa, sending us a postcard from nearly every port. From Spain she wrote that she had just left Morocco and had settled in a villa near Palma for the winter. That simply knocked us out!

Aunt Alice was unbelievably exotic to us—our own resident sophisticated, world-traveled *femme fatale*. We loaded all our intimate adolescent problems on her and loved her visits to our home and our visits to her magical apartment in Brooklyn, which was filled with the treasures of her travels. We would whisper secrets over fenugreek tea (her favorite infusion for preventing colds) in her parlor, which was filled with every green foliage imaginable. We would sit on giant sofas covered with vivid floral prints and lots of bright pillows while her two fluffy white cats (who matched her white throw rugs) stalked around and a pet bluebird (which she had discovered on her windowsill one day) chimed in occasionally.

Besides the opportunity to reveal our souls to her, the added allure of our Brooklyn jaunts were the assorted health and figure tips Aunt Alice would give us. Long before yoga, eating "health foods," and talking to houseplants were popular, Aunt Alice had been advocating these practices. We never could keep up with her well-disciplined beauty and health routine, but she has religiously practiced what she's preached for the last forty years. Every morning she rises at 6 A.M., drinks the juice of half a lemon squeezed into a glass of warm water, and then does her morning exercises (much toe-touching, bicycling, stretching, and headstands). Then she washes her face with uncooked oatmeal blended with a little water in the palm of her hand. She never uses soap on her face and when she has used makeup, she removes it with corn or olive oil, followed by witch hazel. For breakfast she has a vitamin cocktail and a slice of her homemade natural bread. During the day she sips herb teas (rose hips and camomile) and vegetable broths of parsley and watercress steeped in hot water, and lunches on a salad. For her large meal, she rarely eats meat, preferring fish or fowl. And what exciting, tasty, healthful compositions she can create from her natural staples! Aunt Alice feels that her dietary habits hold the secret to her extraordinary good health and high energy level. She is indeed the personification of vim and vigor. So are her plants, which are on a special diet as well.

PLANT FOODS

Aunt Alice takes such special care of her plants that one of them, a species of hastatum, which botanists have not known to bloom, surprised everyone with three blossoms. Aside from giving them love, light, water, attention, and conversation, she supplements their nitrogen and phosphate diets with fish and brew. Taking a tip from Indian farmers who, she read, put fish heads in their rows of corn seed for healthy crops, she feeds her plants the ground-up heads, entrails, and tails of fish. They receive about a teaspoon of this mixture added to their soil once a month, as well as this unusual potion:

Aunt Alice's Plant Beverage

½ teaspoon baking soda

½ teaspoon Epsom salts

½ teaspoon saltpeter

¼ teaspoon clear ammonia

½ gallon warm water

Mix all ingredients and shake well. Feed a teaspoonful to plants once a month. Beverage will keep indefinitely.

Three Tips from Aunt Alice:

Always prune plants on the new moon according to the *Farmer's Almanac.*

For apartment dwellers, bean sprouts and chives, so good in salads, are easy to grow in a window box.

Fishbowls hung inside netted shopping bags make attractive plant hangers.

Vitamin Cocktail

People food.

1 cup skim milk	1 teaspoon honey
½ banana	1 teaspoon brewer's yeast
2 strawberries (or other fresh berries)	1 teaspoon liquid vitamin C
1 egg yolk (save white for a facial)	½ teaspoon liquid vitamin E
1 tablespoon wheat germ	Liquid from 1 vitamin A and D capsule

Blend ingredients in a blender. This drink is loaded with energy.

YIELD: 1 SERVING.

Health Bread

1 tablespoon safflower or corn oil	One ¼-ounce package active dry yeast
1 tablespoon butter	¼ cup warm water
1 tablespoon honey	3 cups whole-wheat flour
1 tablespoon molasses	2 cups soy flour or unbleached white flour
1 tablespoon brown sugar	½ cup wheat germ
2¼ teaspoons salt	½ cup bran
1 cup boiling water	
1 cup scalded milk	

Place oil, butter, honey, molasses, brown sugar, and salt in a large mixing bowl. Pour in the boiling water and scalded milk, stir well, and cool until lukewarm. Mix yeast in warm water and add to bowl of lukewarm liquids (hot liquid will kill the rising action of the yeast, so be forewarned). Stir in flours, wheat germ, and bran, blending well until dough is moist but not sticky. Turn it onto a floured board and let it rest for 10 minutes. Then knead, adding more of any flour if necessary, until dough is an elastic and smooth ball. Place in a greased bowl and turn dough so that the whole ball is oiled, then cover bowl with a tea towel and let dough rise in a warm place (70° to 80°)—in direct sunshine, on the top of a TV, near the stove, etc.—until doubled in bulk. This usually takes from 1 to 2 hours, depending on the available heat. After dough has risen, punch it down, sprinkle with flour, and knead slightly on the board, shaping it into 2 loaves. Place dough in 2 greased 8-inch bread pans, cover, and let rise until again doubled in size. This takes from 45 minutes to an hour. Bake in a preheated 350° oven for 45 minutes to 1 hour or until bread is nicely browned and the edges have shrunk from the sides of pans. Remove from pans and cool. This bread, wrapped in heavy foil, will keep in the freezer for up to 3 months. There are few things in life as satisfying as making one's own bread, or as delicious to eat.

YIELD: 2 LOAVES.

Sunshine Sandwich

Cream cheese

1 slice freshly baked Health Bread (see recipe page 109)

Honey

Walnuts or sunflower seeds

Golden seedless raisins

Spread cream cheese on your homemade bread, trickle a little honey over the cheese, and top with nuts or seeds and raisins.

YIELD: 1 SERVING.

Fresh Herb Butter

1 pint heavy cream

1 teaspoon combined chopped fresh chives, parsley, and dill

¼ teaspoon salt

Place cream in a mixing bowl and beat with electric beater until water separates from a solid mass. Pour off the liquid, season the butter with herbs and salt, and spoon into a decorative dish. Excellent served with fresh vegetables, potatoes, or rice.

YIELD: APPROXIMATELY 8 OUNCES.

Aunt Alice's Health Salad

1 head romaine lettuce

1 carrot, shredded

8–10 fresh raw mushrooms, sliced thin

1 zucchini, sliced

1 cucumber, sliced in rounds, then quartered

1 medium avocado, peeled, pitted, and sliced

2 tomatoes, chopped

2 stalks celery, minced

½ pound raw shrimp, cooked and cleaned (optional)

Handful of sunflower seeds

1 red onion, sliced and separated into rings, for garnish

Sea salt to taste

Toss together all but last 3 ingredients. Sprinkle with sunflower seeds. Garnish with onion rings. Serve with a dressing of sunflower oil and apple cider vinegar. Pleasing proportions are 2 parts oil to 1 part vinegar. Season with sea salt to taste.

YIELD: 4 SERVINGS.

Parsley Salad

1 good-size bunch of parsley

12 cherry tomatoes, quartered

¼ cup wheat germ

¼ cup oil and vinegar dressing (see recipe above), or to taste

Sea salt to taste

Wash parsley thoroughly and drain or pat dry. (If the leaves are slightly wilted, freshen by placing them, stems down, in a glass of water in the refrigerator for an hour or longer.) Holding the parsley in a firm bunch, cut across an inch at a time, including stems. Place in a salad bowl. Add cherry tomatoes and sprinkle wheat germ over salad. Add dressing, sea salt, and toss.

YIELD: 2 SERVINGS.

Chilled Fruit Soup

½ cup dried apricots

¼ cup seedless dark raisins

¼ cup seedless golden raisins

2 cups water

1 cinnamon stick

1 quart apple juice

2 cups mixed fresh sliced mangoes,
  nectarines, purple plums,
  strawberries, blueberries, and
  seedless grapes

Place dried fruits in a saucepan with water and cinnamon stick and simmer for 30 minutes or until soft. Then place half this mixture in a blender and puree. Return to saucepan, add apple juice, and re-heat. When fully heated add mixed fruits. Cook for 5 to 8 minutes or until all fruits are soft, then remove from heat. This delicious nectar can be served hot or chilled, as an appetizer or as a dessert.

YIELD: 6 SERVINGS.

Sautéed Vine Vegetables

1 tablespoon butter

1 tablespoon olive oil

1 large onion, sliced

1 small eggplant, sliced, then slices
  quartered

1 medium yellow squash, sliced

1 medium zucchini, sliced

1 green bell pepper, seeded and diced

2 green tomatoes, chopped

1 red tomato, chopped

½ teaspoon ground savory

1 teaspoon chopped fresh basil

Sea salt and pepper to taste

Aunt Alice

In a large skillet heat butter and olive oil. Add onion and sauté until tender. Then add all the remaining vegetables and toss well. Season with savory, basil, salt, and pepper. Sauté over low heat until all vegetables are tender.

YIELD: 6 SERVINGS.

Vegetable Casserole

1 cup thinly sliced carrots

1 cup fresh green bean halves

1 cup peeled, diced white potatoes

½ cup chopped celery

2 medium tomatoes, quartered

1 small yellow squash, sliced

½ small cauliflower, cut into flowerets

½ Bermuda onion, chopped

½ cup chopped red bell pepper

½ cup frozen green peas

½ cup chicken stock

⅓ cup olive oil

2 cloves garlic, minced

1 bay leaf

2 teaspoons salt

1 teaspoon fresh dill

½ teaspoon ground savory

Preheat oven to 350°. Place vegetables in a large ungreased casserole and toss well. Heat chicken stock in a saucepan with remaining ingredients. Bring to a boil and pour over vegetables. Bake for 1 hour, stirring occasionally.

YIELD: 12 SERVINGS.

The Darden Sisters
Aunt Annie

John and Annie Darden
Barnes in front of their home

Annie Darden was the second oldest child and the oldest daughter of Papa and Mama Darden. Much of the family responsibilities fell on her shoulders, and they couldn't have fallen on stronger or more loving ones. She was highly sensitive to the needs of others and treasured harmony and tranquillity above all things. The slightest argument would upset her, and her main concern was that everyone love one another. She was the family peacemaker, and all the problems of the entire group came her way. She offered solutions and never betrayed a confidence—that's how she got her nickname, "Big Chief."

Annie was as mild-mannered as her mother was fiery, yet the two remained exceptionally close. Even after Annie had left the nest—finished college, was working, married, and had children of her own—she lived right across the street from her parents, continuing to help with the dressmaking and the raising of the younger children. Instinctively she seemed to have realized the toll that continual childbearing and hard work had taken on Dianah, and gladly continued in her role as Big Chief.

Her daughters, Thelma and Artelia, and her son, Elroy, tell us that mothering was so deeply ingrained in her that her tenderheartedness, compassion, and affection were not reserved for friends and family alone. For a while the local hospital was next door, creating great agony for Annie, who couldn't bear to hear people in pain. She never became immune to it and was deeply concerned with each new case, taking flowers, soup, and comfort to the patients.

Annie's husband, John Barnes, was a striking contrast to her. She was plump, he was lean; she was talkative, he was a man of few words; she always had a smile on her face, he was known to cast a stern stare. She collected stray cats and dogs; he shooed them away but carefully cultivated prized Rhode Island Red chickens in his backyard. She was an indulgent mother, he is remembered as a strict disciplinarian. Yet this union was one of deep mutual devotion and respect.

John Barnes was a contractor-mason by trade, and he built Uncle C.L.'s and Aunt Norma's house and the A.M.E. Zion Church, which our whole family attended and where he was the violin soloist. These buildings, as well as banks, stores, and other homes in the east Carolina area, are still standing and are visible testimony to his splendid craftsmanship.

Most evenings, as the sun went down, he could be seen sitting on his front porch in his wicker rocker, chewing a little tobacco and giving passing neighbors a terse: "How do." Some may have found John Barnes a bit forbidding, but Annie knew how to please him. The one thing certain to bring a smile to his lips was her wonderful cooking. Meals were always prepared on time, and the menu never failed to include the two items to which John Barnes attributed his stamina and strength—buckwheat pancakes for his early morning breakfast and sweet potatoes for his evening supper.

Aunt Annie's
Buckwheat Cakes

½ cup buckwheat flour

½ cup whole-wheat or unbleached white
flour

2 teaspoons baking powder

¼ teaspoon salt

¾ cup milk

1½ teaspoons blackstrap molasses (we
prefer sweet unsulfured molasses,
though)

1 egg, well beaten

Sift separately and then measure buckwheat and whole-wheat or white flours. Then sift together with baking powder and salt. Add milk and molasses to beaten egg, stirring until well blended. Pour over dry ingredients, blending well. Fry pancakes on a lightly greased hot griddle. When pancakes are puffed full of bubbles and cooked around the edges, turn and cook on the other side. Serve with butter and molasses or maple syrup.

YIELD: 10 MEDIUM-SIZE PANCAKES.

Baked Sweet Potatoes

John Barnes ate a sweet potato in some form every day of his life. Goodness knows, there is nothing tastier than a steaming hot sweet potato with a pat of melting butter.

Sweet potatoes, as desired   Butter

Vegetable oil

Wash potatoes and pat dry. Rub skins with vegetable oil. Bake in a preheated 425° oven for 45 minutes to an hour or more, depending on size. Test for doneness by squeezing, using a potholder, or piercing with a fork. Serve with a pat of butter.

Baked Stuffed
Sweet Potatoes

For the sake of variety, Annie would sometimes stuff her baked sweet potatoes.

1 teaspoon orange or pineapple juice   Bit of crushed pineapple, mashed

Pat of butter   banana, canned or fresh peaches, or

Dash of brown sugar, ground   applesauce

cinnamon, ginger, or nutmeg

To stuff, remove insides of cooked potato. To each mashed sweet potato add your choice of the above ingredients. Restuff the potato shell or, for a more glamorous presentation, place in a half-orange shell and bake for 15 minutes more in the 425° oven.

Sweet Potato Biscuits

2 cups sifted all-purpose flour

3 teaspoons baking powder

½ teaspoon baking soda

¾ teaspoon salt

3 tablespoons brown sugar

½ teaspoon ground cinnamon

½ cup butter

1 cup baked, peeled, mashed sweet
   potato

½ cup buttermilk

Preheat oven to 425°. Sift together dry ingredients in a medium-size bowl. Cut in butter with a pastry blender (or 2 knives) until mixture resembles coarse crumbs. In a small bowl, stir mashed sweet potatoes and buttermilk together until well blended. Pour into dry ingredients and mix until well moistened. Form into a ball and turn out onto a lightly floured board. Lightly pat top side with flour as well, since it is a rather sticky dough. Gently knead 10 to 12 times until the dough holds together and is smooth. While kneading, add small amounts of flour to prevent sticking. Roll out to ½- to ¾-inch thickness with a floured rolling pin. Cut with a floured biscuit cutter. Bake for 12 to 15 minutes or until lightly browned.

YIELD: 12 TO 14 BISCUITS.

The Darden Sisters

Sweet Potato Bread

⅓ cup butter or margarine

¾ to 1¼ cup sugar, depending on
    sweetness of potatoes

2 eggs

½ cup molasses

1 cup cooked, peeled, mashed sweet
    potato

2 cups all-purpose flour

¼ teaspoon baking powder

1 teaspoon baking soda

½ teaspoon salt

½ teaspoon ground cinnamon

½ teaspoon grated nutmeg

½ teaspoon ground allspice

¼ teaspoon ground cloves

¼ cup seedless raisins

¾ cup chopped walnuts

Preheat oven to 350°. Combine butter or margarine, sugar, and eggs. Beat until light and fluffy. Stir in molasses and sweet potatoes. Sift dry ingredients and spices. Add to sweet potato mixture. Add raisins and chopped walnuts. Blend well. Turn into a greased loaf pan (9-×-5-×-3 inches) and bake for 1 hour, or until the edges have pulled away from the sides of the pan and the bread feels firm to the touch in the center. Turn out of pan and cool completely on a baking rack.

YIELD: 1 SWEET POTATO LOAF.

French Fried Sweet Potatoes

Sweet potatoes, as desired

Salt or sugar to taste

Vegetable oil for frying

Peel and cut sweet potatoes into thin strips. Fry in hot fat until crisp, brown, and tender on the inside. Drain on paper towels. Serve hot, either plain or sprinkled with salt or sugar. This is particularly excellent with breakfast as a substitute for grits or hashed brown potatoes.

YIELD: 1 MEDIUM SWEET POTATO SERVES 2 NICELY.

Sweet Potato Puffs

Sweet potatoes, as needed

Brown sugar to taste

Butter to taste

Pecans or walnuts, ground (a little less than ¼ cup per potato)

Boil the potatoes until tender. Peel and mash. Add brown sugar and butter to taste. Form into 1½- to 2-inch balls. Roll each ball in ground nuts until entire surface is covered. Place in a warm oven until ready to use as garnish for a meat or poultry platter.

YIELD: 6 PUFFS PER MEDIUM POTATO.

Sweet Potato Croquettes

4 medium sweet potatoes

3 tablespoons melted butter

1 teaspoon vanilla extract

½ cup chopped black walnuts

1 cup seedless raisins

2 tablespoons brown sugar

1 egg, beaten

1 cup crushed cornflakes

Preheat oven to 350°. Wash potatoes well and boil them in their jackets until tender. Then peel and mash until lump-free. Add melted butter, vanilla, black walnuts, seedless raisins, and brown sugar. Mold into 2-inch croquettes. Dip in beaten egg. Roll in crushed cereal. Place on a buttered baking sheet and bake for 25 minutes or until light brown. Remove croquettes from sheet with a spatula. Delicious served around a beef or pork roast.

YIELD: 8 CROQUETTES.

Sweet Potato Spoon Custard

1 cup mashed, cooked sweet potatoes

2 small bananas, mashed

1 cup milk

2 tablespoons brown sugar

½ teaspoon salt

2 egg yolks, beaten

3 tablespoons seedless raisins

Preheat oven to 300°. Combine mashed sweet potatoes and bananas. Add milk and blend. Add remaining ingredients and mix well. Pour into a well-greased 1-quart casserole. Bake for 45 minutes, until custard is firm and golden brown. Wonderful served with lamb or pork.

YIELD: 6 TO 8 SERVINGS.

Candied Yams

6 medium yams

¾ cup brown sugar

1 teaspoon grated lemon rind

2 tablespoons flour

¼ teaspoon salt

¼ teaspoon ground cinnamon

¼ teaspoon grated nutmeg

4 tablespoons butter

1 cup fresh orange juice

Preheat oven to 350°. Boil yams in their jackets until tender but firm, about 10 minutes. When cool enough to handle, peel and slice in rounds. To the sugar, add grated lemon rind, flour, salt, cinnamon, and nutmeg. Place half the sliced yams in a medium-size casserole dish. Sprinkle with the spiced sugar mixture. Dot with half the butter. Add a second layer of yams, using the rest of the ingredients in the same order as above. Pour orange juice over all and bake for 45 minutes.

YIELD: 4 TO 6 SERVINGS.

Glazed Sweet Potato and Apple Casserole

4 medium sweet potatoes

2 large apples, preferably Macintosh

½ teaspoon salt

2 teaspoons lemon juice

3 tablespoons butter

⅓ cup molasses

¼ cup brown sugar

¼ cup chopped pecans

Preheat oven to 325°. Boil sweet potatoes until tender but still firm and allow them to cool. Then peel, slice, and place in a shallow baking dish. Core and slice the apples, then sprinkle salt and lemon juice over them. In a skillet bring butter to a slow sizzle and toss apple slices around in the pan until slightly soft. Arrange apples with the sweet potatoes. Then add molasses to butter remaining in pan and bring to a boil. Pour over apples and sweet potatoes, coating well. Sprinkle brown sugar and pecans on top. Bake for 30 minutes or until brown and bubbly on top.

YIELD: 4 TO 6 SERVINGS.

Heavenly Hash
Sweet Potato Salad

4 medium sweet potatoes, cooked and
   chilled

¾ cup drained crushed pineapple

¾ cup marshmallows cut into small
   pieces (or use miniatures)

½ cup chopped pecans

¼ cup diced celery

2 tablespoons fresh orange juice

½ cup mayonnaise

Lettuce of choice, as needed

Red cherries, for garnish

Peel chilled sweet potatoes and cut into small cubes. Add pineapple, marshmallows, pecans, and celery. Mix orange juice with mayonnaise, add to salad, and toss gently. Serve on bed of lettuce and top with red cherries.

YIELD: 4 TO 6 SERVINGS.

North Carolina Grated Sweet Potato Pudding

This was our father's favorite dessert from his childhood.

5 cups coarsely grated raw sweet potatoes

¾ cup brown sugar, packed (or up to 1 cup if using fresh coconut)

1½ cups milk

½ cup melted butter

3 eggs, well beaten

¼ teaspoon grated nutmeg

½ teaspoon ground cinnamon

¼ teaspoon ground allspice

¼ teaspoon ground cloves

½ cup seedless raisins

½ cup fresh or prepared shredded coconut

½ cup chopped pecans

1 teaspoon grated orange rind

Preheat oven to 400°. Mix all ingredients together and pour into a buttered, medium-size casserole or skillet. Bake for 50 to 60 minutes. As crust forms around edges during baking, remove from oven and stir pudding well to mix the crust throughout. Do this several times until cooking is finished. Serve warm or cold, plain or topped with whipped cream or ice cream.

YIELD: 8 SERVINGS.

Sweet Potato Pie

3 large eggs

1¼ cups sugar

Dash of salt

1 teaspoon ground cinnamon

½ teaspoon ground allspice

¼ teaspoon grated nutmeg

1 cup heavy cream

3 cups cooked mashed sweet potatoes

1 unbaked 10-inch pie shell (see page 238)

Preheat oven to 350°. Beat eggs well, add sugar, salt, and spices, and mix thoroughly. Add cream and stir. Add mashed potatoes and mix thoroughly. Turn into pie shell and bake for 1 hour or until firm.

YIELD: 8 TO 10 SERVINGS.

Lizzie Darden, still wearing high-school graduation cap, with date, girl friend, and brother C.L. (seated)

Aunt Lizzie

Every large family has its designated "beauty," and in the Darden household that distinction went to Lizzie. Of all the girls, she was the most impetuous, flirtatious, and popular with the boys. She was reputed to be one of the best dancers in the county, and Mama Darden saw to it that she was certainly one of the best dressed. Papa Darden and sons were very protective of Lizzie and discouraged potential gentlemen callers so that she would finish her education.

Lizzie's distinguishing talent was her dramatic recitation of poetry from memory. Her theatrical gestures and well-timed pauses kept her in demand with church groups and women's clubs in Wilson and neighboring towns, who invited her to perform at their teas, testimonials, and concerts. However, Lizzie never contemplated the stage as a career; when it came time to pick an occupation, she chose nursing.

At the suggestion of her brother John, she enrolled in Tuskegee Institute near his home in Alabama. But shortly after graduation, without waiting for the family's stamp of approval, Lizzie eloped.

She had lost her heart to the school's star athlete, Mr. Randall James, a soft-spoken, well-mannered Texan, and the two set out to seek their fortune. Mr. James tried several occupations in several towns before settling in his native Texas as a mortician. Both he and Lizzie were working for a local undertaker in his hometown when they discovered oil on their land. Thoughts of great wealth dazzled them, but large companies had tight control of the oil fields, and several court battles only served to deplete their meager savings.

After a long sickness and many crushed dreams, Mr. James died, leaving Lizzie with two young sons, Randall and Charles, and a daughter, Johnnie K. Learning of her plight, Uncle C.L. sent for her to return to Wilson, where she settled in Papa Darden's house and worked in the funeral parlor as a female attendant. She and her children also sang at funerals.

But Lizzie was never the same. Old Wilsonians barely recognized the lively beauty who had kicked up her heels just twelve years earlier. Eventually she married Mr. Allen Morgan, and again her dreams were dimmed when old World War I injuries caused him to be confined to a wheelchair. When we knew her, Lizzie had turned the old family home into a boardinghouse where she took the best possible care of her Mr. Morgan and her boarders, all of whom she championed as the finest, most sterling citizens Wilson had ever produced (even the ones who were months behind in their rent and the few who left without paying at all). She was always willing to share—perhaps a bit too generously—what little she had.

As Lizzie grew older, the church became the dominant pillar of her life. In the evenings we would see her, hymnal tucked under her arm, rushing off to choir practice (always a little late). She derived great comfort and strength from religion, and even though her life had never matched her hopes and expectations, she remained loving, gentle, and, above all, tolerant of human frailty.

BRUNCH AT AUNT LIZZIE'S

At least once during the summer Aunt Lizzie would have the family over for brunch after church. She was perhaps the slowest cook in the history of the South. Her after-church Sunday brunches seemed to take hours to prepare. Her famished guests grew impatient, but this never seemed to disturb Lizzie's serenity. Humming to herself, she'd float around the kitchen, unaware of time. But, once she got it all together, a fabulous meal was put on the table and, miracle of miracles, everything was hot!

Menu
Fried Chicken or Broiled Chops
*Homemade Sausage
*Fried Apples
Eggs Scrambled with Green Pepper and Onions
Bacon
*Grits Soufflé
*Soda Biscuits
Compote of Peaches and Figs (Direct from Her Backyard) with Cream

*Recipe appears in this chapter.

Fried Apples

4 apples, preferably green   *2 tablespoons butter*

Core the unpeeled apples, then cut into circles or slices. Cook in the butter, turning often, until soft. If you have a sweet tooth or if the apples are bland in flavor, stir in ⅓ cup brown sugar and 2 tablespoons water. Continue cooking until apples are coated with syrup.

YIELD: ABOUT 4 SERVINGS.

Homemade Sausage

2 pounds fresh ground pork butt   *1 teaspoon black pepper*

1 teaspoon ground sage   *1 small red chili pepper, minced, or ¼*

1½ teaspoons salt   *teaspoon cayenne*

Mix and blend all ingredients using your fingers. Shape into 2-inch patties. Fry until crisp and brown on both sides.

YIELD: 16 TO 18 PATTIES.

Grits Soufflé

2 cups cold cooked grits

1¾ cups milk, heated

¼ cup butter

Pinch of salt

4 egg yolks, beaten

4 egg whites, beaten until soft peaks
  form

Preheat oven to 350°. Mash grits with a masher and add heated milk. Blend well, leaving no lumps. Add butter, salt, and egg yolks. Fold in stiffly beaten egg whites. Pour into a medium-size, greased soufflé dish or casserole. Bake for about 45 minutes or until firm in the center.

YIELD: 8 SERVINGS.

Soda Biscuits

2 cups sifted all-purpose flour

2 teaspoons baking powder

½ teaspoon baking soda

½ teaspoon salt

⅓ cup shortening

⅔ cup buttermilk or sour milk (see
  Glossary, p. 326)

Preheat oven to 450°. Sift flour again with dry ingredients. Cut shortening into flour mixture until fine. Add enough milk to make a soft dough. Turn onto a floured board. Knead dough slightly 10 to 12 times. Roll ½-inch thick. Cut with a small floured biscuit cutter. Place on an ungreased baking sheet and bake for 12 to 14 minutes or until lightly golden.

YIELD: 12 TO 15 BISCUITS.

Sausage Biscuits

1 recipe Soda Biscuit dough (see above)

½ pound soft pork sausage meat

Preheat oven to 450°. Roll out biscuit dough in 1 piece to ¼-inch thickness. Spread on a thin layer of sausage. Roll up as you would for a jelly roll. Slice ½-inch thick. Place on a lightly greased pan and bake for 15 minutes.

YIELD: 15 TO 18 BISCUITS.

MORE BRUNCH FAVORITES FROM AUNT LIZZIE'S KITCHEN

Sweet Milk Griddle Cakes

3 cups sifted all-purpose flour

3 teaspoons baking powder

½ teaspoon salt

¼ cup sugar

¼ teaspoon ground cinnamon

3 eggs

2 cups milk

3 tablespoons melted butter

Sift flour 3 more times together with the baking powder, salt, sugar, and cinnamon. Beat eggs, add milk, and pour slowly into the dry ingredients. Beat thoroughly and add butter. Drop by spoonfuls onto a lightly greased hot griddle. When puffed full of bubbles and cooked on edges, turn and cook on other side.

YIELD: 2 DOZEN SMALL OR 1 DOZEN LARGE GRIDDLE CAKES.

VARIATION:

For blueberry pancakes, add a cup or more of washed, stemmed blueberries to the batter.

Pecan Waffles

2 cups sifted all-purpose flour

3 teaspoons baking powder

2 teaspoons sugar

½ teaspoon salt

¼ teaspoon cinnamon

3 eggs, separated

1¼ cups milk

¼ cup melted butter

¼ cup finely chopped pecans

Sift the dry ingredients together. Beat the egg yolks lightly and mix with the milk. Add to flour mixture, beating until smooth. Stir in melted butter, and gently fold in stiffly beaten egg whites. Add pecans. Bake in a hot and lightly greased waffle iron.

YIELD: 6 WAFFLES.

Banana Doughnuts

2 cups all-purpose flour

2 teaspoons baking powder

½ teaspoon baking soda

½ teaspoon salt

2 tablespoons vegetable shortening such
as Crisco

⅓ cup granulated sugar

1 egg

¼ cup buttermilk

1 medium ripe banana, mashed

⅛ teaspoon each of ground nutmeg and
cinnamon, or mace and cloves

½ teaspoon vanilla extract

Vegetable fat, for frying

Confectioners' sugar

Sift together dry ingredients. Beat shortening until creamy, then add sugar and beat until light. Add egg and beat in well. Then add buttermilk, banana, spices, and vanilla, and blend. Put onto a floured board, knead lightly 6 to 8 times, and roll to ½-inch thickness. Cut dough with a floured 2½-inch doughnut cutter. Fry in hot 2-inch-deep oil for 2 to 3 minutes, turning frequently until nicely browned. Drain on paper towels, and dust with confectioners' sugar.

YIELD: 1 DOZEN DOUGHNUTS AND HOLES.

Fruit Fritters

1 cup all-purpose flour

1½ teaspoons baking powder

2 tablespoons granulated sugar

½ teaspoon salt

1 egg

½ cup milk

1 tart apple, pared, cored, and cut into
    6 sections

1 peach, peeled and sliced

1 orange, sectioned

1 banana, sliced

Handful of pitted cherries, grapes, or
    prunes

1 pear, peeled and sliced

Vegetable oil, for frying

Confectioners' sugar

Grated nutmeg

Mix and sift dry ingredients. Beat egg with milk, add dry ingredients, and mix well. Then dip individual pieces of fruit into the batter and coat evenly. Fry in deep hot oil until brown. Drain on paper towels and sprinkle with powdered sugar and nutmeg. Best served as a dessert for brunch or dinner.

YIELD: 6 TO 8 SERVINGS.

Lizzie's little nieces loved "short'nin', short'nin',"
Lizzie's little nieces loved short'nin' cakes.

Shortcakes

2 cups all-purpose flour

4 teaspoons baking powder

1 teaspoon salt

2½ tablespoons soft brown sugar

⅓ cup vegetable shortening or butter

⅔ cup light cream

1 tablespoon melted butter

1½ quarts combined strawberries or
   raspberries mixed with blueberries
   and sliced peaches

Granulated sugar to taste

Whipped cream, for topping

Preheat oven to 425°. Mix and sift flour, baking powder, salt, and brown sugar. Cut in shortening with a knife or rub into batter with fingertips. Add light cream gradually, mixing to a soft dough. Roll out on a lightly floured board to slightly over ½-inch thickness. Cut 12 circles with a large biscuit cutter. Place 6 circles in a lightly buttered pan or on a cookie sheet. Brush with melted butter and top with the remaining 6 circles. Bake for 15 minutes. Then let the shortcakes cool slightly, remove the top half, and put the fruit, sweetened with sugar to taste, in any combination of your choice between the halves and on top of the cakes. Make sure the fruit has lots of juice. (Add a little orange juice if it doesn't.) Top with a dot of whipped cream.

YIELD: 6 SHORTCAKES.

NOTE: *The same shortcakes can be used with creamed meat or fish filling, omitting the brown sugar.*

Artelia Darden Tennessee
with husband Jessie

Aunt Artelia

Artelia was the youngest Darden girl and the spunkiest. Independence and individuality were always important to her. As a child, she was considered a tomboy since she favored male companionship, enjoyed playing games, and was especially good at baseball.

Always eager to keep up with her brothers, she bravely accepted all their challenges. Once she smoked ten of Arthur's cigarettes in a row, silently suffering the resulting headaches and dizziness for the sake of the backslapping and congratulations she won. Uncle J.B. taught her how to play cards, and she played casino and whist with gusto and abandon, usually winning. Of course these were secret activities, which took place in the back of the shed, for not even Artelia would have dared to smoke or play cards in Papa Darden's house!

Artelia inherited her mother's staunch pride. When she was seven, a new minister in town stopped by her father's store and requested that she deliver some string beans to his home at a later time. However, when she arrived he refused to let her in the front door and ordered her to go around to the back. Many seven-year-olds would have been intimidated into obeying this order from a man of the cloth, but Artelia never cared much about public opinion. She knew she'd been insulted, and she marched home, taking the beans with her.

Like her mother and sisters, Artelia was an excellent seamstress and milliner, but, unlike them, she was never fond of studying. She valiantly struggled through college to please the family and went on to teach elementary school, but she was quite relieved to marry Jessie Tennessee, a blacksmith, and move to Phoebus, Virginia. Everyone held their breath, waiting to see if the former tomboy would be able to cook and keep house. And Artelia had quite a surprise for them—she was not only a housekeeper, but a most inventive cook with a knack for making anything taste good.

Some years later Artelia "surprised" the Darden family once again. She announced her decision to divorce Jessie and remain in Phoebus. At a time when widowed or divorced women took their children and moved back to their parents' home, Artelia characteristically chose to remain where she was. Her romance had been stormy, but after their marital rift, Artelia and Jessie became good friends. Neither remarried and when both were advanced in years, he was still known to accompany her to her lodge meetings and Friday-night card games. Artelia remained very close to her children, Butch, Eugene, and little Artelia, throughout her life, and they remember that she loved to bake and would sing and hum in the kitchen. When they heard her sing out, "Take two and butter them while they're hot," they knew it meant she had prepared one of her best breads. Muffins, biscuits, and fruit loaves were her specialties, and one thing is for sure—no one could stop at just two.

Tea Biscuits

3 medium potatoes, peeled and cut up

2 tablespoons melted lard

½ cup melted butter

⅓ cup sugar

1½ teaspoons salt

1¼ cups milk

1 yeast cake, or one ¼-ounce package
  active dry yeast

1 whole egg plus 1 egg yolk, beaten

6–7 cups all-purpose flour

Boil and finely mash potatoes. Add melted lard, butter, sugar, and salt. Scald milk, then cool to tepid. Dissolve yeast in milk. Add beaten egg and yolk and stir into potato mixture. Then gradually add the flour. Knead 8 to 10 minutes and place in a large greased bowl. Cover with a tea towel, set in a warm place, and allow to rise. When doubled in bulk, remove to a floured board and work into a smooth dough, kneading lightly. Roll out dough about ½-inch thick and cut with a small biscuit cutter. Brush each biscuit with additional melted butter and put in buttered pans. Cover with a tea towel, place in a warm spot, and let rise until doubled in bulk. Preheat oven to 425°. Bake biscuits for 12 to 15 minutes or until golden. These are delicious. Take two and butter them while they're hot!

YIELD: ABOUT 3 DOZEN BISCUITS.

Artelia's Plain Biscuits

3 cups sifted all-purpose flour

3 teaspoons baking powder

1 tablespoon sugar (optional)

¾ teaspoon salt

½ cup butter

Approximately ¾ cup milk

1 egg, well beaten

Preheat oven to 400°. Sift dry ingredients together. Then, using a pastry blender or two knives, cut in butter. Combine milk and egg and slowly add to flour until mixture is wet enough to hold together. Turn onto a floured board. Knead, then roll to ½-inch thickness and cut with a biscuit cutter. Bake for 10 to 12 minutes or until lightly golden.

YIELD: ABOUT 2 DOZEN BISCUITS.

"Sure Nuff Down-Home Cracklin'" Bread

Cracklings are made from the crisp brown skin of ham rind or pork fat. To make your own cracklings, cut rind or fat into small pieces. Place them in a skillet and fry as you would bacon, until all the fat is removed and the remaining pieces are brown and crisp. The same can be done with the skin of a chicken.

2 cups cornmeal

½ teaspoon salt

½ teaspoon soda

1 cup diced cracklings

1 cup buttermilk

Preheat oven to 425°. Sift the dry ingredients together and, using your hands, rub in the cracklings. Then stir in the buttermilk. The batter will be stiff. Shape into 6 round or oblong loaves and put on a greased baking sheet, or use a 9-x-9-inch greased baking pan. Bake for 30 minutes or until lightly golden and firm to the touch. Serve hot.

YIELD: 8 SMALL LOAVES.

Hush Puppies

2 cups white cornmeal

1 teaspoon baking powder

1 medium onion, chopped fine

1 cup milk, more if needed

½ teaspoon salt

2 eggs, well beaten

Vegetable oil, for frying

Mix all ingredients to the consistency of very thick pancake batter. Drop by rounded teaspoonfuls into deep hot oil. Fry until golden brown. Serve hot with fried fish or chicken.

YIELD: 8 TO 10 HUSH PUPPIES.

Blueberry Muffins

2 cups sifted all-purpose flour

¼ cup sugar

3 teaspoons baking powder

½ teaspoon salt

⅓ cup melted butter

1 egg, lightly beaten

1 teaspoon vanilla extract

1 cup milk

1 teaspoon grated orange zest

1 cup fresh blueberries

Preheat oven to 400°. Combine sifted flour with dry ingredients and sift twice again. Stir melted butter, beaten egg, and vanilla into milk. Add to flour mixture along with the orange zest and blueberries, stirring just enough to moisten. Batter should look lumpy. Fill greased muffin cups two thirds full. Bake for 20 minutes or until golden brown.

YIELD: 10 TO 12 MUFFINS.

Peach or Apricot Muffins

2 cups sifted all-purpose flour

3 teaspoons baking powder

¼ teaspoon baking soda

¼ teaspoon ground nutmeg

¼ teaspoon ground allspice

1 egg, beaten

½ cup brown sugar, firmly packed

⅓ cup melted butter

¾ cup milk or sour cream

⅔ cup peeled and chopped fresh ripe peaches or apricots, then mashed with a fork

1 teaspoon vanilla extract

Preheat oven to 400°. Combine sifted flour with dry ingredients in a large-size bowl. In a medium-size bowl, stir together beaten egg, brown sugar, melted butter, milk or sour cream, mashed peaches or apricots, and vanilla. Add to flour mixture, stirring just enough to moisten. Stir only until mixed. Batter should look lumpy. Fill greased muffin cups two thirds full. Bake for 20 minutes or until golden brown.

YIELD: 10 TO 12 MUFFINS.

Pecan Muffins

MUFFIN BATTER:

1 cup sifted whole-wheat flour

1 cup sifted all-purpose flour

4 teaspoons baking powder

½ teaspoon salt

1 cup milk

3 tablespoons chopped pecans

½ teaspoon ground cinnamon

⅓ cup honey

2 eggs, beaten

⅓ cup melted butter

1 teaspoon vanilla extract

TOPPING:

3 tablespoons sugar

¼ teaspoon ground cinnamon

½ cup chopped pecans

Preheat oven to 400°. To prepare batter: Combine sifted flours with baking powder and salt and sift twice more. Scald milk. Stir in cinnamon and honey. Let cool to room temperature. Stir in beaten eggs, melted butter, and vanilla. Add to the flour mixture, stirring just enough to moisten. Add chopped pecans. Stir only until mixed. Mixture should look lumpy. Fill greased muffin cups two thirds full. To prepare topping: Combine the sugar, pecans, and cinnamon in a small bowl. Sprinkle each muffin with some of the mixture, pressing it lightly into the batter. Bake for 20 minutes or until golden brown.

YIELD: 10 TO 12 MUFFINS.

Raisin Bread

1 cup applesauce

¼ cup melted butter

1 egg, beaten

½ cup granulated sugar

¼ cup brown sugar, packed

2 cups all-purpose flour

2 teaspoons baking powder

¾ teaspoon salt

½ teaspoon baking soda

1 teaspoon ground cinnamon

1 teaspoon grated nutmeg

¾ cup seedless raisins

¾ cup chopped walnuts

Preheat oven to 350°. Combine applesauce, butter, egg, and sugars in a bowl. Blend well. Sift other dry ingredients (including cinnamon and nutmeg) together and stir into applesauce mixture until smooth. Add raisins and chopped nuts. Turn into a well-greased 9-×-5-×-3-inch loaf pan. Bake for 1 hour, or until the edges shrink from the sides of the pan and the bread is nicely browned. Serve plain or toasted, with butter or cream cheese.

Banana-Nut Bread

2½ cups sifted all-purpose flour

1 tablespoon baking powder

½ teaspoon salt

¼ cup softened butter

1 cup sugar

1 egg, beaten

1 cup mashed ripe bananas

1 tablespoon grated lemon rind

½ cup milk

1 teaspoon vanilla extract

1 cup chopped walnuts

Preheat oven to 350°. Sift dry ingredients together. Cream butter, gradually adding sugar, then add the egg. Beat until smooth. Add bananas, lemon rind, milk, and vanilla. Add flour mixture. Stir until blended. Then add nuts. Pour into a greased 9-×-5-×-3-inch loaf pan. Bake for 1 hour. Cool for 10 minutes in the loaf pan, then remove and cool completely on a wire rack. This bread is even better the second day.

YIELD: 1 LOAF.

Spoonbread and Strawberry Wine

146

Cranberry-Nut Tea Cake

1½ cups halved fresh cranberries

½ cup confectioners' sugar

2 cups all-purpose flour, sifted

1½ teaspoons baking powder

½ teaspoon baking soda

½ teaspoon salt

¾ cup sugar

¼ cup softened butter, plus extra melted
     butter for topping

1 egg, lightly beaten

¾ cup fresh orange juice

1 teaspoon grated orange zest

½ cup chopped walnuts

Preheat oven to 350°. Combine halved cranberries and powdered sugar in a small bowl and let stand. Sift flour, baking powder, baking soda, and salt together. Then beat sugar, butter, and egg until smooth. Gradually add flour mixture, alternating with orange juice. Blend until smooth. Add cranberry mixture, zest, and nuts. Place in a lightly greased 9-×-5-×-3-inch loaf pan and bake for 50 minutes to 1 hour, or until lightly browned and the sides have pulled away from the pan. When done, remove from pan and brush with melted butter.

YIELD: 1 TEA CAKE.

"Bud"—
Walter T. Darden

Our father, Walter Theodore Darden (affectionately called "Bud"), like the song says, has been a lot of places and seen a lot of things, and has the gift of knowing how to share his experiences. He is a consummate teller of tales (tall and real). His one-man dramas, told in a deep, sonorous voice, and replete with the facial expressions, body gestures, and vocal mannerisms of all the characters, have unfolded on the screens of our minds and kept us laughing as long as we can remember. Bud's is the story of four towns: Wilson, North Carolina, and Opelika, Alabama, where he grew up; Tuskegee, Alabama, where he tried to settle; and Newark, New Jersey, where he did settle.

CULTURE AND HIGH DRAMA
IN WILSON

That Bud was a busy kid. As the youngest child in his large family, he was practically smothered with attention, errands, and jobs. He claims that Mama Darden kept him too dressed up for his taste and that his sisters babied him, while Papa Darden kept him hopping—trimming caskets, selling items in their store, and peddling records and sheet music for his older brother C.L. Perhaps this is why the Chautauqua stands out in his memories. Every summer he was excused from chores when this variety show from far-off New York City came to town. He remembers the high spirits and excitement in small-town Wilson when a large striped tent was erected to house the prominent personalities who participated in the plays, operas, lectures, and acts that comprised each weeklong Chautauqua. "Even the most offensive bigots lost their diabolical sting at that time of year when the town got 'culture,'" he says. Once John Philip Sousa's Marching Band appeared. Bud left that show vowing to become a famous bandleader.

The good feelings the traveling Chautauqua generated were short-lived in 1911. For off a freight train and into Wilson came the well-known and feared black outlaw, Louis West, and his band of desperadoes. They had pulled many daring robberies and, although their actions were deplored by some, they had become underground black folk heroes, on the order of Jesse James and Robin Hood. Word leaked out to the sheriff that Louie was resting up in Wilson, so he and a posse rushed over to their hideout. Louie demanded to see a search warrant, and a shoot-out ensued. When the smoke cleared, the sheriff was mortally wounded. While making their getaway, Louie and his gang were apprehended and jailed. Most Wilson blacks stayed off the streets, fearing reprisals. Bud didn't. He even skipped school to hear Louie's lawyer give an impassioned plea for mercy, to see Louie stoically stand to hear himself sentenced to the electric chair, and Shorty, his sidekick, and the rest of the gang get life. Mama Darden told him to forget the saga of Louie West's defiance and get back to school. She packed his favorite sweet potato biscuits in his lunch pail, but schoolboy Bud was pondering justice and courtroom drama and had decided to become a lawyer instead of a bandleader.

"Bud"—Walter T. Darden

DIVERSIONS IN OPELIKA

After the death of his mother, Bud was sent to live for a while with his oldest brother, John, and his wife, Maude, in Opelika, Alabama. From then on, he divided his time between those two towns. He says that Opelika, a rural town, was more spread out and less populated than Wilson. His routine consisted of a ride by pony to Miss Parish's one-room schoolhouse and then on to John's drugstore for his soda-jerking duties. Excitement was rare; there was no Chautauqua to look forward to. The only annual event Bud remembers at all was Sheriff Moon's Bar-B-Que. It was a two-day affair: the first day for the whites, the second for the "coloreds." Sheriff Moon, he says, was known for his ten-gallon yellow Stetson hat; his red neck; the colorful, long, glistening pearl-handled pistols he carried on each hip; and his general meanness. But his picnic was always a big hit. He served enough food to last the average person a week. Every meat that could be barbecued—squirrel, deer, bird, raccoon, opossum, bear, fish—in short, anything that could swim, fly, or crawl was dumped into barbecue sauce. Bud claims that bicarbonate of soda actually saved his life after such an outing.

Saturday night was Opelika's one time to come alive. All the farmers came to town to get supplies, exchange news, let off steam, and live it up. Bud's arms would be tired at the end of the day from scooping out tutti-frutti ice-cream cones. (That was the most popular flavor for those who were not knocked out from the moonshine that flowed freely from Mason's Shoeshine Parlour around the corner.) Sometimes things got rough. One summer evening when Bud was fourteen, a very beautiful and voluptuous woman many years his senior requested that he deliver some ice cream to her home. Once there, she suggested that he stay and play the phonograph for some guests she was expecting. The guests never arrived, so Bud left. Later it was discovered that a paramour of the lady in question had seen Bud's entrance, clocked the time of his exit, and was plot-

Bud Darden and friend Bud Vick in front of family business

ting his demise. This was his first brush with the intense and often irrational passion that pervaded those hot Saturday nights.

Fortunately, it was time for him to return to high school at Livingston in North Carolina, so he was removed from harm's way.

Like his brothers John and J.B., Bud decided to become a physician and, like them, he held a bevy of jobs to get himself through medical school, which for him was Howard University, in Washington, D.C.

ARTISANS AND THE KLAN IN TUSKEGEE, ALABAMA

Degree in hand, Bud returned to Alabama. "For the grand sum of eight dollars a month, I accepted an internship at John Andrews Hospital in Tuskegee, which was an oasis of black self-sufficiency. One could purchase anything from a house to a pair of shoes that had been made by the hands of black artisans."

Bud might have stayed in Tuskegee had it not been for a local white doctor who, as fate would have it, was a Klan leader. The Klan doctor had wrongly diagnosed a child's fractured arm and sent the child away with only a bandage. Bud put a cast on the child's arm. "Professional pride" forced the Klansman to demand Dr. Darden's immediate departure from town. At first our father rejected the idea, but Brother John, with his sixth sense, encouraged him to go north. It was arranged for him to join Dr. John A. Kenney, who had left under similar forced circumstances and who had opened a hospital in Newark, New Jersey.

Bud during his Atlantic City bellboy days

"Bud"—Walter T. Darden

WORK, MARRIAGE, AND OTHER PURSUITS IN NEWARK, NEW JERSEY

Bud and Jean vacationing in the Caribbean

In a two-tone Nash (yes, his style as well as his skills was too flamboyant for the Klan!) Dr. Bud arrived in Newark to establish his career. His salary at the hospital was $1,800 a year; the days began at 7 A.M., often ending after 11 P.M. He learned a lot from Dr. Kenney, and then decided to open his own office. Among his first patients was a woman who had not walked for years because of a crippling arthritic condition. Four hefty men brought her to his office. She had a fear of needles and began thrashing around, nearly crushing Bud when he tried to give her an injection. To quiet her, and perhaps to protect himself, he said unthinkingly, "Be still so you'll get well and walk." She took him at his word and walked into the waiting room, shocking the four hefty fellows. The power of suggestion might have been at play here, but the story spread and certainly didn't harm his beginning practice.

Bud felt that he didn't have time for marriage and swore he would remain a bachelor like his debonair brother Charles in Los Angeles. However, his brother J.B. in Petersburg, Virginia, introduced him to a lovely schoolteacher, Mamie Jean Sampson. Shortly after they met, she took a job as a community social worker in Buffalo, New York, so weekends found Walter T., the confirmed bachelor, taking a long train ride to visit her. They married and, after honeymooning in Cuba, settled in on the floor above his office, and eventually had us.

Life with Father has never been dull. He has attained some of his boyhood ambitions. He didn't become a bandleader, but for a while he was quite an impresario, bringing to Newark the big bands of Count Basie and Benny Goodman, presenting fashion shows, entertainers, and celebrities (Lionel Hampton, Sammy Davis, Jr., Billy Eckstine, and Sarah Vaughn) for the benefit of various educational, civic, and civil rights groups. He didn't become a lawyer, but he appeared in court as a medical consultant and added a dash of drama to the courtroom scene. Lately, new talents have surfaced. Cosmopolitan Bud has succumbed to a tug back to his Southern heritage and created a garden in his backyard. On weekends one can find him preparing unique concoctions from his homegrown produce or old-time family favorites, such as his version of Papa Darden's Grape Wine, using grapes from his own vines. Every Fourth of July when the garden is in full swing, he gives a picnic for friends, neighbors, and relatives, usually totaling over fifty people. Everyone pitches in, either bringing a dish or setting up the games, picnic tables, and lawn umbrellas. At the end of the day everyone is well fed and exhausted. Bud's chapter is therefore divided into his picnic menus, weekend concoctions, and old-time favorites.

Strolling on the boardwalk in Atlantic City, Bud and Mamie Jean with friends Charlotte Kyle and Marie Kellar

Bud's Fourth-of-July Bash
*Roast Suckling Pig
*Fried Chicken
*Barbecued Spareribs
*Charcoal-broiled Flank or Shell Steak
*Corn on the Cob
*Greens (Collard or Mixed)
String Beans (see page 251)
*Potato Salad or Macaroni and Shrimp Salad
*Jubilee Salad
*Deviled Eggs
*Garlic French Bread
Ice-Cold Watermelon
Homemade Tutti-Frutti Ice Cream (see page 47)
Coconut Cake (see page 242)
*Strawberry Wine Punch
Assorted Sodas and Cold Beer

*Recipe appears in this chapter.

"Bud"—Walter T. Darden

TIPS FOR PICNICS

Steaks: Sprinkle on garlic powder, salt, pepper, and onion salt. Squeeze fresh lemon juice on both sides; this is an excellent tenderizer. Grill over slow-burning coals for 5 to 10 minutes on each side to make a nice medium steak.

Corn on the cob: Shuck corn and remove silk. Cover with cold salted water. Add a little milk, to sweeten corn. When water boils corn is done.

Garlic French bread: Make deep slits across loaves of French bread. Butter each side with softened butter and sprinkle with garlic powder or 1 large clove of garlic, finely minced, per loaf. Wrap in tin foil and heat on top of grill or in moderate oven for 15 minutes.

Jubilee salad: Add fresh-cooked or drained canned corn kernels, sliced cucumbers, and shoestring beets to mixed salad greens and toss with oil and vinegar dressing and seasonings (count on 5 to 7 heads of lettuce for 50 people).

Strawberry Wine punch: Pour 2 bottles of Strawberry Wine (see page 10), or 1 1.5 liter bottle of a dry white wine with 1 cup of strawberry liqueur over a chunk of ice in a large punch bowl. Add a splash of club soda and whole strawberries as a garnish.

Roast Suckling Pig
(Outdoor)

This is a recipe that does not lend itself to strict directions and will require some experimentation on your part. Much depends upon the size of your grilling equipment and what size pig it can accommodate. With the help of a good friend, we made our own grill out of a 50-gallon metal oil drum. The drum was cut in half, hinged together, punctured with air holes, and mounted on a sturdy stand. Coals were placed in the bottom, a grating placed in the middle, and the pig placed on it.

Another method for roasting a pig is to dig a hole in the ground to accommodate hot coals. Cover the hole with some kind of metal grating, and place the pig on top of that.

Now for preparation of the pig itself!

1 suckling pig (allow 1 pound per person)
White vinegar

Salt and pepper to taste
Barbecue sauce

Have pig split in half for faster cooking time. Wash thoroughly and pat dry. Using your hands, rub the outside and the inside cavity with vinegar and a liberal amount of salt and pepper. Let stand for 12 hours in the refrigerator. Begin heating coals about 30 minutes before placing pig on the grill. For added flavor, mix hickory chips with the coals. Place the grill at least 10 to 12 inches from burning coals. Place pig on the grill so that it is opened flat, skin side down. Turn pig every 20 to 25 minutes for even cooking. In terms of cooking time, allow not less than 25 minutes to the pound. In the last two hours of cooking, baste with barbecue sauce. Basting too soon can

"Bud"—Walter T. Darden

cause the pig to burn. The best way to test for doneness is to explore the pig's inner cavity for any pink spots. The pig must be served well done. Fortunately, it is almost impossible to overcook a pig. We found this out the hard way when our first attempt, a 35-pound pig, caught fire when placed too near the coals and cooked in 4 hours instead of 10. It appeared to be a disaster, but much to our surprise, it turned out to be delicious anyhow. So give it a try! There's enough room to make mistakes and still produce a success. Garnish the pig by placing an apple in its mouth and cherries in the eyes.

Fried Chicken for 4

Norma Jean's specialty.

One 2½- to 3-pound chicken, cut into serving pieces

Salt and pepper to suit taste

One 3-pound can solid vegetable shortening

IN A BROWN PAPER OR PLASTIC BAG PLACE:

1 cup flour

1 teaspoon paprika

1 teaspoon dry mustard

¾ teaspoon grated nutmeg

½ teaspoon garlic powder

½ teaspoon cayenne pepper

1 teaspoon salt or to taste

Wash the chicken pieces in cold water, leaving some moisture. Sprinkle with salt and pepper. Place a few pieces of chicken at a time in bag and shake until evenly coated. Melt the vegetable shortening in a Dutch oven or large skillet. If fat sizzles when a drop of water hits it, drop in the coated chicken pieces. Fry until golden brown, then drain on paper towels.

Fried Chicken Gravy

Strain 2 tablespoons of the shortening used to fry chicken in a skillet. Add 2 tablespoons flour. Stir over medium heat until brown. Add salt and pepper to taste and ¾ cup milk or cream, stirring continuously until it thickens. Pour over chicken, rice, or potatoes.

Fried Chicken for 50

When frying chicken for 50, use 12 chickens. Be sure to change the frying fat at least 3 times, since the crumbs at the bottom of the kettle will burn and eventually affect the flavor. Mix the flour coating in the small amount indicated in the above recipe so that it won't become gummy, and repeat as needed. Use 2 large kettles, so you can fry several pieces at a time.

Cousins Kelly and Artelia Bryant's Barbecued Spareribs

We allow 3 ribs per person, since we serve other meats as well.

FOR 4 TO 6:		FOR 50:
4 pounds	spareribs	30 pounds
¼ cup	white vinegar	1½ cups
½ cup	water	3 cups
2 tablespoons	brown sugar	¾ cup
1 tablespoon	prepared mustard	6 tablespoons
1½ teaspoons	salt	3 tablespoons
½ teaspoon	black pepper	1 tablespoon
¼ teaspoon	cayenne pepper	1½ teaspoons
1 whole	lemon, juiced, or 2 tablespoons bottled lemon juice	6 lemons or ¾ cup
1 whole	onion, chopped	6
½ cup	ketchup	3 cups
2 tablespoons	Worcestershire sauce	¾ cup
2 tablespoons	butter (optional)	1 stick
1½ teaspoons	liquid smoke (optional)	3 tablespoons
½ cup	crushed pineapple, drained (optional)	3 cups
Splash of	beer	One 12-ounce can

Place spareribs in a roasting pan, cover with tin foil, and bake in a preheated 425° oven for 45 minutes. Mix vinegar, water, brown sugar, mustard, salt, pepper, cayenne, lemon juice, onion, and ketchup, and bring to a boil. Lower heat and simmer for 20 minutes in an uncovered pan. Add Worcestershire sauce and any of the optional items you wish. After 45 minutes, pour off excess grease from ribs, pour on half the barbecue sauce, and reduce heat to 350°. Baste with additional sauce and bake covered for 40 minutes longer. Uncover and continue baking for 20 minutes or until ribs are nicely browned and fork tender. To grill, marinate the prebaked ribs for 1 hour or longer in the sauce, place on grill, and turn frequently over slow coals until fork tender, basting occasionally.

Mixed Greens

Bud eats greens every day, so he always makes them in quantity and reheats them during the week. For the picnic, he doubles the proportions.

2 ham hocks, or 1½ pounds salt pork

2 quarts water

5 pounds mustard greens

5 pounds turnip greens (with the small turnips attached to the greens, peeled and quartered)

Salt and pepper to taste

Boil ham or salt pork in water for about 1 hour. In the meantime, prepare greens, removing damaged parts and stems. Wash 3 or 4 times or until rinse water is clear. The leaves of mustard and turnips are fairly small and do not require cutting before cooking. Instead, add whole leaves, turnips, and seasoning to the boiling water; cover and cook rapidly, about 25 minutes or until tender. When done, cut greens with a knife and two-pronged fork while still in pot. Ham hocks or salt pork can be eaten or discarded.

YIELD: 12 TO 15 SERVINGS.

Collard Greens

1½ quarts water

1 teaspoon crushed red pepper

1½ pounds pork neck bones, or 2 ham hocks

About 8 pounds collards

2 teaspoons sugar

½ cup cider or white vinegar

Salt and pepper to taste

Place water in a large pot. Add red pepper and bones or hocks and simmer for about 1 hour while preparing greens. To prepare greens, discard damaged or yellow parts of leaves. Cut away tough stems from each leaf and wash collards thoroughly until rinse water is clear of dirt and grit. Collard leaves are large and usually require cutting before cooking. To do so, fold leaf in half at its center vein, fold over once or twice, then cut in half with scissors or a knife. Add remaining ingredients to bones in boiling water, then the greens. Cover and cook rapidly for about 30 minutes or until greens are tender but firm. Best served with diced raw onions and vinegar.

YIELD: 16 SERVINGS.

NOTE: *The liquid in which greens have been cooked is called "pot liquor." It is renowned for its nutritional value and can be used as an excellent vegetable stock for soups, as a soup in its own right, or, traditionally, to dunk corn bread. Pot liquor can be enriched by tying several mustard and turnip stems in a bunch and cooking them with the greens. Discard stems when the greens are done.*

Cousin Johnnie K.'s Macaroni and Shrimp Salad

FOR 6:

		FOR 50:
8 ounces	macaroni	Three 16-ounce packages
½ cup	diced celery	3 cups
½ cup	chopped onion	3 cups
¼ cup	chopped green bell pepper	1½ cups
1 pound	small shrimp, cooked and shelled	6 pounds
½ cup	mayonnaise	3 cups or more
	Salt and pepper to taste	
	Pimentos, for garnish	
	Paprika, for garnish	

Add 1 tablespoon salt to 4 quarts rapidly boiling water for each pound of macaroni. Add macaroni and cook, uncovered, until tender, stirring occasionally. Drain and rinse in cold water. Toss vegetables, shrimp, and mayonnaise thoroughly with macaroni. Season with salt and pepper, and garnish with pimentos and paprika.

"Bud"—Walter T. Darden

Potato Salad

Carole makes a glorious potato salad.

FOR 6:		FOR 50:
6	medium potatoes	Four 5-pound bags
2 teaspoons	salt	5½ tablespoons
¼ teaspoon	paprika	2 tablespoons
¼ teaspoon	dry mustard	2 tablespoons
5 tablespoons	salad oil	2½ cups
2 tablespoons	apple cider vinegar	1¾ cups
2	eggs, hard-cooked and chopped	20
1 small	onion, coarsely chopped or grated	5 medium
½ cup	diced celery	4 cups
½ cup	mayonnaise	3½ cups
1 tablespoon	prepared mustard	½ cup
1 tablespoon	pickle relish	½ cup
1 teaspoon or more	celery salt	3 tablespoons or more
	Pimento, stuffed olives, green pepper rings, for garnish	

Boil potatoes in their jackets until tender. Cool, peel, and cut into coarse chunks. In a small bowl mix the salt, paprika, dry mustard, salad oil, and vinegar. Stir this into the potatoes, mixing lightly. Chill for several hours. Then add the chopped eggs, grated onion, and celery. Stir in mayonnaise, prepared mustard, and pickle relish. Season liberally with celery salt. Garnish with pimento, stuffed olives, and green pepper rings.

Carole's Deviled Eggs

FOR 4:		FOR 50:
5	eggs, hard-cooked	30
2 tablespoons	mayonnaise	¾ cup
1½ teaspoons	prepared mustard	3 tablespoons
1½ teaspoons	apple cider vinegar	3 tablespoons
1 teaspoon	lemon juice	2 tablespoons
	Salt and pepper to taste	
	Paprika to taste	

Peel hard-cooked eggs and halve lengthwise. Remove yolks and mash them with a fork. Briskly stir in mayonnaise, mustard, vinegar, and lemon juice until mixture forms a smooth paste. Add salt and a few grains of pepper to taste. Fill egg whites with yolk mixture and dust with paprika. Refrigerate for at least 30 minutes before serving.

Bud's Sunday Roast Chicken

Bud with Norma Jean

Two 2½–3-pound roasting chickens
2 lemons, halved
2 tablespoons prepared mustard
2 cloves garlic

1 tablespoon fresh rosemary, chopped
Salt and pepper to taste
1 cup dry white wine

Preheat oven to 375°. Rinse chickens thoroughly and pat dry. Rub each chicken inside and outside with lemon halves. Mix prepared mustard with garlic and rosemary and rub over chickens. Sprinkle with salt and pepper. Then stuff each cavity with the lemon halves. Place chickens on a rack in a roasting pan. Cover with lemon juice or wine. Bake for about 1¼ hours, or until it registers 165° on a meat thermometer, basting from time to time with the pan juices. Add water or more wine if additional basting juices are needed.

YIELD: 8 SERVINGS.

NOTE: *If desired, serve with Chestnut and Rice Stuffing, recipe follows.*

Chestnut and Rice Stuffing

Hester White, Bud's wonder secretary, sometimes makes this savory stuffing to serve with his roast chickens.

1 cup chopped onions

½ cup chopped celery, including leaves

2 tablespoons melted butter

1½ teaspoons poultry seasoning

1 teaspoon salt

2 tablespoons chopped fresh parsley

½ cup chopped canned chestnuts

½ cup chopped cooked giblets (from chicken in recipe above)

2 cups cooked rice

Preheat oven to 375°. Sauté onions and celery in melted butter until tender. Remove from heat and add poultry seasoning, salt, and parsley. In a bowl blend together chestnuts, giblets, and rice. Add sautéed mixture and blend well. Bake in a lightly greased casserole dish for 25 minutes.

YIELD: STUFFING FOR 2 CHICKENS.

"Bud"—Walter T. Darden

Bud's Saturday Seafood Stew

This dish is a family affair, with everyone chopping and Daddy supervising the results.

1 pound raw shrimp

½ cup vegetable oil

2 onions, chopped fine

2 cloves garlic, minced

4 unshelled lobster tails, cut into thirds

3 cups clam juice

6 ripe tomatoes, peeled and quartered

2 cups peeled and cubed potatoes

Salt and pepper to taste

1 bay leaf

1 teaspoon dried thyme

1 teaspoon dried basil

2 tablespoons fresh parsley

1½ cups white wine

1 pound haddock fillets, or any firm white fish, quartered

1 dozen clams, washed and scrubbed

Shell shrimp, leaving the tails intact. Wash and devein shrimp and set aside. Place vegetable oil in a large pot. Add onions and garlic, and sauté until tender. Add lobster and sauté until pieces turn red. Remove lobsters and reserve. Add clam juice, tomatoes, potatoes, salt, pepper, bay leaf, thyme, basil, and parsley. Bring to a boil, lower heat, and simmer, covered, for 25 minutes. Then add wine, shrimp, haddock, and lobster. Simmer for 5 minutes longer. Add clams and continue simmering until they open. Add salt and pepper to taste. Serve as a main dish in large soup bowls.

YIELD: 5 TO 6 SERVINGS.

NOTE: *Discard any clams that do not open.*

Bud's Stewed Fruit Compote

1 dozen fresh kumquats if in season; or
    1 whole orange, unpeeled, seeded
    and chopped

Juice of 1 lime

Juice of 1 lemon

Rind of half a lime, chopped

Rind of half a lemon, chopped

1½ cups water

2 cups unpitted dried prunes

2 cups dried apricots

1 cup dried peaches

Sugar to taste (about 4 heaping
    teaspoons—optional)

Combine kumquats or orange with lime and lemon juices and rinds. Cover with the water. Bring to a boil, lower heat, and simmer, covered, for 30 minutes. Add remaining ingredients. (Bud never uses sugar, preferring a very tart mixture.) Continue cooking until all fruits are tender, about 1 hour. Use as a breakfast fruit, a dessert, or a bedtime snack. Serve hot or cold.

YIELD: 6 SERVINGS.

OLD-TIME FAVORITES

Tipsy Cake

4 eggs

2 cups sugar, plus extra

⅛ teaspoon salt

1 quart milk

1 pint dark rum or whiskey

1 very large sponge cake, dried out by
    leaving uncovered on a cake rack for
    8–24 hours

1 pint heavy cream

¼ pound blanched slivered almonds,
    lightly toasted

1 small jar each of red and green
    Maraschino cherries

"Bud"—Walter T. Darden

Beat eggs one at a time until they are light and fluffy. Add sugar and salt and beat thoroughly. Scald milk and stir into mixture. Return to the pot and cook until thick enough to coat the spoon, but not long enough to curdle mixture. Remove from stove and cool. Then add 1¾ cups of rum or whiskey to the custard.

Break cake into coarse pieces and line bottom of a large bowl with a layer of cake. Cover with a layer of custard and continue alternating until all the cake and custard are used. Whip cream until it forms stiff peaks; add ¼ cup more rum or whiskey and additional sugar to taste. Cover cake with whipped cream and decorate with slivered almonds and Maraschino cherries. Place in the refrigerator for about 2 hours to ripen. It is even better the second day.

YIELD: 12 SERVINGS.

Syllabub

2 cups heavy cream

½ cup sugar

¼ cup rum or brandy

Grated nutmeg

Whip the cream until stiff. Fold in sugar and rum or brandy. Cover and chill in the refrigerator for 1 hour or so. Serve in sherbet glasses or punch cups with a faint dusting of nutmeg.

YIELD: 6 SERVINGS.

The Sampsons

16 Noble Street in Delaware,
Ohio—the house Granddad
built for his family

Granddad Sampson

Granddad Sampson was the only grandparent we ever met, and although he died when we were young, we remember him well. He was a strikingly handsome man with a long white flowing beard, which in later years reached almost to his waist. He had six fingers on each hand, which might have made a lesser man self-conscious. But Granddaddy would say that this only made his hands more powerful, and what a powerful man he was! His incredible physical strength, which lasted until his death at nearly one hundred years of age, made an indelible impression on all who knew him. He was a man of few words, but his presence carried more weight than words ever could. His was not the silence of diffidence but of many weathered storms and deep inner reserves, rooted in a difficult childhood and the constant struggle to ensure the survival of his family in adulthood. Somewhat eccentric in later years, he once replied when chided for talking to himself, "I can't think of a more interesting person to talk to."

William Sampson was born in Kentucky in approximately 1865. He lived with the Percivals, a wealthy white family who had taken him into their home to be raised as a houseboy. He had no knowledge of his own family except a vague memory of being part of a large family. He was told that he had been given away by his mother to a stranger who appeared at their door when he was three years old. Granddaddy assumed that he was given away in this manner because his family could not afford to care for him. But he was never able to gather any information from the Percivals about his true origins, nor the identity of the stranger who brought him to their home, or even if William Sampson was his true name. These factors were to haunt him all of his life. As a young boy, he was aware of unconfirmed rumors among the townsfolk that he was actually the son of one of the Percivals and a servant. The day before the will of old Mr. Percival was to be read, the courthouse mysteriously burned down, destroying the document and intensifying rumors that William Sampson, who had been summoned to the dying man's bedside, may indeed have been an heir.

As a boy, "Pony," as he was called, was raised with a mixture of affection and abuse that characterized such master-servant relationships. In the summer he was forced to go barefoot, and in the winter he was given the same shoes to wear for four years. As a result, his feet were stunted and pained him all his life. He was not allowed to go to school but learned whatever he could through his duties as a playmate for the Percival children, who shared their school lessons with him until he was ten. Then it was decided that he had received enough education, and he was given the workload of a man. He had to work from sunrise to sunset, had no contact with other children, and was frequently beaten if he became fatigued or made a mistake. He received no medical care. Once he fell from a horse and, though in excruciating pain, he was still required to work. It was not discovered that his hip had been fractured until he was hospitalized after a fall from his cherry tree at the age of eighty. Though he suffered a second fracture from this fall, miraculously he recovered.

William Sampson was an amazingly tough, resilient, and self-

Granddad Sampson
at home

reliant man. He could make his own clothes and prepare his own food. He built most of the homes in which his family lived, as well as the furniture, and he also made some of his own farming tools. At different times throughout his life, he was a migrant farm worker, a butcher, the manager of a dairy farm, and a railroad construction worker. For the latter part of his life, he was the boiler man as well as night chef at a hospital in Delaware, Ohio, where he finally settled with his family. But Granddaddy's first love remained farming. He was profoundly rooted to the earth, was happiest when working with his hands, and often seemed in closer harmony with things of nature than with people. Yet he was a deep and loving man. He taught us that when doves coo mournfully, it will rain within hours; when maple leaves turn upward, it will rain in a day; and when the bark of trees is thicker than usual, it will be a bad winter. He could look at the sky and predict the weather, feel the soil and tell you what it would and would not yield. Plant and animal life thrived under his care. He raised bees, cows, rabbits, chickens, vegetables, and fruits. From his beehives, Granddad Sampson would extract the most delicious honey. It was one of his favorite foods, and he used it for everything from home remedies to baking his favorite cakes. Frequently he would send our family honey in the comb with advice on how to use it. The following recipes were inspired by his suggestions.

Fruited Honey Chicken

One 3-pound chicken, cut up for frying

Salt and pepper

¾ cup apple cider or juice

½ cup orange juice

¼ cup lemon juice

1 onion, chopped

½ cup vegetable oil

1 fresh unpeeled apple, sliced (or a
handful of dried apples)

Handful of seedless raisins

Handful of dried apricots

Handful of pitted prunes

2 tablespoons honey

Salt and pepper the chicken pieces, then marinate chicken in fruit juices and onion for 1 hour or so (reserve marinade). Preheat oven to 350°. Brown both sides of all chicken pieces in oil. Place chicken in a covered casserole and cover with marinating juices plus the remaining ingredients. Bake for 45 minutes, basting occasionally with marinade and pan juices.

YIELD: 4 TO 5 SERVINGS.

Granddad Sampson

Honey Duck

One 4-pound duck, quartered

1 clove garlic, minced

1 teaspoon salt

1 orange, peeled, and quartered or
    sectioned

¼ teaspoon ground ginger

¼ cup lemon juice

2 tablespoons honey

½ cup seedless grapes (if not in season,
    use 1 small can black cherries)

Preheat oven to 325°. Place duck skin side up on a rack in a baking dish. Bake for 1 hour. Drain off the fat and arrange the duck in a casserole. Add garlic, salt, orange, ginger, lemon juice, and honey. Cover and bake for 30 minutes more. Add grapes (or drained canned cherries) and bake, uncovered, for another 10 minutes.

YIELD: 4 SERVINGS.

Honey Custard

3 eggs

½ cup honey

⅛ teaspoon salt

2¾ cups milk

½ teaspoon lemon extract

½ teaspoon grated orange rind

Grated nutmeg

Preheat oven to 350°. Beat eggs until light. Add honey and salt. Continue beating until well blended. Scald milk. Slowly pour milk over egg mixture, stirring constantly. Add lemon extract and orange rind. Pour into buttered custard cups. Sprinkle nutmeg on top. Set in a shallow pan filled with an inch of hot water. Bake for 45 minutes or until set.

YIELD: 5 TO 6 SERVINGS.

Old-fashioned Honey Sponge Cake

1 heaping cup sifted cake flour

¼ teaspoon salt

5 large eggs, separated

½ cup granulated sugar

½ cup honey

¼ cup hot water

1½ teaspoons vanilla extract

1 teaspoon grated lemon rind

¾ teaspoon cream of tartar

Confectioners' sugar or Honey Icing (recipe follows)

Young Granddad Sampson

Preheat oven to 325°. Sift flour and salt together and set aside. Beat egg yolks until frothy. Stir in sugar, honey, hot water, vanilla, and lemon rind until well blended. Add flour mixture and blend well. In a separate bowl beat egg whites until foamy. Add cream of tartar. Continue beating until stiff peaks form. Fold into batter mixture. Pour batter into a lightly greased 9-inch tube pan and bake for 50 minutes, or until the edges shrink from the sides of the pan and it is firm to the touch in the middle. When cool, dust with powdered sugar or frost with Honey Icing.

YIELD: 10 TO 12 SLICES.

NOTE: *Stale honey cake can be used for Tipsy Cake (see page167).*

Granddad Sampson

Honey Icing

2 tablespoons softened butter

2 tablespoons honey

2 cups confectioners' sugar

Drop of vanilla extract

Pinch of salt

1 egg white

Cream the butter and honey together, adding ½ cup of the sugar, the vanilla, and the salt. Stir well. Add unbeaten egg white and remainder of sugar. Beat until smooth and use as icing for Honey Sponge Cake (see preceding recipe).

YIELD: ENOUGH FOR 1 HONEY SPONGE CAKE.

Honey Punch

1½ quarts water

1 cup honey

Juice of 3 lemons

Juice of 3 oranges

3 cups pineapple juice

1 cup unsweetened grape juice

1 cup canned or fresh crushed pineapple
with its juice

Fresh mint springs, for garnish

Heat 2 cups of the water so that it is warm enough to dissolve the honey easily. Cool. Then mix in remaining 2½ cups of water, juices, and crushed pineapple. Pour into tall glasses filled with ice. Garnish with mint sprigs.

YIELD: ABOUT 3 QUARTS.

HONEY REMEDIES

A doctor was a luxury to Granddad Sampson, and he was suspicious of them anyway, so he blended his own cold preventatives. He believed in the curative health-giving properties of honey, and even advocated warm beeswax for relieving stiff joints.

Gargle

Blend equal parts of honey, glycerin, and vinegar. Use as needed.

Cough Syrup

His children don't remember the proportions but do know the ingredients.

Honey

Tea brewed from horehound leaves and
   stems

Lemons

Onions

Vinegar

Few drops of turpentine

Old-fashioned Lye Soap

When we were children, we used to watch Granddad making soap in a big black pot in his backyard. This was an economical, all-purpose soap that was used for almost anything in life that ever needed washing—laundry, floors, hair, and in a pinch the body. It was even said to soothe insect bites.

1 gallon old leftover grease   *3 boxes Red Devil lye*
About 4 gallons water

Strain crumbs from grease and place it in a large iron kettle or washpot. To start, add 2 gallons of water. Add lye. Boil for about 30 minutes, stirring constantly until lye "eats" up grease (mixture will become lighter and lighter). Then add 2 more gallons of water. Continue boiling, stirring constantly, until mixture is the consistency of molasses or honey. Remove from fire and let harden in pot for 2 to 3 days. Then cut soap out of pot in usable blocks.

Granddad Sampson making soap in his backyard

Grandmother Corine Johnson Sampson

Corine Sampson with husband William and sons William and Glen in Elizabethtown, Kentucky, around 1908

Grandmother Corine was known for her religious zeal. One church was not enough for her. She was an active member of two—the Baptist Church and the Holiness Church. For the Baptist, she taught Sunday school, and for the Holy Tride Stone Church, she was a "home missionary," which meant that she traveled to neighboring towns to "save souls" and recruit members. She saw no conflict between the two faiths but adopted what she considered the more Christ-like approach of the Holiness members: conservative dress (long sleeves and skirts), no personal adornment (makeup or jewelry), no body defilement (smoking or drinking), and strict observance of the Sabbath at all costs (no working or cooking on Sunday). Mom Sampson was in church on Sunday literally from dawn to midnight, yet she led by example rather than decree, allowing religious freedom. Therefore, some of her children remained Baptist even after the Holiness Church finally absorbed her full attention.

Without any doubt, Mom Sampson was the most vocal personality in her household. She held strong opinions about most things and led her family in an austere life where cleanliness was next to godliness, where the rod was not spared for fear of spoiling the child, where children were expected to be seen and not heard, and where hard, honest work was the order of the day.

She was an excellent manager, and when Dad Sampson brought in his salary, she gave him 35 cents for chewing tobacco and proceeded with the weekly budget. This was in no way meant to demean him, but she had a strong sense of herself and her capabilities, and they both recognized her uncanny ability to stretch a dollar as far as it could go—and then some. Pursuit of worldly goods did not interest Corine, but she was concerned that her family have proper food, good shelter, and adequate clothing. The one luxury she possessed was a piano. Dad Sampson traded a cow for it, and she patiently gave each of her children music lessons and taught them hymns.

Little is known about Corine's early days. She was born in Camden, Alabama, one of five brothers and sisters, graduated from Tuskegee Institute, and was a schoolteacher by profession. She went to Elizabethtown, Kentucky, to live with her sister Rutelia and to teach. There she met and married William Sampson. He was quite a few years her senior, but this did not bother her. She said that she would rather be "an old man's darling than a young man's slave."

Early in their married life Corine's mother died, leaving two small children, Clyde, nine, and Mamie Jean, our mother, four. Corine and Mr. Sampson took them in and raised them as their own children, never telling William and Glen, who were infants at the time, or Asa, who came later, that they were not their natural siblings. It was her feeling that this would make the family "more harmonious."

Corine felt strongly that a woman's role should not be limited to the home, and was very appreciative of the support and understanding she got from Dad Sampson concerning her religious convictions, even though he was less active in the church. Without his cooperation, she couldn't have functioned as actively as she did in her religious pursuits and evangelistic missions. For while she was doing God's work, he was often called upon to run the household and cook the meals. They held each other in high esteem and were never known to utter one harsh word between them.

Corine advised her only daughter to be self-sufficient, not to marry early, and to find a man who would encourage her to pursue her own individual interests. With this in mind, she would greet all of her daughter's suitors at the door with a lecture (sometimes lasting for an hour) on the importance of education before romance, and religion above all.

Grandmother Corine pricked herself while sewing and died of blood poisoning before we were born. The most vivid image we have of her is the description our mother used to give us of Corine's annual Christmas celebration. Her memory also came through to us in the many so-called wholesome foods we were required to eat, such as liver and creamed spinach and, among our favorites, spoonbread and tapioca. Our mother explained to us that since the Sampsons had lived on a dairy farm, many of their dishes utilized milk and cream, which were fresh and plentiful. We have therefore divided this chapter into two quite different sections—Corine's Christmas preparations and our favorite "dairy" dishes inherited from her.

Mom and Dad Sampson on their way to church in Delaware, Ohio

THE SAMPSON CHRISTMAS

Every year Corine organized the Christmas celebration. Granddaddy Sampson would chop the Christmas tree, and the whole family made the decorations. It was a very big event. For many days everyone would string cranberries to make long chains, and pop and string popcorn. Large red apples were shined and hung. Oranges were punctured with cloves until no skin showed, and these were suspended from ribbons on the tree. Peppermint sticks

Grandmother Corine Johnson Sampson

and painted cookies dangled tantalizingly from the branches. Granddaddy could whittle wood, so there were miniature wooden toys hanging along with paper angels and snowflakes. But the crowning glory of the Sampson Christmas tree was a sprinkling of little brass candleholders filled with white candles made from the beeswax from Granddaddy's hives.

The family did not exchange gifts with one another but invited the two Sunday-school classes that Corine taught to share their Christmas spirit. Corine would lead the caroling while her son William played the piano. Punch and frosted cake were served, then each child was given a treat from the tree to take home.

Painted Christmas Cookies

Rose water and orange-flower water, favorite flavorings at the turn of the twentieth century, can still be purchased in some drugstores and gourmet shops.

COOKIE DOUGH:

- *1 cup butter*
- *1 cup sugar*
- *1 egg*
- *3 cups sifted all-purpose flour*
- *Pinch of salt*
- *1 teaspoon rose water*
- *1 teaspoon orange-flower water*
- *½ teaspoon almond extract*
- *½ teaspoon lemon extract*
- *Red, orange, green, and yellow food coloring*

COATING:

- *2 cups confectioners' sugar*
- *1 teaspoon vanilla extract*
- *3 tablespoons heavy cream*
- *Various food colorings*
- *Granulated sugar*
- *Nuts, citron, red cherries, raisins*

Cream butter and sugar well, then add egg. Stir in flour and salt. Divide dough into 4 parts. To first part add rose water, to the second orange-flower water, to the third almond extract, and to the last lemon extract. A drop of red food coloring in the rose, orange in the orange-flower, green in the almond, and yellow in the lemon will differentiate the flavors. Chill dough for 1 hour. Preheat oven to 375°. Then roll each section of dough separately on a well-floured board to ¼-inch thick. Cut with Christmas tree, star, animal, Santa Claus, or snowflake cookie cutters and place on an ungreased cookie sheet. Prick a hole in the top of each cookie if you plan to string them on the tree. Bake for about 10 minutes. Meanwhile, make coating: Blend all ingredients together and divide into sections. Using food coloring, tint each section a different hue. When cookies have cooled, paint them with a small paintbrush. Use granulated sugar, also tinted, for accent, as well as small bits of nuts, citron, slivered red cherries, and raisins. Have fun.

YIELD: 5 DOZEN COOKIES.

CORINE'S "DAIRY" DISHES

Kidney Stew

2 large beef kidneys

2 tablespoons apple cider vinegar

2 tablespoons butter

1 medium onion, chopped

¼ cup flour

1½ cups beef stock (or 2 cubes beef
   bouillon dissolved in 1½ cups water)

Juice of 1 lemon

1 cup sour cream

Salt and pepper to taste

Cooked rice

Parsley, for garnish

Grandmother Corine Johnson Sampson

Soak kidneys for 1 hour in a bowl of water to which the vinegar has been added. Rinse well and place in a saucepan with fresh water to cover. Parboil for 5 to 10 minutes. Remove from pan, cool a bit, then chop into small pieces. In a frying pan heat butter, add onion, and sauté until tender. Then add kidney pieces. Sprinkle the flour over this and brown the mixture well, stirring frequently. Add beef stock and lemon juice. Simmer for 10 minutes. Add sour cream, stir, and simmer for 1 minute more. Season to taste. Serve over steaming rice, garnished with parsley.

YIELD: 4 SERVINGS.

Creamed Sweetbreads

4 pairs sweetbreads	2 cups light cream
3 tablespoons butter	1 dozen small mushrooms, sliced
4 teaspoons grated onion	Salt and pepper to taste
1 tablespoon flour	Paprika

Soak sweetbreads in cold water for 1 hour. Parboil for 5 minutes. Let cool. Remove skin and cut into small pieces. Put butter in a frying pan and heat until hot and bubbly. Add sweetbreads and grated onion. Fry until sweetbreads are slightly brown, stirring frequently. Sprinkle flour over mixture and blend. Then add cream and mushrooms, mixing thoroughly. Cook over low heat for about 10 minutes. Season with salt and pepper. Dust with paprika. Serve over hot toast or in heated patty shells.

YIELD: 6 SERVINGS.

Liver with Cream Gravy

4 strips bacon

¼ cup flour

¼ teaspoon salt

⅛ teaspoon pepper

4 slices beef or calf's liver

1 medium onion, chopped

½ cup sweet or sour cream

Fry bacon to a crisp and drain on paper towels. Mix together flour, salt, and pepper and dredge liver in mixture. Fry for 5 minutes on each side or until nicely browned. Add onion to pan for last 5 minutes. Remove liver when done and add crumbled bacon and sweet or sour cream to pan juices and onion. This makes a nice gravy for hominy grits (breakfast) or rice (dinner).

YIELD: 3 TO 4 SERVINGS.

Tongue with Horseradish Sauce

TONGUE:

One 4- to 5-pound beef tongue

1 medium onion, quartered

2 celery tops

1 carrot, coarsely chopped

1 clove garlic

¼ teaspoon salt

6–8 peppercorns

HORSERADISH SAUCE:

1 tablespoon grated onion

1 tablespoon butter

1 tablespoon flour

1 cup light cream

4 tablespoons white prepared horseradish

Grandmother Corine Johnson Sampson

For tongue: In a pot cover tongue with water, and add remaining ingredients. Bring to a boil, lower heat, and simmer, loosely covered, for 20 minutes per pound or until a fork pierces the tongue easily. Remove from pot and skin carefully. For sauce: Sauté onion in butter until slightly browned. Add flour and blend well. Slowly add cream, stirring constantly. Add horseradish and heat thoroughly. Serve with sliced tongue. This also makes an excellent sauce for corned beef or boiled beef.

YIELD: 6 SERVINGS.

Mom Sampson's Spoonbread—Our Favorite

1 cup yellow cornmeal

2 cups boiling water

3 tablespoons butter

1 teaspoon salt

3 large eggs, well beaten

1 cup milk

Preheat oven to 375°. Slowly add cornmeal to the boiling water, stirring constantly until thick and smooth. Add butter and salt and cool to lukewarm. Then add eggs and milk. Beat for 2 minutes, then pour into a greased casserole and bake for 35 minutes or until golden brown. Spoon out while piping hot and pass the butter!

YIELD: 8 SERVINGS.

Pineapple Syllabub

2 tablespoons sugar

1 teaspoon vanilla extract

3 egg whites, stiffly beaten

1 cup heavy cream, whipped

1 cup drained crushed pineapple

Add the sugar and vanilla to the stiffly beaten egg whites. Fold in the whipped cream and crushed pineapple. Chill and serve in punch cups.

YIELD: 4 TO 6 SERVINGS.

Orange Tapioca

¼ cup tapioca

5 tablespoons sugar

⅛ teaspoon salt

2⅓ cups milk

1 egg, separated

1 teaspoon orange extract

6 fresh orange sections, peeled (or drained canned mandarin), for garnish

Add tapioca, 4 tablespoons of the sugar, and the salt to the milk. Stir in lightly beaten egg yolk. Cook over low heat, stirring occasionally, until thick. Remove from heat. Beat egg white until soft peaks form. Add remaining 1 tablespoon of sugar and continue beating until stiff and glossy. Fold into tapioca mixture. Add orange extract. Pour tapioca into sherbet glasses. Garnish with orange sections. Serve warm or chilled.

YIELD: 4 TO 6 SERVINGS.

Grandmother Corine Johnson Sampson

The Sampson Brothers

Clyde

On a recent visit to Cincinnati, we asked our mother's brother, Uncle Clyde, to share some of his childhood reminiscences with us, but he found it difficult to talk about the past. We left disappointed, but a few days later we received this letter telling us about his life.

"My earliest memories are of being in a log cabin with my mother, older half-brother, Sam; and your mother, in Camden, Alabama. We had no stove, in fact, no conveniences. Out back was a garden, though, where we grew vegetables, and a spring where we drew water. I had a little job delivering groceries to two old maids who had a turkey farm on the edge of town. Every Sunday we had fried chicken and rice for breakfast and that was considered a very good breakfast. Fireworks were exploded at Christmastime in those days. Then, one Christmas, I remember the neighbors telling me not to play; that it wasn't appropriate because our mother was very ill. Soon after that, she died. The church women laid her out and since there was no funeral parlor in those days, we purchased a simple casket in the furniture store. Our sister, Tiny, came from Kentucky and packed us up to go with her. The white man who ran the grocery store in Camden asked her to leave me with him to work but she said "no," that we wouldn't split up the family. We took the train from Camden to Birmingham, Alabama, and when I looked out the window I saw a man with a wagon selling milk. He had a white horse and every time he would go into a home the horse would walk to the next house and wait for him. It's funny the things you remember. When we reached our destination, Elizabethtown, Kentucky, we had trouble locating the house where Rutelia and Corine, our older sisters lived. We knocked on the wrong door and a man answered. I thought he said his name was "Jesus" and I ran back and told Mamie that we had moved to a town where "Jesus" lived. At the time I was about eight or nine years old. It was decided that since Sam was old enough to work, he would stay with Rutelia and Tiny. Because they were not married, and Corine was, we would live with her and her husband, Dad Sampson. Corine said to cut down on confusion, we would all be called Sampson and from then on we were just like any other family.

"I don't remember the reason for it, but we left Elizabethtown a couple of years later and stopped on a farm where we all picked strawberries and weeded the onions for a farmer. They did not have proper living conditions there and we were housed in an abandoned chicken coop. Mom Sampson saved every penny and from there we went to Xenia, Ohio, where Dad opened a small meat market. A competitor up the street lowered his prices drastically and we soon went broke. Mother, anxious to settle where good schools were, decided to locate on a dairy farm in Wilberforce, Ohio. We worked for Farmer Brice and I never will forget the day he installed indoor plumbing. I had never seen anything like that before, and I said to Mamie, "One day we're going to have it too." It was here that Mamie and I started grade school. I had to get up at 4 A.M. to milk the cows and check the traps and go through deep snow to do it sometimes. Then I'd have my breakfast and Mamie and I would walk to school. We carried our lunch pails and Mamie, being liberal and generous, many times allowed me to eat most of

Uncle Clyde as a child

her lunch before we reached school. We had to walk a mile and a half each way. Mother used to make cracklin' bread and bran bread for us to carry. After school we had to work then do our lessons. When I finished grade school, that was considered a very good graduation. Mother had a revelation that we should resettle in Delaware, Ohio. This we did. It was a small college town, Ohio Wesleyan is there, and work opportunities were good. We had chores to do in the house and jobs in the community. Mamie did not like to clean the lamp chimneys, so she paid me ten cents a week to clean them and not to tell. I would pull her braids if we had a scrap. I always regretted when the church had its annual hayride as mother insisted that I chaperone Mamie. This I disliked. Mamie earned her first monies from the sale of ice cream cones. She and another girl, Elsie Austin, who was my first girl friend, had a pony and a cart which they drove from door to door. She also shucked corn for tuition money. William was a clerk in a novelty store, Glen did everything, but mainly dug for freshwater clams and oysters. He once found a pearl that he sold for forty-two dollars—big money in those days. Asa cleaned out the movie house. I used to hunt and trap fur-bearing animals—mink, muskrats, coons, polecats, etc. The money saved went for my tuition at Tuskegee Institute where I studied plumbing and incidentally happened to install new fixtures for Maude Darden in Opelika, long before anyone knew there would be a connection between the Sampson and Darden families. William graduated from Wilberforce; Glen, Ohio State; Mamie from Ohio University; and Asa attended Fisk. I think our family did all right, considering our beginnings as migrant workers and the hard times we saw. It has taken me all this time to see the power of our mother's religious convictions."

Until his retirement, Uncle Clyde worked for an insurance company in Cincinnati. Hunting was his main pastime then, and he took his son Lowell as well as the boys to whom he was a Big Brother on camping and hunting trips. Often he cooked in the "bush," but sometimes he brought his game home for his wife Marie to prepare. He emphasizes that one must be inventive, use the ac-

Clyde Sampson after a good day's hunting

companiments and garnishes that the seasons provide, and employ common sense in the proportions given, as they will vary according to the size of the catch. Here, then, are a few recipes from Uncle Clyde's "wild" days.

Brunswick Stew

This dish can also be made with a 4- to 4½-pound stewing chicken as a substitute for rabbit and squirrel.

1 medium-size rabbit

1 squirrel

2 quarts water

1½ tablespoons salt

1 large onion, chopped

1½ cups fresh baby lima beans, or 1 package frozen

2 slices bacon, diced

4 medium potatoes, peeled and cubed

3 cups chopped fresh tomatoes

½ teaspoon pepper

1 teaspoon sugar

2 cups fresh corn kernels

2 tablespoons flour

2 tablespoons butter

Skin and clean the rabbit and squirrel, and wash in several changes of water. Cut in serving pieces. Bring the water to a boil and add the rabbit and squirrel. Boil for 1 hour. Add salt, onion, lima beans, bacon, potatoes, tomatoes, and pepper. Cover and cook slowly for another hour or until tender. Then add sugar and corn. Continue cooking for 15 minutes. Mix flour and butter to a paste and add to stew to thicken. Adjust seasoning. Cook about 15 minutes longer. Serve hot.

YIELD: 4 TO 6 SERVINGS.

Fricasseed Rabbit or Squirrel

1 medium-size rabbit, or 2 squirrels

1 teaspoon salt

½ teaspoon pepper

1 cup flour

¾ cup bacon fat

2 cups boiling water

Skin, clean, and cut rabbit into 6 pieces. Roll the pieces in salt, pepper, and flour. Place bacon fat in a large, heavy skillet and heat. Fry rabbit until it is brown on all sides. Pour off most of the fat and add the boiling water, then cover and simmer for 20 to 30 minutes. Serve with gravy from the pan.

YIELD: 2 TO 3 SERVINGS.

Roast Rabbit

1 rabbit

Apple cider vinegar

Ground cloves or dried sage

Salt and pepper

1 onion, sliced

4 bay leaves

3 tablespoons bacon fat

2 teaspoons grape or mint jelly (optional)

Preheat the oven to 300°. Skin and clean rabbit and wash in cold water. Pat dry and rub with vinegar. Rub rabbit with ground cloves or sage, salt, and pepper. Place in a shallow pan and lay sliced onion and bay leaves on top. Drizzle bacon fat over meat, then cover with aluminum foil. Cook slowly (30 minutes to the pound) until tender. Grape or mint jelly may be stirred into the pan juices before serving.

Deer Steaks

6 venison steaks

½ cup white vinegar

½ cup vegetable oil

1 clove garlic, minced

1 bay leaf

½ teaspoon prepared mustard

¼ teaspoon black pepper

Butter

Cut venison into slices about 1 inch thick. Combine the rest of the ingredients except the butter and marinate the steaks in this sauce for 3 hours. Then remove from the marinade, rub with butter, and broil under a hot fire for roughly 8 minutes on each side.

Leftover venison makes a good hash, says Uncle Clyde.

The Sampson Brothers

Roast Opossum with Yams

1 opossum	4 bay leaves
Salt and pepper	2 cups boiling water
Ground sage, to taste	6 yams, peeled and sliced
Juice of 1 lemon	Butter

Preheat oven to 350°. Skin and clean the opossum. Take out the intestines, etc., being careful to remove musk glands from the small of the back and beneath the front legs. Rinse well. Rub inside and out with salt, pepper, sage, and lemon juice. Place in a roasting pan on top of bay leaves and pour the boiling water over it. Cover and cook for 45 minutes. Turn meat and add yams dotted with butter. Continue cooking for another 45 minutes or until tender, removing cover for final 10 minutes to brown meat.

YIELD: 3 TO 6 SERVINGS, DEPENDING ON SIZE OF OPOSSUM.

Clyde's son Lowell,
with game

Roast Quail

6 quail

½ cup apple cider vinegar

¼ cup butter

½ pound chicken livers, quartered
    (optional)

1 onion, chopped

1 clove garlic, minced

2 cups chicken broth

1 cup port wine

1½ cups raw rice

½ teaspoon salt

Cover plucked and cleaned quails with cold water to which vinegar has been added and leave to soak overnight in the refrigerator. Then rinse in cold water. Pat dry. Preheat oven to 375°. Melt butter in a large pan and brown quail on all sides. Remove from pan. In same pan, sauté chicken livers, if using them. Add the onions and garlic, and sauté about 1 minute, until limp. Pour in chicken broth and return quail to pan. Add wine and stir in rice and salt. Cover and bake for 30 minutes.

YIELD: 6 SERVINGS.

The Sampson Brothers

Pheasant with Pecan Stuffing

PHEASANT:
1 good-size pheasant
Salt and pepper
1 clove garlic, halved
2 tablespoons butter
½ cup sherry
Blueberries (optional), for garnish

PECAN STUFFING:
¼ cup minced celery
¼ cup minced onion
½ cup seedless raisins
2½ cups bread crumbs
1 cup chopped pecans
¼ cup honey
¼ cup melted butter
1 egg, well beaten
¼ cup heavy cream
¼ cup water

*Uncle Clyde in his
ROTC uniform at
Tuskegee Institute*

For the pheasant: Preheat oven to 350°. Pluck and clean bird, then rub inside cavity with salt, pepper, and garlic. For the stuffing: Place the celery, onion, raisins, bread crumbs, and pecans in a medium-size bowl. Mix honey, butter, egg, cream, and water together in a small bowl. Stir into celery mixture and combine well. (You should have 4 cups of stuffing.) Stuff pheasant. Place bird in a roasting pan, rub with butter, moisten with sherry, and roast, allowing 25 minutes per pound. Baste often with pan juices, adding more sherry if necessary. Wild blueberries swirled around in the natural gravy make a nice garnish.

YIELD: 2 TO 3 SERVINGS.

Roast Goose

A Sampson Christmas treat.

One 8- to 10-pound goose

STUFFING:

½ pound pitted prunes

Apple cider

5 medium tart apples, peeled and sliced

½ cup slivered almonds

1 teaspoon grated orange rind

For the stuffing: Soak prunes in enough apple cider to cover for several hours. Remove prunes from cider and combine with apples, almonds, and grated orange rind. Reserve cider. Preheat oven to 400°. Wash goose well, removing any extra fat from the inside. Place in a roasting pan on a rack and stuff with fruits. Prick the skin all over with a sharp knife point, so that the fat drips freely and the skin will become crisp. Roast goose in the preheated oven for 20 minutes, then reduce temperature to 350° and roast for a total of 3 hours. Baste with reserved apple cider.

YIELD: 8 SERVINGS.

Uncle Clyde and his wife, Marie

The Sampson Brothers

Jeannie's Bran Bread

Uncle Clyde's daughter, Jean Marie, has learned to bake this much-loved bread from her father's school-pail days.

1 egg

1⅔ cups buttermilk

½ cup honey or molasses

2 cups coarse bran

2 cups unbleached white or whole-wheat flour

2 teaspoons baking powder

1 teaspoon salt

1 teaspoon baking soda

½ cup seedless raisins or chopped dates (optional)

Preheat oven to 350°. In a large bowl beat egg until light. Add buttermilk and honey or molasses. Mix dry ingredients and add to egg mixture, blending well. Add raisins or dates (if you like them) and pour batter into a greased 9½-×-5½-inch loaf pan or 12 muffin cups. Bake for 50 to 60 minutes, or until the edges pull away from the sides of the pan and the center feels firm to the touch.

YIELD: 1 LOAF OR 1 DOZEN LARGE MUFFINS.

William

Unfortunately, we never got to know Uncle Bill as well as we would have liked before he died. Our mother had always told us about her brother in Chicago who was an accountant for the government, and one hot summer she took us to visit him and his wife, Ruth. Beside the intense Chicago heat, the standout of the trip for us was Uncle Bill's ham radio set. He told us he had started out in 1916, at the age of twelve, with a crude crystal set, and little by little had advanced to the sophisticated equipment that then monopolized his entire den. Right after dinner he checked his watch and invited us to join him for a call from Hamburg, Germany. We told a thick German accent that we were Uncle Bill's nieces from New Jersey and told the same to a ham radio buff in Alaska.

We made only one other trip to his home but were again impressed by the many friends Uncle Bill, a somewhat reserved man, had made through his radio.

Recently his brother Asa told us that, as a boy, William played the organ for his mother's religious gatherings and served as choir director for the Baptist Church, but quite unbeknownst to puritanical Mom Sampson, he also moonlighted with a local dance band. And though the churchgoers were always tattling on the "sinners," lucky for him the news never traveled home!

William's widow, Ruth, told us that their romance had actually started in the dining room at Wilberforce University in Ohio, where they were both students. She had a part-time job in the cafeteria and caught Bill's attention by giving him extra portions at suppertime.

Shortly after their marriage, Ruth's sister died, leaving two orphaned sons. Just as his father and mother had done with Clyde and Mamie, Bill took the children in and happily raised them as his own. The two boys, Gerald and Thomas, tell us that their father got a big kick out of being a Boy Scout leader and commissioner of the Maywood, Illinois, Civil Defense Unit, and that for recreation he loved to bowl and had taught them the game. The family bowled often, and after an invigorating game Bill Sampson's favorite and most requested meal was Aunt Ruth's pot roast dinner with bread pudding for dessert.

Uncle Bill and Aunt Ruth at
Wilberforce University

Aunt Ruth's Pot Roast

One 2- to 3-pound round roast

Salt and pepper

1 tablespoon brown sugar

2 tablespoons butter

2 tablespoons vegetable oil

1 large onion, chopped, plus 8 tiny white onions

1 tablespoon tomato ketchup

¼ teaspoon ground cloves

1 cup water

4 medium white potatoes, peeled and cubed

4 carrots, sliced

Season meat with salt and pepper and rub with brown sugar. Melt butter and oil in a heavy pot. Add meat and brown quickly on all sides. Add chopped onion and brown also. Stir in ketchup, cloves, and water. Cover tightly. Cook over a very low flame for 1½ hours. Then put in potatoes, white onions, and carrots, and continue cooking for 30 minutes. To serve, slice thin and spoon pan juices and vegetables over the meat.

YIELD: 4 MAN-SIZE SERVINGS.

Mama Jenny's Bread Pudding

Ruth inherited this recipe from her mother.

CUSTARD:

   3 egg yolks

   Pinch of salt

   ¼ cup sugar

   1¾ cups scalded milk

   ¼ teaspoon vanilla extract

   Butter

   Approximately 8 slices white bread

   ¼ cup apple jelly

   ⅓ cup seedless raisins

TOPPING:

   3 egg whites

   ⅛ teaspoon cream of tartar

   ¼ cup sugar

   ¾ teaspoon vanilla extract

Preheat oven to 325°. For the custard: Beat egg yolks until frothy, then stir in salt and sugar. Add milk slowly and cook in the top of a double boiler until the mixture coats a spoon. Add vanilla. Butter bread on both sides and toast each side under the broiler until brown. Cut into ½-inch cubes. Line the bottom of an 8-inch-square pan with a third of the toast cubes. Dot with apple jelly and sprinkle with raisins. Add a layer of custard, then alternate layers of toast, apple jelly, raisins, and custard until pan is full. Bake for 30 minutes or until almost firm. For the topping: Beat egg whites until foamy, add cream of tartar, and beat until stiff but not dry. Add sugar and vanilla, and beat until well blended. Pile the meringue lightly over pudding and bake for about 8 minutes or until meringue is golden brown.

YIELD: ABOUT 9 SERVINGS.

Glen

Members of our family have told us that when Glen was a grade-school boy in Delaware, Ohio, doing odd jobs—mainly tending lawns and caring for the elderly who couldn't get about—someone requested that he change a tire. The Sampsons had never owned a car, so Glen replied that it was a little out of his line and he didn't know how. Dad Sampson, who was standing nearby, took him aside and advised him to remove "can't" and "don't know how" from his vocabulary and to replace them with "I will do it tomorrow." Dad Sampson reasoned that, given time, one could master almost anything. This was a lesson Glen took to heart. He has always been a jack-of-all-trades and a master of many.

Glen's savings just barely got him through Ohio State, where he graduated as a pharmacist. He was practically down to his last quarter when his sister, in Buffalo, Mamie Jean, heard about a long-ailing banker who was looking for a man Friday who was a dietitian, masseur, and landscaper. She put in a word for Glen, who brushed up on nutrition on the train ride, improvised the massage,

already knew landscaping, and was hired. The banker's health took an upward swing so he put Glen in charge of supervising the meals for the sixty people (staff and family) who lived and ate on the family compound. More fish, fresh vegetables, fruits, and no rich sauces was Glen's simple idea.

At night Glen took on a full-time position at the post office, and he maintained these two jobs until retirement. Through the banker, he gained access to rare coins, and, through his post-office career, access to rare stamps, and that's how he began two collections that are highly prized today. He knows the complete history of every coin and stamp in his collection—where they were minted or printed, as well as their origins and political implications, and on occasion he has testified as an expert in cases of fraud.

Uncle Glen has a quiet gentle manner that can be deceptive. The family remembers that when a man demanding payment of a bill got carried away and pushed Dad Sampson, fifteen-year-old Glen, who happened to witness the incident, jumped out of the second-floor window and landed on his feet with fists up, ready to defend his father. The ferocity of his approach—to say nothing of the velocity or uniqueness—startled the bill collector so much that he hotfooted it down the street, never to return.

Glen tells us that even he doesn't know how he accomplished this Superman flight and that most of his Delaware days were far less dramatic. Pure heaven for him were Mom Sampson's orange and lemon peel candies and Dad Sampson's sun-dried fruits. But unfortunately these recipes were not handed down, and none of the Sampsons can remember how they were done. The old family custom that Uncle Glen does continue today is fruitcake baking. He and his wife, Cassie, always have several different kinds on hand at Christmas, and we can testify that all his cakes will have you jumping for joy and flying for more.

Uncle Glen's 8-Year Black Fruitcake

1 pound butter

1 pound brown sugar

10 eggs

1 teaspoon ground cinnamon

1 teaspoon ground nutmeg

1 teaspoon ground cloves

1½ teaspoons ground mace

1 wineglass (½ cup) red wine

1 wineglass (½ cup) brandy

1 cup rose water

1 pound sifted all-purpose flour

2 pounds seedless black raisins

2 pounds currants

¾ pound citron and mixed candied
   fruit (pineapple, orange, etc.)

1 cup chopped black walnuts

½–1 cup dark rum

Preheat oven to 350°. Cream butter and brown sugar, then add eggs, one at a time, beating each before adding. Mix in spices, wine, brandy, and rose water. Sift in half the flour, blending well. Mix the other half of the flour with the raisins, currants, citron, and nuts. Add this mixture last. Pour into three 9-inch loaf pans or two 10-inch tube pans, lightly greased, and bake for 20 minutes. Then turn oven down to 275° and bake for 1 to 1½ hours, or until firm. Remove from pans, cool to room temperature, and place individual cakes in rust-proof lidded cake tins. Pour 5 to 6 tablespoons of dark rum evenly over each cake, seal tightly, and store in a cool, dark place. Every 3 months, continue to add 5 to 6 tablespoons of rum for the next 2 to 4 years, depending upon your patience. Then thoroughly wash and dry the cake tin. Wrap cakes securely in wax paper, replace in cake tins, and seal. The cake can be eaten at any time but improves with age. The longest Uncle Glen waited to serve this holiday treat was 8 years.

YIELD: THREE 9-INCH LOAVES, OR TWO 10-INCH TUBE CAKES.

Ora Witte's White Fruitcake

Glen's wife, Cassie, got this recipe from a friend.

1 cup butter

2 cups sugar

1 teaspoon lemon extract

2½ cups sifted cake flour

2 teaspoons baking powder

½ teaspoon salt

1 cup milk

¼ pound white raisins

¼ pound candied citron, pineapple, and orange and lemon peel

¼ pound dried light figs

¼ pound almonds, blanched and chopped

¾ cup grated coconut

7 egg whites, stiffly beaten

¼ pound candied cherries, halved

½ cup rum (optional)

Uncle Glen and his wife, Cassie

Preheat oven to 275°. Cream butter and sugar together and add lemon extract. Sift 2 cups of flour with baking powder and salt. Add to creamed butter and sugar, alternating with milk. Mix remaining ½ cup of flour with fruits, almonds, and coconut, and blend into the batter. Last, gently fold in beaten egg whites. Decorate the top with candied red cherries and bake in a well-greased and floured 10-inch tube pan for 2½ hours until firm. Remove from pan, cool, and moisten with rum if desired.

YIELD: ONE 10-INCH TUBE CAKE.

No-Bake Fruitcake

If you like, rum can be used in place of citrus juices or sprinkled on top.

*1 cup assorted candied fruits
(pineapple, lemon, orange, citron,
red cherries)*

1 cup golden raisins

½ cup chopped dates

¾ cup chopped walnuts

*3½ cups graham cracker crumbs
(1 pound of crackers)*

½ teaspoon ground cinnamon

¼ teaspoon grated nutmeg

⅛ teaspoon ground cloves

*1 cup miniature marshmallows,
packed*

1 tablespoon lemon juice

3 tablespoons orange juice

⅔ cup evaporated milk

2 tablespoons honey

Whipped cream, for topping

In a large bowl mix candied fruits, raisins, dates, nuts, cracker crumbs, and spices. In a separate bowl mix marshmallows, citrus juices, milk, and honey, and stir well. Blend everything together until crumbs are moist, then press into an 8-inch loaf pan. Chill for several days before slicing, and top each slice with a dollop of whipped cream.

Asa

Asa was the "baby" of the Sampson family. In fact, he was ten years younger than his nearest brother, Glen. Although quite loquacious now, Asa tells us that the motto of the house when he was growing up was "Silence is golden," and, in dealing with the community, "Stick to your own business." That meant you were in no way to keep up with the Joneses or do what they were doing. This was a point Corine made crystal clear to Asa one Sunday. When some playmates, who knew he couldn't play on the Sabbath, asked to borrow his baseball gear, Asa readily lent them his bat, ball, and mitt. But when they were returned, Corine made Asa burn them up in the backyard. Moral: Thinking about or abetting an act is as damning as participating in it.

Cards were considered the Bible of the devil, and movies and dancing were equally taboo. But Asa's curiosity got the better of him once. He found a partner and, with two other couples, learned to dance by listening to Arthur Murray's instructions over the radio. After Corine accelerated her Sunday-school activities by presenting Easter pageants with the neighborhood children, Asa began to feel that his dancing was a poor reflection on her and eliminated it from his agenda. He has been a serious member of his mother's Holiness Church ever since.

Asa says that although Mom Sampson was strict, she had a lovely smile and a teasing sense of humor. He recalls with a chuckle that after he had sold nine piglets and come home from a shopping spree wearing a new shirt, she inquired about the price. When told it cost seventy-five cents, she laughingly shook her head and said, "Seventy-five cents! Imagine that, a seventy-five-cent shirt on a twenty-five-cent boy!" and gave him a hug.

Although Asa remembers more toil than pleasure in his childhood, there were happy days. During the spring street carnivals came to town; in summer there was boating or swimming in the stone quarry; and then there were birthdays. Dad and Mom Sampson gave each child a large apple or orange and a penny for every year.

Asa literally married the girl next door, Gertrude. They raised four children in the house that Dad Sampson built, and now play host to visiting grandchildren. Everyday Asa walks three and three-quarter miles to and from the telephone company where he works. "Neighbors used to set their clocks by Dad's walk to work along the railroad," Asa told us, "but I now have to vary my route, because I've been robbed twice. That's one difference between today and yesterday. Folks didn't have to lock anything and no one was afraid to feed a stranger."

Asa is a photography buff and, while rummaging through some old negatives, discovered a quaint recipe for Devil's Food Cake in Corine's handwriting. Gertrude has added her own touch to another dish Mom Sampson used to prepare on Saturday for Sunday supper—Chicken in the Pot. Chicken and cake are still their favorite Sunday-night fare.

Gertrude's Chicken in the Pot

One 4- to 5-pound stewing hen, or two
   2½-pound chickens

Salt to taste

2 slices lemon

8 small potatoes, unpeeled

4 carrots, scraped and diced

2 stalks celery, chopped

1 medium onion, chopped

½ pound string beans, cut into thirds

1 bunch parsley, chopped

¼ teaspoon dried thyme

Pepper to taste

Place game hen or chickens in a big pot (a Dutch oven will do nicely). Cover with water. Add a dash of salt and bring to a full boil. Skim the surface and reduce flame. Add lemon slices, cover, and simmer for 30 minutes (1 hour for stewing hen). Add vegetables, herbs, and salt and pepper to taste, and simmer for another 30 minutes or until fork tender. Serve in soup bowls with plenty of broth.

YIELD: WILL SERVE 4 TO 5 RAVENOUS PEOPLE.

Devil's Food Cake

¾ cup cocoa

1⅓ cups sugar

⅔ cup vegetable shortening, such as
   Crisco

1 teaspoon salt

1 teaspoon vanilla extract

1 cup buttermilk

3 eggs

1¾ cups sifted cake flour

1¼ teaspoons baking soda

White Mountain Cream Icing (recipe
   follows)

Preheat oven to 350°. Combine cocoa and sugar. Place shortening, salt, and vanilla in a mixing bowl. Add sugar-cocoa mixture in fifths, creaming 100 strokes (about 2 minutes in an electric mixer) after each addition and adding 2 tablespoons of the buttermilk after the third addition of the sugar-cocoa mixture. Add eggs, one at a time, beating 100 strokes after each addition. Sift flour and baking soda together 3 times. Add flour in fourths, alternating with remaining milk in thirds, beating 50 strokes for each addition of flour and 25 strokes for each addition of milk. Pour into two greased and floured 9-inch layer pans and bake for 25 to 35 minutes. Prepare icing and spread on each layer and sides of cooled cake.

YIELD: 8 TO 10 SERVINGS.

White Mountain Cream Icing

1 cup sugar

½ teaspoon cream of tartar

¼ cup water

1 egg white

½ teaspoon vanilla extract

Boil the sugar, cream of tartar, and water together. Beat egg white until stiff. Remove sugar syrup from fire when little threads spin off a spoon, and pour over beaten egg white. Beat vigorously with sweeping strokes until cool. Add vanilla extract and spread on cooled cake.

YIELD: 1 CUP.

Mamie Jean Sampson Darden

Our mother was a rare combination of femininity and strength. She admired beauty in art and in nature and radiated a special beauty of her own. She was fond of poetry, of harp and organ music, and would sing in the oddest little light voice. Yet, if the lights went out, if a pipe burst or a tire went flat, she could fix them. Flowers grew in profusion in her matchless flower garden, and she always gathered them around her and gave them generously as gifts. So at home with nature was she that we can remember bees flying in and out of her hair without her fearing a sting. She had been the only girl growing up with four brothers on a farm, and could ride a horse, swim, bicycle, and play an aggressive game of tennis. In appearance, she was unassuming and modest, but we never knew her to back down when she thought she was in the right. When she held a little girl's hand the universe seemed safe and secure.

Mamie Jean loved nothing better than giving or receiving a surprise. She was always embroidering or crocheting a gift for someone and always cooked a little something extra in the pot for any unexpected guest. We remember how surprised she was when we drew a mural all over her bedroom wall for her birthday present. It took her a moment to regain her composure, but she kept our scrawlings a week before calling in the painters. And how proud she was when we loaded strawberries from our garden into our red wagon and sold them door to door, earning our first money.

Mother never ever forgot her family's early struggles to survive, and she shared her time and knowledge unselfishly. After graduation from Ohio University, she immediately went to where the greatest educational challenges were at that time—the rural South. There she taught elementary school in West Virginia; North Carolina; and Petersburg, Virginia, where she met her future husband—Bud, our father. A new job in Buffalo, New York, as a social worker for the Urban League, brought her closer to him and to the altar.

Out of a concern for the quality of life for all people, she became a devoted community worker after her marriage. She was a member of the New Jersey Emergency Relief Administration, a YWCA board member, worked with the League of Women Voters and Planned Parenthood, and served on the board for youth consultation at the Friendly Neighborhood House. We remember the countless PTA and Town Hall meetings she attended, and the many camping expeditions she led with her Girl Scout troop, but most of all we remember the annual skit she and her friends put on at Christmastime at the old folks' home. None of the ladies could sing, but that didn't put a dent in their spirits or the amusement of the senior citizens.

Many of Mother's friends and relatives depended on her advice because her keen insight always got to the heart of the problem and because her sense of justice and logic was unfailing. In her youth she had been her family's inspiration, smoothing all ruffled feathers and charting everyone's course. We called her "the answer woman" because our phone was always ringing with someone wanting to consult on a problem—personal or financial. It seemed so incongruous that little ex-schoolmarm Mamie Jean was quite a businesswoman, but she read the *Wall Street Journal*, studied economics with zeal, and attended many classes and lectures on real estate and investment. In her later years she regretted not having used her financial acumen in a professional capacity, yet we still hear praise for the sound tips and business knowledge she gave to others. Her theory was that poverty and war were like weeds in a garden, enemies that must be removed from our world. The last task she completed before her death was, appropriately, plucking weeds from around her prized rose tree.

We feel blessed to have had her as our mother. She taught us to live adventurously; to love rain; to suck the nectar from honeysuckle; to make a garden; to fashion dolls from corn silk; to color Easter eggs with plant dyes; and to recognize birds, flowers, leaves, and trees. She instilled in us a spirit of independence and taught us to stand firm in whatever we thought was right, and to pursue our own dreams until they became realities, without losing sight of the fact that how the struggle is waged is as important as the victory. In the best sense of the word, she was the most "liberated" woman we ever knew.

For many years she had been childless, so when we finally arrived, she liked nothing better than feeding us. We were poor eaters, so she had to be creative with food, and she was. Surprises, sherbets, soups, and basics—oh, what lovely treats we remember from Ms. Mamie Jean!

Mother's first class in
the rural South

Mamie Jean Sampson Darden

Egg Surprise

Mother and us

1 slice whole-wheat bread   *1 egg*
1 pat butter

Using a small teacup or biscuit cutter, cut out a circle in the center of the bread. In a frying pan put butter and let it sizzle. Add hollowed slice of bread and crack egg into the hole over the butter. Fry until egg is firm and gently turn over. Also toast the circle part of the bread on both sides and use this to cover the egg. This "surprise" will delight a child.

YIELD: 1 EGG SURPRISE.

Snow Ice Cream

On the first big snow of the year, our mother would collect some freshly fallen snow in a big pan. Then she would add a little sugar and some heavy cream, along with a few drops of vanilla extract, and stir it up. You had to eat fast before it melted. We called it "nature's ice cream" and loved it.

Rose Petal Jelly

1 cup tender rose petals, well packed
(see Note)

¼ cup rose water, or 1 teaspoon rose
extract

¾ cup water

1⅓ cups sugar

1 tablespoon honey

1 teaspoon lemon juice

Cut petals into fine pieces and wash in a colander or large strainer. Place petals, rose water, and water in a saucepan and simmer for 5 minutes or until petals are soft. Strain petals and measure ½ cup of remaining liquid (add water if you have less). Return liquid to saucepan. Add sugar and honey and bring to a rapid boil. Return petals to saucepan and reduce heat. Simmer very slowly for 20 minutes, then add lemon juice and cook for 5 minutes more. Pour into heated jars and seal with paraffin (see page 37).

Once we accidentally overcooked this recipe and made a delicious discovery. The mixture had become too stiff to make a jelly, so we dropped it by spoonfuls on a greased cookie sheet and enjoyed rose petal candy instead!

YIELD: 2 SMALL JARS.

NOTE: *Use only roses that have not been treated with pesticides. Do not use commercial roses.*

Lollipops or Hard Candy

2 cups sugar

¾ cup clear corn syrup

1 cup water

⅛ teaspoon salt

2 teaspoons fruit-flavored extract, such as cherry, lemon, or orange

¼ teaspoon food coloring

Lollipop sticks

Grease a cookie sheet, then combine the sugar, corn syrup, water, and salt in a medium-size saucepan. Cook over medium heat, stirring constantly, until the hard crack point of 300° is reached on a candy thermometer, or a drop of the mixture placed in a cup of cold water turns into a brittle ball. Promptly remove from heat and stir in the extract and food coloring of your choice. Work fast, as candy hardens quickly. Pour little circles of candy on the cookie sheet and leave enough room for the sticks, which you must push in immediately, making sure that ½ inch of the end is well covered. When lollipops are cool, jiggle loose from cookie sheet and wrap in wax paper. If lollipop sticks are unavailable, Dixie cup spoons split in two work well. Without a stick, you will still have delicious hard candy. (You can put Popsicle sticks into 4 large apples, dip them in this mixture, and make candied apples too.)

YIELD: 2 DOZEN LOLLIPOPS.

Watermelon Cake

3 cups sifted all-purpose flour

3 teaspoons baking powder

¼ teaspoon salt

4 egg whites

1 stick (½ cup) butter

1½ cups sugar

1 cup milk

1 teaspoon vanilla extract

¾ teaspoon red food coloring

⅓ cup seedless black raisins, floured

Dark Green Frosting (recipe follows)

Preheat oven to 350°. Sift flour, baking powder, and salt together. Beat egg whites until stiff, then set aside. Cream butter and sugar until fluffy and add dry ingredients, alternating with the milk. When well blended, add vanilla and carefully fold in the beaten egg whites. Pour half of the batter into another bowl, add red food coloring and floured raisins. Grease and flour a 9-inch spring-form or tube pan and pour half the white batter into the bottom of the pan. Gently spread the red batter on top (the raisins will look like watermelon seeds). Then cover with the other half of the white batter (the rind). Bake for 40 to 50 minutes, or until the edges shrink from the sides of the pan and the center is firm to the touch. When cool, frost with Dark Green Frosting.

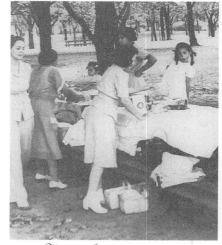

Mamie Jean at family reunion picnic in Delaware——Jean Marie, Gertrude (back row), Cassie (foreground)

Dark Green Frosting

2 tablespoons butter

2 cups confectioners' sugar

2 tablespoons heavy cream

1 teaspoon green food coloring

Mamie Jean Sampson Darden

Cream butter, and add remaining ingredients. Mix until smooth and spread on Watermelon Cake (recipe above).

YIELD: 2 CUPS.

VARIATION:

As kids, we were so thrilled with this recipe that we added 2 tablespoons of real watermelon juice to the red batter for authenticity and even attempted a cantaloupe cake by using an orange center with golden raisins for the seeds and Honey Icing (see page 176) for the rind.

YIELD: ENOUGH FOR 1 WATERMELON CAKE.

Peach Tea

A refreshing twist on regular iced tea.

3 cups chilled tea

6 tablespoons sugar

½ cup lemon juice

3 cups peach nectar

2 cups ginger ale

Ice, orange slices, cloves, and fresh mint sprigs

Combine first 5 ingredients in a large pitcher. Pour into tall, ice-filled glasses. Decorate each glass with an orange slice studded with cloves and a sprig of mint.

YIELD: 8 SERVINGS.

Ginger Ale Salad

The name always intrigued us.

1 cup sliced fresh peaches, grapefruit, and cherries

½ cup canned crushed pineapple, drained

¼ cup seedless grapes

¾ cup drained juice from fruit

2 envelopes unflavored gelatin

2 tablespoons lemon juice

½ teaspoon ground ginger

Pinch of salt

Pinch of paprika

½ cup mayonnaise

2 cups ginger ale

¼ cup slivered almonds

Combine fruits in a mixing bowl. Measure ¾ cup of the juice that has accumulated and place it in a saucepan. Sprinkle gelatin over the juice and let it sit for 2 minutes, then simmer until dissolved. Add lemon juice, ginger, salt, paprika, mayonnaise, and ginger ale. Blend well, and chill until mixture is the consistency of egg whites. Then stir in fruit and almonds. Mix well and turn into a 1½-quart circular mold or individual ones. Chill until set. To remove salad, immerse mold in warm water for 1 minute. Then gently run a knife around the rim and invert onto a platter. Serve on a bed of lettuce.

YIELD: 6 TO 8 SERVINGS.

Mamie Jean Sampson Darden

Chocolate Punch

We enjoyed serving this to the neighborhood gang.

Four 1-ounce squares semisweet
   chocolate
½ cup sugar
2 cups hot water
2 quarts milk
1½ teaspoons vanilla extract

1 quart vanilla ice cream
1 quart club soda
½ pint heavy cream, whipped
Ground cinnamon

In a large saucepan combine the chocolate and sugar with the hot water. Bring to a boil, stirring for 2 minutes. Add milk, and continue heating. When hot, beat in vanilla with a rotary egg beater or whisk. Remove from heat. Chill, then pour into a punch bowl over ice cream. For sparkle, add club soda. Top with whipped cream and dust with cinnamon.

YIELD: 12 SERVINGS.

Who could ever forget Mother's favorite Girl Scout classics?

Jungle Stew

2 large onions, chopped

1 green bell pepper, seeded and chopped

1 clove garlic, minced

¼ cup vegetable oil

2 pounds ground beef

1 cup uncooked elbow macaroni

Two 15-ounce cans red beans

Two 1-pound cans stewed tomatoes

Salt and pepper to taste

Sauté onions, pepper, and garlic in the oil in a pot until onion is wilted. Add meat and brown. Then add all other ingredients and simmer until macaroni is tender.

YIELD: 8 SERVINGS FOR HUNGRY CAMPERS.

Mother camping out with friends Clara, Bea, and Olivia in Buffalo

Mamie Jean Sampson Darden

Some Mores

2 marshmallows   1 milk chocolate bar
2 whole graham crackers

Toast marshmallows over the campfire. Then place them on top of a graham cracker. Add milk chocolate bar, top with the second graham cracker, and press down to form a sandwich.

YIELD: 1 SERVING.

SHERBETS

Orange Jack-O'-Lanterns

Sherbet was one of Mother's favorite snacks, and she loved making her own.

At Halloween, she would cut off the tops and scoop out the insides of oranges, make little mouths, eyes, and noses, and fill them with homemade Orange Cream Sherbet (recipe follows).

Orange Cream Sherbet

1 teaspoon unflavored gelatin

2 tablespoons cold water

1 cup orange juice

½ cup milk

½ cup heavy cream

Juice of 1 lemon

½ cup sugar

In a small saucepan soak gelatin in cold water. Stir over medium heat until completely dissolved. Let cool. Combine all other ingredients and add gelatin. Pour into an ice tray, cover with wax paper, and put in freezer. When frozen, put into a mixing bowl and beat until light. Return to ice tray and refreeze.

YIELD: 3 TO 4 SERVINGS, OR FILLING FOR 4 ORANGES.

Mother enjoying ice cream she sold with friend Elsie

Easy Grape Sherbet

1 cup unsweetened grape juice

½ cup sugar

2 cups milk

Warm grape juice. Dissolve sugar into it. Let cool and add cold milk. (See Note.) Pour into 2 ice trays and freeze. When solid, remove from trays and beat briskly with an egg beater. Return to trays, cover with tin foil or wax paper, and refreeze. For some reason this sherbet tastes like violets.

YIELD: 6 TO 8 SERVINGS.

NOTE: *Mixture may curdle but will become smooth during the freezing process.*

Mamie Jean Sampson Darden

Mint-Lime Ice

1½ cups boiling water

One 8-ounce jar mint jelly

1 pint ginger ale

Juice of 3 limes

½ cup honey

2 egg whites, stiffly beaten

Pour boiling water over jelly in a bowl. Stir until dissolved. Let cool. Add ginger ale, lime juice, and honey. Pour into 2 ice trays, cover with wax paper, and put in freezer. Chill to the semisolid stage. Remove from freezer and mix in beaten egg whites. Replace in freezer and serve when solid.

YIELD: 6 TO 8 SERVINGS.

Watermelon Sherbet

2 cups watermelon puree (either mash through a sieve or use a blender)

2 teaspoons unflavored gelatin

¼ cup water

½ cup sugar

½ teaspoon lemon juice

⅓ cup milk

¼ cup heavy cream

Place watermelon puree in a large bowl. Soak gelatin in the water for about 5 minutes. Place in a small saucepan over medium heat, and stir until completely dissolved. Let cool. Stir into watermelon puree. Add sugar, lemon juice, milk, and cream. Blend well. Pour into 2 ice trays, cover with wax paper or aluminum foil, and freeze. When frozen, remove from trays, beat briskly with an egg beater, return to trays, and refreeze.

YIELD: 6 TO 8 SERVINGS.

Cranberry-Orange Sherbet

1 cup heavy cream

One 1-pound can jellied cranberry
    sauce

One 6-ounce can frozen orange juice

¼ cup sugar (optional)

Dash of ground cinnamon

Dash of salt

Place heavy cream in a mixing bowl and beat with an egg beater until stiff peaks form. Gradually beat in cranberry sauce and frozen juice. Add sugar if desired, cinnamon, and salt. Beat until well blended. Pour into 2 ice trays, put into freezer. Freeze until solid.

YIELD: 6 TO 8 SERVINGS.

Mamie Jean Sampson Darden

Our winters were warmed and summers cooled with Mother's soups.

Vegetable—Bone Marrow Soup

Mother and friends

Two 1-inch-thick slices beef shinbone, meat and marrow intact

3–5 meaty beef neck bones

1 teaspoon pepper

5 quarts boiling water (do not hesitate to use any vegetable stock available)

2 large onions, quartered, then sliced

Two 28-ounce cans whole tomatoes and their juice

¼ cup dried green split peas

¼ cup dried yellow split peas

¼ cup small dried lima beans

¼ cup small-grain barley

½ pound okra, cut into ¼-inch rounds

2 carrots, scraped and cut into rounds

2 celery stalks, sliced thin

1 cup corn, fresh if possible, but one 8-ounce can will suffice

1 cup fresh string beans

2 medium parsnips, peeled and cut into small rounds

Salt to taste (about 2–3 tablespoons)

Add shinbone, neck bones, and pepper to boiling water. Simmer briskly for 1 hour, skimming foam as it forms. Add onions and tomatoes. After an additional 30 minutes, add peas, lima beans, and barley. Continue cooking for 1½ hours, stirring occasionally. Add remaining vegetables and salt to taste. Cook a final 45 minutes to 1 hour, or until meat falls from the bones. Remove meat to trim fat and unpalatable gristle. Then return meat to pot and adjust seasonings. Total cooking time should be 3½ to 4 hours. This soup is best when cooked in quantity, so if you don't have a 10- to 15-quart pot, now is the time to buy or borrow one.

This hearty soup, which is a meal in itself, can be refrigerated for several days, or frozen and used throughout the winter months.

YIELD: SERVES MULTITUDES!

Turkey Soup

Since a turkey means a feast for our family and friends, this recipe is based on a 24-pound turkey or heavier. If you begin with a smaller bird, feel free to experiment and adjust the proportions. At any rate, this is how ours is made.

1 large turkey carcass

½ cup turkey stuffing, if you have some left over

2 fairly large onions, chopped

2 bay leaves

Salt and pepper to taste

3 carrots, sliced into rounds

5 large stalks celery, halved (includes tops and leaves)

Cut as much turkey as possible from the carcass, dice the meat, and set this aside. Place carcass, including wings, drumsticks, and stuffing, in a large pot. Add water to cover, bring to a boil, and lower heat. Add onions, bay leaves, and seasonings. Simmer for 2 hours. Then remove large bones and strain broth through a sieve into a clean pot. Add carrots and celery and continue cooking for 45 minutes. Remove the celery stalks with a slotted spoon and puree in a blender. Then stir puree into the soup to thicken it. Add reserved diced turkey, adjust seasonings, and cook at a slow simmer for 15 minutes more.

YIELD: ABOUT 10 SERVINGS.

Tomato Bisque

10 large ripe tomatoes

2 tablespoons butter

2 medium onions, chopped

1 cup chicken broth

1 bay leaf

Pinch of sugar

Salt and pepper to taste

1 cup light cream or milk

Croutons (optional)

Reserve 1 tomato and coarsely chop the rest. Melt butter in a large saucepan and sauté onions until tender. Add chopped tomatoes and cook about 15 minutes or until tender. Puree chopped tomatoes and onions in a blender (or food mill) and return to saucepan. Add chicken broth and bring to a slow boil. Add bay leaf, sugar, salt, and pepper and simmer for 20 minutes. Peel and chop reserved tomato into small bits. Add to saucepan along with milk. Simmer for 5 minutes and serve. Sprinkle with croutons if desired.

YIELD: 6 SERVINGS.

Cold Buttermilk Soup

1 quart buttermilk

½ cucumber, peeled and diced fine

½ tomato, peeled and diced fine

One 6-ounce can baby shrimp, drained,
or ½ pound cooked fresh shrimp

Fresh dill, for garnish

Combine first 4 ingredients. Chill. Sprinkle with dill and serve cold.
This is a refreshing soup on a hot summer day.

YIELD: 6 SERVINGS.

MOTHER'S BASICS

Mamie Jean's Chicken Fricassee

One 4- to 4½-pound stewing chicken,
cut into eight pieces

1 quart water

3 carrots, halved

2 large stalks celery, cut into thirds

1 small onion, quartered

1 bay leaf

2 pinches of rosemary

2 teaspoons salt

⅛ teaspoon pepper

2 cups uncooked elbow macaroni, or
batter for Drop Dumplings (recipe
follows)

Wash chicken thoroughly, removing any visible pieces of fat. In a Dutch oven bring water to a boil. Add carrots, celery, onion, bay leaf, and rosemary. Drop the chicken, piece by piece, into this so as not to lower the boiling point. Cover pot, lower heat, and simmer for 1 hour. Add salt and pepper and continue simmering for 30 minutes or until chicken is tender. Adjust seasoning, then add the macaroni, if using it. If there is not enough broth to cover the macaroni, add more water. If making dumplings, remove the celery, puree it in a blender with a small amount of liquid, and add it to the pot to thicken the broth. Then ease teaspoonfuls of batter into the boiling liquid so that they rest partially on the chicken. Cover and continue cooking for 18 minutes.

YIELD: 5 TO 6 SERVINGS.

NOTE: *If you wish a fricassee with more liquid, cook noodles separately in 5 cups of chicken broth made from boiling the neck, gizzard, liver, and heart with a small onion, a carrot, a celery stalk, salt, pepper, and a bay leaf.*

Mother, ready to serve

Drop Dumplings

1 cup flour

½ teaspoon salt

2 teaspoons baking powder

1½ tablespoons melted butter

⅓ cup milk or chicken stock

Sift together dry ingredients. Add melted butter and milk or stock, and mix. Batter should be moist but stiff. Drop by teaspoonfuls into boiling liquid. Cover and cook for about 18 minutes.

YIELD: 1 DOZEN DUMPLINGS.

On wedding anniversaries, when we were put to bed early and romance was in the air, Mother pulled out her special dishes for two.

Stuffed Red Snapper (or Striped Bass) with Shrimp and Raisin Stuffing for 2

Have fish prepared for stuffing at the fish market. Request that the head and tail be left on so as to preserve fish juices.

One 2-pound red snapper

Salt

1 tablespoon heavy cream, sour cream, or melted butter

1 tablespoon dried bread crumbs or dry stuffing

Paprika

⅓ cup white wine

Lemon slices, for garnish

STUFFING:

5 raw jumbo shrimp, shelled and deveined

1 tablespoon butter

2 tablespoons diced celery

2 tablespoons minced onion

⅛ teaspoon dried thyme

¼ teaspoon salt

¼ teaspoon garlic powder

2 dashes of pepper

1¼ cups dried bread cubes or prepared stuffing mix

1 egg, lightly beaten

2 tablespoons milk

1 tablespoon raisins

Preheat oven to 375°. Wash fish thoroughly. Pat dry and place in a shallow baking dish. Salt fish liberally inside and out. For the stuffing: Wash shrimp, and cut into ¼-inch slices. Set aside. In a small saucepan melt butter. Add celery and onion and sauté until tender. Add shrimp, sauté until slightly pink, and remove from heat. Stir in thyme, salt, garlic powder, and pepper. Mix the dried bread cubes or stuffing mix with the egg, milk, and raisins and add to the sautéed mixture. Mix thoroughly. (You should have about 1½ cups of stuffing.) Fill fish cavity, including the head area. Rub the top of the fish with the cream, sour cream, or melted butter. Sprinkle with dried bread crumbs and paprika. Pour wine into the baking dish but not over fish. Bake for 35 to 40 minutes. Garnish with lemon slices.

YIELD: A FILLING MEAL FOR 2, SERVED WITH ONLY A SALAD
OR A VEGETABLE.

NOTE: *Shrimp and raisin stuffing is excellent for turkey and chicken as well. Adjust the quantity according to the size of the bird to be stuffed. You may also add soft sausage that has been cooked in small lumps, about ¼ cup or less to every 1½ to 2 cups of stuffing.*

*Mother in Delaware, Ohio,
with her best friend, Elsie*

Crab-Stuffed Fillet of Flounder for 2

⅓ cup diced onion

⅓ cup finely chopped celery

1 tablespoon butter

¼ pound crab meat, picked over to
    remove any shells, and flaked

¾ cup prepared stuffing mix

1 egg, lightly beaten

4 medium flounder fillets

SAUCE:

2 tablespoons butter

¼ cup thinly sliced fresh mushrooms

3 tablespoons flour

½ cup fish stock or ½ cup water and
    1 fish bouillon cube

½ cup white wine

¾ cup heavy cream

Paprika

Preheat oven to 350°. Sauté onion and celery in butter until tender. Add crab meat and continue cooking for 2 or 3 minutes. Remove from heat. Add stuffing mix and beaten egg. Mix well. Spread equal amounts in center of fillets, and roll, starting with the smaller end. Lay each rolled fillet on its flap so that it does not come apart. For the sauce: Melt butter in a small saucepan. Add mushrooms. Stir in flour. Add stock or water and bouillon cube and stir constantly over low heat until mixture thickens. Add white wine and continue cooking for 3 to 4 minutes. Add cream and cook until slightly reduced and thickened. Pour sauce over fillets, and sprinkle with paprika. Bake for about 25 minutes.

YIELD: 2 SERVINGS.

Mamie Jean Sampson Darden

Fresh Green Peas
at Their Best

Fresh green peas are also delicious as a raw vegetable served in salads.

2 pounds green peas in their pods

1½ tablespoons butter, plus
    1½ teaspoons (optional), for
    topping

1 medium onion, sliced

Salt and pepper to taste

A few sprigs parsley, chopped fine

Shell peas, place in a saucepan, and add just enough water to cover. Bring to a boil and cook rapidly, uncovered, for about 20 minutes or until peas are just tender. Drain and set aside. In a frying pan melt 1½ tablespoons butter, add onion slices, and sauté until they are browned and tender. Add peas and seasonings. Stirring frequently, sauté lightly until reheated. Top with extra butter if you wish, and sprinkle with chopped parsley.

YIELD: 4 SERVINGS.

Fried Green Tomatoes

2 large green tomatoes, unpeeled

3 tablespoons bacon fat or vegetable oil

1 egg, beaten with 1 tablespoon water

Dry bread crumbs, lightly salted

Slice tomatoes a little over ¼-inch thick. Heat bacon fat or oil in a heavy skillet. Dip tomato slices in egg. Place bread crumbs on wax paper and coat each side of the slices. Fry over medium heat until golden brown on both sides and tender throughout when pricked with a fork. Drain on paper towels. Serve hot as a dinner or breakfast vegetable.

YIELD: 4 SERVINGS.

Yellow Squash and Onions

2 medium yellow squash

Salt and pepper to taste

1 medium onion, sliced thin

2–3 tablespoons bacon fat or butter

Cut squash into ¼-inch slices. Sprinkle with salt and pepper. Place ¼ inch of water in a heavy skillet. When water boils, add squash. Lay onion slices on top. Cover and steam over medium-high heat until all the water has evaporated, watching carefully so that squash doesn't burn. Add bacon fat or butter, stirring so that squash is well coated. Cook uncovered over low heat for about 30 minutes, or until tender, stirring occasionally.

YIELD: 4 SERVINGS.

Mamie Jean Sampson Darden

Strawberry Pie

Carole's most requested dessert.

One 9-inch baked pie shell
(see following recipe)

2 pints fresh strawberries, stemmed
and washed

1 cup sugar

2 tablespoons cornstarch

1 cup water

2 tablespoons strawberry Jell-O powder

1 pint heavy cream

1 teaspoon vanilla extract

Prepare pie shell. Drain the berries and set aside. Combine sugar, cornstarch, and water. Cook over medium heat until thick and clear. Remove from heat and add Jell-O. Mix well. Cool slightly. Fill pie shell with whole berries. Pour mixture evenly over them. Chill for at least 4 hours. Just before serving, whip cream to form stiff peaks. Beat in vanilla, and mound on top of pie. Since this is a fairly sweet pie, we prefer unsweetened whipped cream, but you may like a little powdered sugar blended in. Delicious!

YIELD: 6 TO 8 SERVINGS.

Excellent Single Pie Shell

1½ cups flour

½ teaspoon salt

½ cup solid vegetable shortening

3 tablespoons ice water

Preheat oven to 475°. Sift flour and salt into a bowl, reserving 4 tablespoons. Cut shortening into flour and salt mixture until lumps the size of small peas form. Blend the reserved flour and ice water to form a paste. Add to flour and mix lightly and quickly until mixture can be formed into a somewhat flaky ball. Put dough on wax paper, placing a second sheet of wax paper over it. Roll, with short, light strokes, to ⅛-inch thickness. Remove top layer of wax paper. Place dough in a 9- or 10-inch pie plate, using a knife to loosen dough gently from wax paper. Trim edges, leaving about ½ inch overlapping. Flute edges as desired. If pie shell is to be baked before being filled, prick dough in several spots over its surface with a fork. Bake for 8 to 10 minutes.

YIELD: ONE 9- OR 10-INCH PIE SHELL.

Apple Brown Betty

Carole's second most-requested dessert.

2 cups fresh whole-wheat bread crumbs

¼ cup melted butter

½ cup sugar

1 teaspoon ground cinnamon

Juice and grated rind of ½ lemon

5–6 tart apples, peeled, cored, and sliced

½ cup orange juice

Heavy or light cream

Preheat oven to 350°. With a fork, lightly toss bread crumbs with melted butter. Combine sugar, cinnamon, lemon juice and rind to form a paste. Line the bottom of a buttered casserole dish with approximately one third of the bread-crumb mixture. Spread half the apples over the crumbs, then half the paste over the apples. Repeat this process, with crumbs as final layer. Pour orange juice evenly over apple mixture. Cover and bake for 30 minutes. Uncover and bake for another 15 minutes, or until apples are very tender. Serve hot or cold with whipped or plain cream.

YIELD: 6 SERVINGS.

Aunt Marjorie Palmer's Every-Kind-of-Cookie Dough

Aunt Marjorie, a close friend of Mother's, gave her this basic recipe, and we have used it to make at least nine varieties of crunchy cookies.

¾ cup equal amounts butter and solid
    vegetable shortening

½ cup brown sugar

½ cup granulated sugar

1 egg

1 teaspoon vanilla extract

2 cups sifted all-purpose flour

½ teaspoon baking soda

¼ teaspoon salt

Preheat oven to 400°. Cream the butter and shortening together with the sugars until fluffy. The butter is for flavor and the shortening adds crispness. Then add the egg and vanilla and blend well. Sift the flour with the soda and salt, then resift. Add to butter mixture, blending well. Divide dough in half and, using your finger tips, roll each half into a long roll about 2 inches in diameter. (One roll may be frozen for future use if you so choose.) Chill dough ½ hour, then cut roll into ¼-inch slices or press through a cookie press. Bake on a greased cookie sheet for 6 to 8 minutes or until cookies are golden around the edges.

YIELD: 5 DOZEN COOKIES.

VARIATIONS:

1. Peanut butter—combine ½ cup peanut butter with ½ cup butter, omitting shortening and using ½ cup less flour.

2. Chocolate chip—add ½ cup chocolate chips, ¼ cup chopped nuts, and 2 tablespoons milk.

3. Lemon wafers—add 1 tablespoon freshly grated lemon rind and replace vanilla with lemon extract.

4. Molasses-spice—add 2 tablespoons molasses, 1½ teaspoons more baking soda, and replace vanilla with 1 teaspoon each ground ginger, cloves, and cinnamon.

5. Honey—replace granulated sugar with ½ cup honey; add ½ cup more flour.

6. Pumpkin—add 1 tablespoon pumpkin pie spice.

7. Apple—add 1 tablespoon apple pie spice and 1 small apple, peeled, cored, and chopped.

8. Eggnog—add 1 tablespoon rum and 1 teaspoon grated nutmeg.

9. Fruitcake—add 1 tablespoon brandy and ½ cup chopped citron and nuts.

Coconut Cake

3 cups sifted cake flour

3 teaspoons baking powder

½ teaspoon salt

3 eggs, separated

1¼ cup sugar

1 cup butter

¼ cup milk

¾ cup coconut milk (see Note)

1 teaspoon vanilla extract

¼ cup finely grated fresh coconut (see Note)

Seven-Minute Frosting (recipe follows)

Preheat oven to 350°. Sift the flour, baking powder, and salt together twice. Beat egg whites until stiff, then add ¼ cup of the sugar and set aside. Cream butter until fluffy and add remaining 1½ cups of sugar and the egg yolks, mixing well. Add flour, alternating with milk and coconut milk, and blend until smooth. Add vanilla and grated coconut. Last, fold in egg whites. Bake in three well-buttered 8-inch cake pans for 30 minutes, or until the edges shrink from the sides of the pans and the cakes are firm to the touch in the center. Loosen the cakes by running a knife around the edge of the pans. Turn onto cake racks and cool. When cool, cover with Seven-Minute Frosting.

YIELD: SERVES 12.

NOTE: *Prepare the coconut by drilling a hole in the "eye" and draining the milk. Hammer it open, remove the white meat, and grate it. Coconut milk can also be bought in cans at most supermarkets.*

Seven-Minute Frosting

2 egg whites

1½ cups sugar

5 tablespoons cold water

¼ teaspoon cream of tartar, or
    1½ teaspoons light corn syrup

¼ teaspoon salt

1 teaspoon vanilla extract

1½ cups finely shredded coconut

Mother at University of Ohio in Athens with friend Marie

Place egg whites, sugar, cold water, cream of tartar or corn syrup, and salt in the top of a double boiler. Then place over rapidly boiling water, beating constantly with an egg beater, for 7 minutes, or until icing will stand in peaks. Remove from heat, add vanilla, and continue to beat until thick enough to spread. When entire cake has been frosted, sprinkle coconut generously over the top and sides.

YIELD: ENOUGH FOR ONE 8-INCH CAKE.

VARIATION:

This huge production was Norma's birthday cake every year, and one year it somehow evolved into Ambrosia Cake when we ate too much of the coconut and had to stretch it with ¼ cup grated orange rind and decorate the top with mandarin orange sections.

Indian Pudding

Delicious, nutritious, makes you feel ambitious.

1 quart milk	1 teaspoon ground cinnamon
⅓ cup yellow cornmeal	¼ teaspoon ground ginger
2 tablespoons butter	2 eggs
½ cup molasses	1 cup cold milk
½ cup brown sugar	Light cream
½ teaspoon salt	

Preheat oven to 350°. Scald the quart of milk in the top of a double boiler. Add cornmeal and cook for 15 minutes, stirring frequently.

Then add butter, molasses, sugar, salt, spices, and eggs. When well blended pour into a buttered medium-size casserole dish. Pour cold milk on top without stirring it in and bake for 1 hour, or until it is browned on top and the consistency of custard. Serve warm, topped with cream.

YIELD: 6 SERVINGS.

Brownies

Two 1-ounce squares unsweetened chocolate

⅔ cup butter

1 cup sugar

½ cup flour, sifted

½ teaspoon baking powder

⅛ teaspoon salt

2 eggs, beaten

⅔ cup chopped walnut meats

1 teaspoon vanilla extract

Preheat oven to 375°. Melt chocolate and butter in top of a double boiler and cool slightly. Then add all other ingredients in the given order. Mix well and pour into a greased 8-inch-square pan and bake for 25 minutes or until firm when touched in the center.

YIELD: 16 BROWNIES.

Holiday Time with the Winner Sisters

Lucy, Waltine, Mattie

When the holidays roll around, there is one event we look forward to with much anticipation—gorging ourselves silly at Mattie's house. She has our family over every Thanksgiving or Christmas for a dinner prepared with the help of her sisters, Waltine and Lucy. It's so delectable that we hate to finish eating. The sisters have shared their entire menu, along with their thoughts on work, food, and fun in the thirties.

Mattie Winner was a nursing student at Tuskegee while our father was interning there. After he settled in Newark, he sent for Mattie from her native Texas to be his nurse. She joined him in New Jersey, and later arranged for Waltine and Lucy to follow.

In the early 1930s, Newark was not ready for the sisters. Even though they arrived qualified to teach, black teachers were not being hired. So Waltine became Daddy's secretary, and Lucy took a job at Kellar's Drugstore in those preautomation days, taking photographs of people who posed in a little booth. Three for a dime and a dollar for a blowup were the prices.

"Newark was a doozie in the thirties," says Mattie. "The Southern migration brought a lot of people from the South here looking for a better life. But the Depression hit. People had to create their own jobs—and so the numbers racket and speakeasies were going strong. Contagious disease was common, and the increase of cases was alarming. We had to deliver babies at all hours of the night in the home, sometimes by candlelight. If hard work could kill you, we'd all be gone by now."

The sisters agree that World War II changed life for black people in Newark. Defense jobs opened up, the Army absorbed many jobless men, and new welfare systems were initiated. Waltine, who later worked for the Welfare Department, feels that relief did a lot of good for those in need at the time, but when much of the new-found employment disappeared after the war only the welfare system was left for many.

Waltine and Lucy used to eat regularly at Father Divine's Restaurant. He was a colorful and controversial religious cult leader of the time. They remember his delicious and cheap (25 cents for all you could eat) banquets and describe how steaming hot dishes flowed from the kitchen, all perfectly prepared in great abundance and served on long tables covered with white linen, sparkling silver, and bright and fragrant bouquets. No doubt these sumptuous affairs must have been the inspiration for the sisters' own holiday feasts.

Lucy, who eventually did teach in the Newark school system, recalls her early years in Newark as "hard times," but feels that "somehow the town was jumping and we just had a lot of fun. All the big bands and top singers came here. Jimmy Lunceford and Billie Holiday were my favorites, along with Ella and Sarah. Plus, we had local revues and house parties. Rent parties were being given left and right. When the jitterbug hit, that was right up my alley, and don't forget the hukabuck."

Mattie married a dance promoter, Carl Jones, now a nightclub and restaurant owner. Lucy married a handsome undertaker,

Arthur Russell. And Waltine married a GI, Joe Thomas, now a printer. When we were children, they were the most glamorous people in the world. And now that we are older, they still are.

Holiday Dinner, Texas Style, for 12
*Roast Turkey with Corn Bread Stuffing and Giblet Gravy
*Barbecued Ham
*Cranberry Sauce
*Green String Beans
Mixed Greens (see page 159)
*Mashed Yellow Turnips and Carrots
*Creamed Onions
*Sweet Potato Pudding with Marshmallows
*Baked Macaroni with Cheese
*Tossed Green Salad with Homemade Mayonnaise
Refrigerator Rolls (see page 287)
Fruitcake (see pages 205–7)
*Mincemeat Pie
*Ambrosia
*Eggnog
Fresh Fruit
Nuts and Mints

*Asterisk indicates that recipe appears in this chapter.

Mattie's Roast Turkey with Corn Bread Stuffing and Giblet Gravy

One 18–20-pound turkey (oven ready)

Salt and black or white pepper

1 recipe Corn Bread Stuffing (recipe follows)

Vegetable oil (approximately ½ cup)

1 recipe Giblet Gravy (recipe follows)

Preheat oven to 350°. Rub the inside of turkey's cavity with salt and pepper. Rub skin with salt. Fill turkey loosely with Corn Bread Stuffing. Place turkey in a large brown paper bag.° Pour vegetable oil freely on bag and rub while pouring. Tie a cord loosely around open end of bag. Place in a roasting pan and do not cover with lid. Roast turkey for 4½ hours. Serve with Giblet Gravy.

° Please be sure the bag is not made from recycled materials. During the holidays, baking bags are available in most supermarkets.

YIELD: 10 TO 12 SERVINGS.

Corn Bread Stuffing

1 cup chopped onion

1 cup chopped celery

3 teaspoons poultry seasoning

½ cup margarine or vegetable oil

4 cups corn bread crumbs

4 cups white bread crumbs or cubes

1 tablespoon chopped parsley

½ teaspoon salt

½–¾ cup water or turkey giblet broth

Sauté onion, celery, and poultry seasoning in melted margarine or vegetable oil until tender. Do not brown. Combine with corn bread crumbs, white bread crumbs or cubes, and parsley. Add salt and water or turkey giblet broth, and toss lightly with a fork until well mixed.

YIELD: 8 CUPS, OR ENOUGH STUFFING FOR A
15-POUND TURKEY.

VARIATION:

If oyster stuffing is desired, 1 pint of shucked oysters, drained well and coarsely chopped, may be added to recipe.

Giblet Gravy

Turkey neck, liver, gizzard, and heart

1 teaspoon salt, plus extra to taste

½ cup flour, plus enough water to make
   a watery paste

Pepper to taste

Place turkey neck and giblets in a saucepan. Add 1 teaspoon salt and enough water to cover. Boil for 1 hour or more, until giblets are tender. Discard neck and cut giblets into small cubes. After turkey has cooked, puncture bag immediately, remove turkey, and place on a platter. Remove bag, leaving drippings in roasting pan. If there is not enough liquid for 3 cups, add enough stock from giblets to make that amount. Bring this to a rapid boil. Stir in flour and water paste for thickening. Add giblets and cook slowly for about 10 minutes. Adjust seasoning with salt and pepper to taste.

Waltine's Barbecued Ham

One 5-pound precooked ham

1 bottle, or about 2 cups, of your favorite barbecue sauce (we prefer Cousin Kelly Bryant's —see page 158)

Preheat oven to 300°, place ham in a small roasting pan. With a pastry brush or spoon, moisten the ham with sauce. Cook ham for 1½ hours, basting with sauce every 20 minutes. May be served hot or at room temperature.

Cranberry Sauce

1 pound (4 cups) fresh cranberries

1½ cups sugar

1 cup water

1 whole orange, unpeeled, seeds removed and chopped fine

¼ teaspoon ground cloves

½ cup crushed pineapple, drained

½ cup chopped walnuts

Sprinkle of ground cinnamon

Wash cranberries and set aside. Bring sugar and water to a boil. Add cranberries, orange, and cloves. Simmer over a high flame, stirring frequently, until berries pop open. Add crushed pineapple, walnuts, and cinnamon, and blend. Cool and serve, or pack in hot jars and process for 15 minutes, according to canning directions beginning on page 20.

YIELD: ABOUT 2 PINTS.

Mattie's Green String Beans

3 slices bacon

2 cups water

1 small onion, halved

½ teaspoon salt

2 pounds green beans, whole, with tips removed

1 small pimento, cut into small cubes

Place bacon in a quart saucepan and add water. Bring to a boil and cook for 10 minutes. Add onion and salt. Cook for about 3 minutes. Add string beans. Boil for 15 to 18 minutes. Drain beans and discard bacon. Mix beans with pimento cubes for decoration.

YIELD: ABOUT 8 SERVINGS.

Waltine's Mashed Turnips and Carrots

1 large yellow turnip, peeled and quartered

6 large carrots, peeled and halved

¾ stick butter

1 medium onion, diced fine

2 tablespoons sugar

Salt and pepper to taste

Bring a large pot of water to a rapid boil and toss in the vegetables. Partially cover and cook rapidly for approximately 35 to 40 minutes until completely tender. Drain and mash with a potato masher. In a second pan, melt butter and add diced onion. Sauté until onion is tender and translucent. Add butter and onions, sugar, salt, and pepper to the mashed vegetables, blending well. Reheat if necessary.

YIELD: 8 SERVINGS.

Lucy's Creamed Onions

2 pounds pearl onions, peeled
¾ cup water

½ teaspoon salt

CREAM SAUCE:
1 tablespoon margarine
1 tablespoon flour
1 cup evaporated milk

1 bay leaf
½ teaspoon salt
Paprika

Place onions in a small saucepan, add water and salt and simmer until tender. Don't overcook. Drain water and set aside. For the cream sauce: Melt margarine in top of a double boiler, add flour and stir until smooth. Stir in evaporated milk. Cook until thickened, stirring constantly. Add bay leaf and salt. Cook for 5 minutes. Remove bay leaf. Combine sauce and onions, and simmer for 5 minutes. Sprinkle with paprika just before serving.

YIELD: 8 SERVINGS.

Mattie's Sweet Potato Pudding Topped with Marshmallows

2 pounds sweet potatoes

½ stick (¼ cup) butter or margarine

1 cup sugar

3 eggs

¾ cup evaporated milk

2 teaspoons vanilla extract

1 teaspoon ground cinnamon

3 tablespoons dark rum (optional)

1 pound marshmallows

Preheat oven to 375°. Wash and boil sweet potatoes in their skins until fork tender. Peel, then add butter or margarine while potatoes are still hot, and mash with a potato masher until mixture is smooth. Add sugar, stirring until well mixed. Then add eggs, one at a time, beating mixture well until all eggs have been added. Stir in evaporated milk, vanilla, cinnamon, and rum if desired. Pour into a buttered 2-quart casserole and bake for 30 minutes. Top with whole marshmallows and continue baking for about 5 minutes or until melted and nicely browned. Serve hot.

YIELD: 8 SERVINGS.

Mattie's Baked Macaroni with Cheese

1 tablespoon salt

2 cups uncooked elbow macaroni

½ stick (¼ cup) melted butter or margarine

12 ounces sharp Cheddar cheese, grated

2 eggs, lightly beaten

1½ cups evaporated milk

Paprika

Preheat oven to 375°. Fill a 3-quart saucepan with water and place over a high flame. When water comes to a rapid boil, add salt and, gradually, the elbow macaroni, so that the water does not stop boiling. Cook, uncovered, for 8 to 9 minutes. Remove from stove, pour into a colander to drain, then place colander with macaroni under cold running water for a few seconds. Put macaroni in a 2-quart casserole and add melted butter or margarine, 8 ounces of the grated cheese, the eggs, and the milk. Mix lightly. Sprinkle the remaining cheese over the top and dust with paprika. Bake for 30 minutes.

YIELD: 8 SERVINGS.

Winner Tossed Green Salad

1 head iceberg lettuce, broken into
    pieces

1 head romaine lettuce, chopped

3 stalks celery, chopped

1 cucumber, peeled and sliced

3 tomatoes, sliced

2 carrots, cut into julienne strips

12 radishes, cut into rounds

1 green bell pepper, seeded and cut into
    rings

In a large salad bowl place all the ingredients. Toss and serve with your favorite dressing or with Mattie's Mayonnaise (recipe follows).

YIELD: 8 SERVINGS.

Mattie's Mayonnaise

1 egg yolk

2 tablespoons white vinegar

¾ teaspoon salt

¼ teaspoon pepper

¼ teaspoon dry mustard

1 cup salad oil

Beat egg yolk and 1 tablespoon of vinegar with salt, pepper, and mustard in an electric mixer at high speed. Add oil, 1 teaspoon at a time, for the first ¼ cup, then slowly add remaining salad oil and vinegar, beating continuously throughout.

YIELD: ABOUT 1 CUP.

NOTE: *The elderly, small children, and anyone with a compromised immune system should avoid eating raw eggs. Pasteurized eggs can be substituted in such cases, and are now available in many markets.*

Lucy's Mincemeat Pie

Lucy cans her mincemeat in the summer months, but you can, of course, make it for instant use.

MINCEMEAT:

8 cups chopped green tomatoes

8 cups chopped green apples

1 cup golden raisins

1 cup black raisins

1 cup chopped mixed dates, prunes, and figs

Chopped fruit and grated rind of 1 orange

2½ cups brown sugar

½ cup molasses

½ cup dark corn syrup

1 cup cider vinegar

1 tablespoon ground cinnamon

2 teaspoons salt

1 teaspoon ground cloves

½ teaspoon ground allspice

½ teaspoon ground ginger

½ teaspoon ground mace

½ teaspoon grated nutmeg

½ teaspoon pepper

HOT WATER DOUBLE PIE CRUST:

1 cup solid vegetable shortening

⅓ cup hot water

1 tablespoon milk

2½ cups flour

½ teaspoon salt

For the mincemeat: Combine all ingredients in a large saucepan. Bring to a boil, then lower heat and simmer for 2 hours, stirring frequently. Use one quarter of the mixture for your pie and process the rest (see page 23) for 20 minutes to keep for later use. For the crust: Preheat oven to 350°. Put shortening in a bowl, pour hot water over it, and stir, adding milk until the mixture is thick and creamy. Sift the flour and salt together and beat into the shortening mixture until a dough is formed. Pat into 2 balls. On a floured board with a floured rolling pin, roll out 1 of them, and place in the bottom of a 9-inch pie plate. Put in mincemeat filling, and cover with rolled-out second ball of dough. Flute the edges and cut slits in the top. Bake for 50 minutes or until crust is golden.

YIELD: ONE 9-INCH PIE, PLUS EXTRA MINCEMEAT
FOR CANNING.

Waltine's Ambrosia

8 oranges, peeled, seeded, and sliced

Grated meat from 1 fresh coconut

1 medium pineapple, peeled, cored, and cut into chunks

In a large crystal bowl place a layer of sliced oranges, a layer of fresh grated coconut, a layer of pineapple chunks. Continue layering until bowl is filled. Top with a layer of coconut. Pour extra orange juice, if desired, over mixture. Chill and serve.

YIELD: 10 TO 12 SERVINGS.

Mattie's Christmas Eggnog

12 eggs, separated

1½ cups sugar

1 cup rye whiskey

1 cup dark rum

1 cup brandy

1 pint heavy cream

1 cup milk, or to taste

Grated nutmeg

Beat egg yolks until light and frothy, adding ¾ cup of sugar while beating. To this mixture add the rye whiskey, rum, and brandy. Beat egg whites until stiff, adding ½ cup sugar while beating. Whip heavy cream until light and fluffy, adding ¼ cup of sugar near the end of whipping. Fold egg whites and whipped cream into the egg yolk mixture. Pour mixture into a large punch bowl. Chill before serving. If mixture has been allowed to sit for a while, beat with a rotary egg beater just before serving. Sprinkle nutmeg on top of each cup of eggnog when served. If a thinner consistency is desired, add 1 cup milk to the mixture, or to taste.

YIELD: ABOUT 2 DOZEN SERVINGS.

New Year's Eggnog

NOTE: *Use the second set of instructions for New Year's Eggnog (see page 270) if you prefer not to use raw eggs, or use pasteurized eggs, now available in many markets.*

Waltine, Mattie, and Lucy with their father in their adopted town, Newark, New Jersey

New Year's Day Dinner at Our House

On New Year's Day we always have Open House at our father's home in Montclair, New Jersey. It is a leisurely day, designed to give us an opportunity to unwind from the frenzy of New Year's Eve, to reflect on the passing year, and to make our resolutions for the coming one. As friends and family drop by, we find it is the perfect time to rekindle old friendships, solidify new ones, reciprocate past hospitalities, and draw our family together. What better way to bring in the New Year than with warm friends and hot food?

Black folklore has it that Hoppin' John brings good luck and greens bring monetary blessings in the coming year, so we always serve this traditionally Southern meal with all the essential trimmings.

Our Menu for 10
*Pigs' Feet
Sliced Turkey and Ham Platter
*Hoppin' John (Black-Eyed Peas and Rice)
Mixed Greens (see page 159)
*Stewed Tomatoes
Baked Sweet Potatoes (see page 118)
*Apple-Walnut Salad
*Corn Bread
*Company Pies
Fruitcake (see pages 205–7)
*Eggnog
Champagne
Assorted Winter Fruits: Persimmons, Pomegranates, Pears, Apples,
Tangerines, Tokay Grapes, and Kumquats

*Asterisk indicates that recipe appears in this chapter.

Spoonbread and Strawberry Wine

Pigs' Feet

12 large pigs' feet, halved

1 quart cider vinegar

4 stalks celery, cut into thirds

4 large onions, quartered

4 carrots, halved

4 bay leaves

12 peppercorns

3 teaspoons crushed red pepper flakes

3 tablespoons salt

Carefully inspect pigs' feet and singe off any remaining hairs. Wash feet thoroughly. Place them in a large saucepan or kettle. Cover with water and add remaining ingredients. Bring to a boil, lower heat, cover, and simmer slowly for about 3 hours. When done, pigs' feet should be fork tender and no longer pinkish in color. Adjust seasoning and serve with additional vinegar and hot sauce.

YIELD: 10 SERVINGS.

Hoppin' John
(Black-Eyed Peas and Rice)

2 ham hocks

1 bay leaf

2 onions, chopped

1 stalk celery, diced

½ teaspoon crushed red pepper

Salt and pepper to taste

2 cups black-eyed peas

2 cups raw rice

Place ham hocks in a large saucepan. Add water to cover and simmer for about 30 minutes. Add bay leaf, onions, celery, and seasonings. Sort out and discard any discolored or damaged peas, rinse remainder well, and add to the pot. If necessary, adjust water level so that the peas are well covered. Cover pot and simmer slowly until peas are tender and liquid level is low, about 1½ hours or until tender. Cook rice separately according to package directions, steaming it until dry. Fluff into peas. Adjust seasoning and cook over low heat until all the liquid is absorbed. If in doubt about the exact amount of liquid needed to prevent the rice from becoming gummy, reverse the process: Fluff the drained peas into the cooked rice and add a small amount of liquid.

YIELD: 10 SERVINGS.

Stewed Tomatoes

¼ cup butter

2 medium onions, minced

12 large ripe tomatoes, peeled and
    coarsely chopped

2 teaspoons salt

2 teaspoons brown sugar

¼ teaspoon pepper

1 teaspoon dried basil

In a large saucepan melt butter and add onions. Sauté until onions are tender. Add remaining ingredients. Bring to a boil, lower heat, cover, and simmer slowly for about 25 minutes. Adjust seasoning if necessary.

YIELD: 10 SERVINGS.

Apple-Walnut Salad

12 apples, peeled and cored

2 stalks celery, diced

1½ cups chopped walnuts

¼ cup seedless raisins

1½ cups mayonnaise

1 teaspoon lemon juice

½ teaspoon grated nutmeg

Lettuce

Purple grapes, halved and seeded, for garnish

Dice apples into small cubes. Add celery, walnuts, and raisins. In a small bowl blend mayonnaise, lemon juice, and nutmeg. Gently fold mayonnaise mixture into apples, coating evenly. Serve on a bed of lettuce and garnish with grape halves.

YIELD: ABOUT 10 SERVINGS.

Corn Bread

1 cup sifted all-purpose flour

1½ tablespoons sugar

2½ teaspoons baking powder

½ teaspoon baking soda

½ teaspoon salt

1 cup yellow cornmeal

2 eggs, beaten

1½ cups buttermilk

¼ cup melted butter

Preheat oven to 425°. Sift together flour, sugar, baking powder, soda, and salt. Add cornmeal. In a medium-size bowl mix eggs, buttermilk, and butter. Add flour mixture. Mix enough to moisten. Pour into a greased 8-inch-square baking pan or 12 muffin tins. Bake for 20 to 25 minutes (15 to 20 minutes for muffins), or until golden and firm to the touch in the center. Cut corn bread into squares.

YIELD: 1 DOZEN SQUARES OR MUFFINS. DOUBLE RECIPE FOR
10 TO 12 GUESTS.

VARIATION:

Blend a small cooked sweet potato or mashed banana into the corn bread batter, for an interesting change.

COMPANY PIES

We always serve one of Uncle Glen's special fruitcakes, but not everyone is a fruitcake enthusiast, so for abstainers we go into our store of recipes gathered from friends and prepare one of our special "company pies."

Lemon Meringue Pie

This is from Suzie Walker, one of Carole's godmothers and a close neighbor of ours. Suzie told us that her twin uncles had been given as slaves to Abraham and Mary Todd Lincoln for a wedding present.

FILLING:

- 4½ tablespoons cornstarch
- 1¼ cups sugar
- ¼ teaspoon salt
- 1½ cups water
- 4 egg yolks, lightly beaten
- ⅓ cup lemon juice
- 2 teaspoons grated lemon rind
- 2½ tablespoons butter

MERINGUE:

- 4 egg whites
- ¼ teaspoon cream of tartar
- ½ cup sugar
- One 9-inch pie shell, baked (see page 238)

For the filling: In the top of a double boiler combine cornstarch, sugar, and salt. Gradually add the water, stirring until smooth. Place directly over medium heat and bring mixture to a boil, stirring constantly until it thickens. Then place over the bottom of the double boiler filled with 1 inch of boiling water. Continue stirring and cook the mixture for 5 minutes longer. Place egg yolks in a bowl and beat with an egg beater. Working quickly, pour about half the cornstarch mixture into the yolks, beating well with a fork. Return entire mixture to the double boiler. Cook and stir for about 3 minutes over the boiling water. Stir in lemon juice, rind, and butter. Remove from the heat and cool, stirring occasionally. Preheat oven to 400°. For the meringue: Beat egg whites with cream of tartar until soft peaks form. Add the sugar, a couple of tablespoons at a time, beating after each addition. Continue beating until stiff peaks form. Pour custard into pie shell. Top with meringue, making peaks here and there. Bake for 8 to 10 minutes, until meringue is a golden brown. Cool and refrigerate until ready to serve.

YIELD: 8 SERVINGS.

Lemon Chiffon Pie

From Grandma Boyd—our adopted grandmother. Since we never knew either of our grandmothers, we were close to Sarah Boyd, who lived to be 101. Her husband, Sam, was a son of Thomas Jefferson and a slave woman. Sam and his mother later settled in Petersburg, Virginia.

½ cup lemon juice

¼ cup orange juice

⅔ cup sugar, plus 1 tablespoon

1 envelope unflavored gelatin

½ cup cold water

3 eggs, separated

One 9-inch pie shell, baked (see page 238)

1½ cups heavy cream, whipped

Grated nutmeg

Mix juices and ⅔ cup sugar in a saucepan and bring to a boil. Dissolve gelatin in the cold water and blend into juice mixture. Lower heat, cook for 3 minutes, then add beaten yolks, stirring vigorously. Reheat entire mixture to the boiling point and strain into a bowl. Let it cool down a bit, then chill. When mixture begins to set, beat egg whites with remaining 1 tablespoon sugar until stiff. Fold into gelatin mixture, pour into cooked shell, and refrigerate. When ready to serve, cover with whipped cream and sprinkle with nutmeg.

YIELD: 8 SERVINGS.

Triple-Decker Butterscotch Pie

From Cousin Alice Scarborough in Belpre, Ohio.

CRUST:

2 cups flour

¾ teaspoon salt

⅔ cup shortening

6–8 tablespoons ice water

FILLING:

2 cups milk

1¼ cups brown sugar

⅓ cup flour

⅛ teaspoon salt

2 egg yolks, beaten

2 tablespoons butter

½ teaspoon vanilla extract

MERINGUE:

2 egg whites

¼ cup granulated sugar

½ teaspoon vanilla extract

Sprinkle of salt

For the crust: Preheat oven to 450°. Sift flour and salt and cut in shortening. Add enough ice water to hold ingredients together. Divide dough into 3 parts and roll into three 9-inch circles. Place separately on baking sheets, pricking each well. Bake for 8 to 10 minutes or until delicately browned. Cool. For the filling: Scald milk in the top of a double boiler. Mix sugar, flour, and salt and add to milk, stirring constantly until thick. Add a little of the mixture to the beaten egg yolks, then return to the double boiler. Cook 4 minutes more. Stir in butter until melted, add vanilla, then cool. Put together with the 3 crusts like a layer cake, alternating crust with filling and ending with filling on top. For the meringue: Reduce oven to 325°. Beat egg whites until soft peaks form. Gradually add sugar, then vanilla and salt. Continue beating until stiff peaks form. Pile meringue lightly on top and sides of pie and bake for 15 minutes, until light brown. Cool and refrigerate. Serve chilled.

YIELD: 8 SERVINGS.

Orange Pie

From Spaulding Berry, Mother's friend and our minister's wife.

1 tablespoon unflavored gelatin

1½ cups fresh orange juice

⅔ cup sugar

¼ teaspoon salt

¼ cup lemon juice

1 teaspoon grated orange rind

1 cup heavy cream

One 9-inch graham cracker pie shell (see Rum Pie, recipe follows)

Mint sprigs and orange slices, for garnish

In the top of a double boiler place the gelatin and ½ cup of orange juice. Cook until dissolved, stirring frequently. Add sugar and salt. Remove from heat. Add the remaining orange juice, lemon juice, and rind. Chill until mixture begins to thicken, then beat until light. Whip cream and fold into mixture. Pour into pie shell. Chill until firm. Garnish with sprigs of mint and orange slices.

YIELD: 8 SERVINGS.

Rum Pie

From Vicki Foster Harris, Aunt Alice's daughter from Brooklyn, New York, who has carried on her mother's mystique.

PIE SHELL (9 OR 10 INCH):

1½ dozen graham crackers

1 stick (½ cup) melted butter

⅓ cup sugar

¼ teaspoon ground cinnamon

FILLING:

Two 8-ounce packages cream cheese, softened

2 eggs, well beaten

½ cup sugar

2 tablespoons dark rum

TOPPING:

1 cup sour cream

3 tablespoons sugar

1½ tablespoons dark rum

Preheat oven to 375°. For the pie shell: Place graham crackers on wax paper and crumble with a rolling pin. Place in a bowl, add butter, sugar, and cinnamon. Mix lightly with a fork until well blended. Place in a 10-inch pie plate and press with a spoon to form a solid crust. For the filling: Blend softened cream cheese with eggs and sugar until smooth. Stir in rum. Pour into graham cracker shell. Bake for 20 to 25 minutes. For the topping: Combine topping ingredients. Remove pie from oven and spread evenly with topping mixture. Return to the oven for 5 minutes. Cool, refrigerate, and serve chilled.

YIELD: 8 TO 10 SERVINGS.

New Year's Eggnog

1 dozen egg yolks

1 heaping cup sugar

1 quart milk

A fifth dark rum

6 egg whites

3 cups heavy cream

Grated nutmeg, for garnish

NOTE: *The elderly, small children, and anyone with a compromised immune system should proba-bly avoid eating raw eggs. In such cases, a pasturized egg product would be more suitable, or you can follow the second set of instructions, which cooks the eggs to form a custard base and in no way compromises the flavor.*

INSTRUCTIONS #1

In a large bowl beat yolks with egg beater until light. Add sugar and beat until thick. Stir in milk, then rum. Beat egg whites until peaks form. Fold into mixture. Pour into a punch bowl and chill (outdoors if cold enough) for at least 2 hours. Beat cream until it peaks softly, then gently fold into chilled mixture. Chill again for at least 2 more hours. When serving, garnish with nutmeg.

INSTRUCTIONS #2

Bring 1 inch of water to simmer in the bottom of a double boiler. Combine the egg yolks and whites in the top of the double boiler. Beat with an egg beater until light. Add sugar and beat until well combined. Stir in 3 cups of the milk and place the mixture over the bottom of the double boiler. Heat the mixture, stirring constantly, until it is thick enough to coat the spoon or until it registers 170 degrees on a candy thermometer. Remove from heat and pour into a large bowl. If the mixture begins to curdle, pour it through a sieve. Stir in the remaining cup of milk. Bring the mixture to room temperature, stir in the rum, and refrigerate for at least 2 hours. Prepare the heavy cream and chill the mixture according to the recipe above.

YIELD: 24 SERVINGS.

Funerals

Russell Darden's grieving sweetheart

As granddaughters, nieces, and cousins of morticians, we have attended our share of funerals and wakes. Surprisingly, we have found that some of the best Southern cooking is to be had during these times of sorrow. The custom of caring for the bereaved in this manner goes back to ancient Africa, where the family of the deceased was given not only food but items of value, including clothing and household items, by the entire community in an effort to offset the loss in a practical manner. This was particularly important if the deceased was the head of a household and the continuation of family stability was a concern. In the antebellum South, churches, fraternal orders, and burial societies took over a similar function, and to a significant extent this continues today. Friends and neighbors also play an important role, each preparing and donating food to those who are grieving so that they need not have the burden of cooking for themselves or the many guests who will be visiting their home. Those closest to the bereaved family take up vigil in the home from morning till night to clean and prepare for visitors and to receive their gifts of food. Tables are arranged and the food tastefully displayed for the dinner following the funeral, when family and friends will come together to mourn, to comfort, and to share their feelings and recollections with one another.

It is a simple act of thoughtfulness to the living, but it takes the form of a feast. Turkeys, hams, roasts, and casseroles are given, but as children, we had a natural interest in the sweets and hot breads that were offered, and to this day we find it particularly appropriate to take a cake, a pie, or bread to the family of the departed.

Chocolate Chip Cake

Courtesy Sister Reta Rapp of New York, New York.

3 cups sifted cake flour

3 teaspoons baking powder

½ pound lightly salted butter

2 cups sugar

4 eggs

1 cup milk

2 teaspoons vanilla extract

Two 1-ounce squares unsweetened chocolate, grated

Preheat oven to 350°. Combine flour and baking powder and sift 3 times. Cream butter and sugar until fluffy. Add 1 egg at a time, beating well after each addition. This mixture must be kept at a very light, fluffy consistency. Fold in dry ingredients, alternating with the milk. Add vanilla. Then fold in grated chocolate. Pour into a greased and lightly floured 10-inch tube or 8-×-10-×-2½-inch square pan. Bake for 1 hour (tube) or 40 minutes (flat pan), or until edges shrink from the sides of the pan and cake is firm to the touch in the center. Serve plain or with Chocolate Frosting (see recipe page 274).

YIELD: 12 TO 14 SERVINGS.

Chocolate Layer Cake

Courtesy Cousin Lilly Tennessee of Plainfield, New Jersey.

2 cups sugar

3 sticks (1½ cups) butter

One 3-ounce package cream cheese

6 eggs

4 cups all-purpose flour

1 heaping tablespoon baking powder

¼ teaspoon baking soda

¾ cup milk

1 teaspoon vanilla extract

Chocolate Frosting (recipe follows)

Preheat oven to 350°. Cream sugar, butter, and cream cheese together. Beat eggs in a small bowl at high speed for about 5 minutes. Add to butter mixture and mix well. Sift flour, baking powder, and baking soda. Add half the flour mixture to the batter and mix at low speed until well blended. Gradually add the milk. Then add the remaining flour, mixing thoroughly. Finally, add the vanilla. Mix thoroughly. Grease two 9-inch cake pans with butter. Distribute batter evenly between pans and bake for about 30 minutes, or until edges shrink from the sides of the pans and the cakes are firm to the touch in the center. Invert onto cake racks and frost with Chocolate Frosting when completely cool.

YIELD: 12 SERVINGS.

Chocolate Frosting

Seven 1-ounce squares unsweetened
chocolate

½ stick (¼ cup) butter or margarine

2½ cups confectioners' sugar

½ cup milk

A few drops of vanilla extract

Melt chocolate squares in a saucepan. Add butter or margarine and simmer for about 1 minute over low heat. Add powdered sugar. Then add milk, and, stirring continuously, simmer for about 2 to 3 minutes. Remove from heat. Stir in vanilla. Let cool before frosting cake.

YIELD: ENOUGH FOR 1 CHOCOLATE LAYER CAKE.

Chocolate-Cherry Upside-Down Cake

Courtesy Deacon Cyrus Rogers of San Francisco.

2 pounds black cherries, or two
20-ounce cans pitted black cherries

9 tablespoons butter

¾ cup brown sugar

½ cup granulated sugar

1 egg, separated

Two 1-ounce squares unsweetened
chocolate, melted in the top of a
double boiler over simmering water

1 cup flour

1½ teaspoons baking powder

¼ teaspoon salt

½ teaspoon ground cinnamon

¾ cup milk

1 teaspoon vanilla extract

½ pint heavy cream

Preheat oven to 350°. Carefully pit the black cherries, leaving them as close to whole as possible. This is painstaking. In a saucepan put the uncooked cherries, add a few tablespoons of water, and simmer for a few minutes until the cherries are a little soft but retain their shape. Remove from heat. Place 6 tablespoons of the butter in a heavy 9-inch skillet (preferably of cast iron), add ¼ cup of the brown sugar, and set on low heat until butter and brown sugar are melted. Blend and spread evenly over the skillet and remove from heat. Carefully place the pitted cherries (fresh or canned) close together in the butter-sugar, with the uncut side down, because that is the side that will show when the cake is served. Reserve the cherry juice. Cream together the remaining butter, remaining brown sugar, and the granulated sugar until very light. Add the egg yolk and melted chocolate, and mix thoroughly. Sift together the flour, baking powder, salt, and cinnamon, and add to the butter-sugar mixture alternating with the milk. Add the vanilla and mix thoroughly. Fold in stiffly beaten egg white. Carefully spoon the cake batter into the skillet so as not to disturb the cherries. Bake for 45 minutes. When the cake is springy to the touch, remove it from the oven, loosen the sides from the edge of the skillet if necessary, and let the cake stand for 10 minutes. Place the cake serving plate upside down over the skillet, hold the skillet handle with one hand, the cake plate with the other, and flip the whole thing upside down. Leave the inverted skillet on the cake plate for 10 minutes, then slowly lift it off. Let the cake cool. Whip the cream until thick, adding a teaspoon of reserved cherry juice every few seconds to give a rich flavor and a bright pink color. Spoon the whipped cream thickly around the edge of the top of the cake, leaving most of the cherries exposed. Cut with a sharp knife.

YIELD: 8 SERVINGS.

Papa Darden's widow visiting his grave

Carrot Cake

Courtesy Sister Effie Artis of Wilson, North Carolina.

1½ cups sugar	1 teaspoon baking soda
3 eggs, separated	½ teaspoon salt
1 cup vegetable oil	½ teaspoon grated nutmeg
2½ tablespoons hot water	1 teaspoon ground cinnamon
1½ cups all-purpose flour	1 cup grated carrots
1 teaspoon baking powder	1 cup chopped black walnuts

Preheat oven to 350°. Beat together the sugar, egg yolks, and oil along with the hot water. Sift together dry ingredients. Add to egg yolk mixture. Then add carrots and walnuts. Beat egg whites until stiff and gently fold into mixture. Bake in a well-greased tube pan for about 55 minutes. Let cool for 10 minutes before removing from pan.

YIELD: 12 SERVINGS.

Angel Pound Cake

Courtesy Sister Corrine Steele of Opelika, Alabama.

1 pound butter

1 pound confectioners' sugar

8 eggs

1 box flour, loosely packed (use the
1-pound sugar box to measure)

1 tablespoon vanilla extract

1 tablespoon lemon extract

Preheat oven to 325°. Cream butter and sugar together. Add eggs, one at a time, beating after each addition. Sift flour and add slowly, stirring at intervals. Add vanilla and lemon extracts. Pour into a greased and lightly floured 10-inch tube or bundt pan. Bake for 1 hour, or until edges shrink from the sides of the pan and the center springs back when touched in the middle. Loosen cake from the pan by running a knife around the edge. Invert onto a cake rack and cool.

YIELD: 10 TO 12 SERVINGS.

Heaven Cake

Courtesy Sister Hilda Lockett of Montclair, New Jersey.

4 eggs
½ pint heavy cream
1½ cups granulated sugar
1½ cups self-rising flour

1 teaspoon vanilla extract
Confectioners' sugar or frosting for topping

Preheat oven to 350°. Break eggs into a mixing bowl and beat until light and foamy (at least 5 minutes). Add heavy cream and beat for another 5 minutes. Pour in sugar, continuing to beat well. Last, blend in flour and vanilla. Bake in a greased tube pan for 50 minutes or in two 8-inch cake pans for 30 minutes, or until edges shrink from the sides of the pans and the centers spring back when touched in the middle. Loosen cake from the pan by running a knife around the edge. Invert onto a cake rack and cool. Dust with confectioners' sugar or frost as desired.

YIELD: 10 TO 12 SERVINGS.

Cold Oven Cake

Courtesy Sister E. Mae McCarroll, M.D., of Newark, New Jersey.

2 cups all-purpose flour	*3 cups sugar*
1 cup self-rising cake flour	*1 cup milk*
2 sticks (1 cup) butter	*6 eggs*
½ cup solid vegetable shortening	*3 teaspoons lemon extract*

Sift flours together 5 times. Cream butter and shortening well and add sugar gradually. Add flour, a small portion at a time, alternating with the milk. Add eggs, one at a time, beating after each addition. Add lemon extract. Turn into a greased, floured 10-inch tube pan. Put in a cold oven. Light oven and set at 325°. Bake for 1 hour and 15 minutes.

YIELD: 12 SERVINGS.

Jiffy Nutmeg Cake— a One-Bowl Cake

Courtesy Sister Virginia Savoy, Mother's best friend, from Montclair, New Jersey.

2 cups sifted all-purpose flour	1½ cups heavy cream
1½ cups sugar	3 eggs
1 teaspoon salt	2 teaspoons grated nutmeg
2 teaspoons baking powder	2 tablespoons dark rum or brandy

Preheat oven to 350°. Sift flour, sugar, salt, and baking powder into a mixing bowl. Add cream, eggs, and nutmeg, and beat for 3 minutes. Add rum or brandy and beat for 1 minute longer. Then pour into a greased and floured 9-×-5-×-3-inch loaf pan and bake for 1 hour, or until a toothpick inserted in the center comes out clean. Cool on cake racks and frost or enjoy uniced.

YIELD: 10 SERVINGS.

Sheet Cake with Yellow Frosting

Courtesy Sister Georgia Dupree of Wilson, North Carolina. This is a good cake to feed a large group.

CAKE:

1 cup butter

2 cups granulated sugar

4 eggs

3¼ cups all-purpose flour, sifted

½ teaspoon salt

6 teaspoons baking powder

1 cup milk

1 teaspoon vanilla extract

YELLOW FROSTING:

½ cup butter or margarine

Pinch of salt

1 egg white

3 cups confectioners' sugar

1 teaspoon vanilla or lemon extract

1–2 tablespoons milk, depending upon desired consistency

A few drops of yellow food coloring

Preheat oven to 350°. For the cake: Cream butter and sugar until light. Beat in eggs, one at a time. Sift flour, salt, and baking powder together. Add dry ingredients to the butter mixture, alternating with milk. Stir in vanilla and blend well. Bake in two greased 16-×-11-×-2-inch sheet pans for 25 minutes. For the frosting: With an electric beater, whip butter or margarine, salt, egg white, and 1½ cups of confectioners' sugar until fluffy. Add vanilla or lemon extract, then remaining sugar, milk (if needed), and yellow food coloring until desired shade is reached. Let cake cool in its pan and frost the top. Cut into squares and serve.

YIELD: 48 SERVINGS.

Peach-Blueberry Pie

Courtesy Cousin Helen James of Goldsboro, North Carolina.

3 cups sliced fresh peaches

1 cup blueberries

¾–1 cup sugar, depending on sweetness of peaches

3 rounded tablespoons flour

¼ teaspoon salt

½ teaspoon ground cinnamon

⅛ teaspoon grated nutmeg

One 9-inch pastry shell, unbaked (see page 238)

¾ cup heavy cream

2 tablespoons butter

Preheat oven to 450°. Mix peaches and blueberries in a bowl. Combine sugar, flour, and spices, and stir into fruits. Spoon into the unbaked pie shell. Pour heavy cream over fruit. Dot with butter. Bake for about 15 minutes or until center of pie bubbles, then reduce heat to 350° and continue baking until nicely browned and set in the middle, about 45 minutes. Serve warm or cold.

YIELD: 6 TO 8 SERVINGS.

Deep Dish Plum Pie

Courtesy Sister Judy Haynes of Montclair, New Jersey.

CRUST:

2½ cups sifted all-purpose flour

1 teaspoon salt

¾ cup solid vegetable shortening

¼ cup ice water

FILLING:

3 cups drained canned plums, pitted,
    juice reserved

¾ cup reserved plum juice

2½ tablespoons tapioca

⅛ teaspoon salt

1 tablespoon lemon juice

¼ teaspoon almond extract

1 tablespoon butter

For the crust: Combine sifted flour with salt and sift into a mixing bowl. Cut in shortening with a pastry blender or 2 knives until mixture is the texture of small peas. Sprinkle with ice water, stirring with a fork. Using your hands, pat dough into a ball, wrap in wax paper, and refrigerate until ready for use. Preheat oven to 425°. For the filling: Halve the plums and set aside. Pour plum juice into a small bowl. Add tapioca, salt, lemon juice, and almond extract. Blend well, then let stand for 10 minutes. Divide dough in half, roll out to ⅛-inch thickness. Line a deep pie dish with half of the pastry dough. Fill with plums. Pour plum juice mixture over plums and dot with butter. Top with upper crust and flute edges to seal. Cut a crisscross design in center of pie so that steam can escape. Bake for 50 minutes or until crust is golden.

YIELD: 8 SERVINGS.

NOTE: *For a less crusty pie, this recipe works well with a single top-layer crust.*

The Very Best
Pumpkin Pie Ever

Courtesy Cousin Thelma Byers of Charlotte, North Carolina.

3 large eggs

1 cup sugar

Pinch of salt

1 stick (½ cup) melted butter

*1 teaspoon each ground cinnamon,
nutmeg, and allspice*

*2½ cups cooked, mashed fresh or
canned pumpkin (see Note)*

*One 9-inch single-crust pie shell (see
page 238)*

Preheat oven to 350°. Beat eggs well. Add ¾ cup of the sugar, salt, and half the melted butter to the eggs; add spices and blend. Then add mashed pumpkin and mix thoroughly. Turn into pie shell and pat pumpkin mixture even with edges of pastry. Sprinkle remaining ¼ cup of sugar over top of pie and dribble remaining melted butter over sugar. Bake for about 45 minutes. The top of this pie is lightly browned and crunchy. Even if people don't like pumpkin pie, we suspect they'll decide this one is delicious.

NOTE: *If using fresh pumpkin, peel pumpkin, cut in thin slices, and put in a heavy saucepan with water to cover over low heat. Cook slowly until all water is absorbed. Stir often when the water is almost absorbed to prevent sticking. Mash and set aside.*

YIELD: 8 SERVINGS.

Deep Dish Rhubarb Crunch

Courtesy Sister Ossie Mae Royal of Wilson, North Carolina.

⅓ cup sifted all-purpose flour	4 cups diced fresh rhubarb
¾ cup oatmeal	¾ cup granulated sugar
1 cup brown sugar	2 tablespoons cornstarch
½ cup melted butter	1 cup water
1 teaspoon ground cinnamon	1 tablespoon strawberry Jell-O

Preheat oven to 350°. Mix flour, oatmeal, brown sugar, butter, and cinnamon. Then press half into the bottom of a buttered 9-inch deep pie dish or casserole. Cover with the rhubarb. Combine granulated sugar, cornstarch, and water and cook over low heat, stirring often, until smooth, clear, and thick. Add Jell-O and pour over rhubarb. Cover with remaining crumb crust and bake for 40 minutes or until mixture is bubbly and golden.

YIELD: 8 SERVINGS.

Pear-Cranberry Pie

Courtesy Cousin Mary Sampson of Montclair, New Jersey.

8 medium Anjou or Bartlett pears

½ cup fresh cranberries

1 cup sugar

1 heaping tablespoon flour

1 teaspoon ground cinnamon

¼ teaspoon ground ginger

⅛ teaspoon salt

Juice of 1 orange

2 teaspoons grated orange zest

Double crust for 10-inch pie (see page 283)

2 tablespoons butter

Preheat oven to 425°. Peel and slice pears into a large bowl. Add cranberries, sugar, flour, cinnamon, ginger, salt, orange juice, and zest. Mix well and pour into a pastry-lined 10-inch pie plate. Dot with butter, then cover with top crust and make air vents in an attractive design in the center. Bake for 15 minutes. Lower heat to 350° and bake for 30 minutes more, or until pie is nicely browned.

YIELD: 8 LARGE WEDGES.

Refrigerator Rolls

Courtesy Sister Corrine Steele of Opelika, Alabama.

1 cup mashed white potatoes

⅔ cup solid vegetable shortening

1½ teaspoons salt

⅔ cup sugar

2 eggs, beaten

*1 yeast cake, or two ¼-ounce packages
active dry yeast*

½ cup lukewarm water

1 cup scalded milk, cooled to lukewarm

6–8 cups sifted all-purpose flour

Butter, melted

While mashed potatoes are still warm, add shortening, salt, and sugar. Cream well, then beat in eggs. Dissolve yeast in the lukewarm water. Stir lukewarm milk into potato mixture, then add yeast. Add enough sifted flour to make a stiff dough. Place on a floured board and knead well. Then place in a large greased bowl and let rise until double in bulk. Knead slightly on a floured board. Place back in the bowl and rub top with melted butter. Cover tightly and place in the refrigerator until ready to use (will keep for 5 to 6 days, supplying you with fresh rolls for the week). About 1½ hours before baking time, pinch off desired amount of dough and shape into cloverleaf or pocketbook rolls. To make cloverleaf rolls, form 1-inch balls and place 3 in each cup of a well-oiled muffin tin. To make pocketbooks, roll out a portion of the dough to ¼-inch thickness. Cut with a biscuit cutter and brush with melted butter. With a knife make an indentation across each roll just left or right of center. Fold the smaller half almost to the edge of the lower and pinch together. Place in a greased pan. Cover rolls with a tea towel and let them rise in a warm place for about 1½ hours, or until they double in size. Preheat oven to 400°. Brush rolls with melted butter. Bake for 15 to 20 minutes or until nicely browned.

YIELD: 3 DOZEN ROLLS.

Tiny Butter Rolls

Courtesy Sister Georgia Dupree of Wilson, North Carolina.

Two ¼-ounce packages active dry yeast

2 cups lukewarm water

2 eggs, well beaten

1 cup sugar

1 tablespoon salt

2 cups scalded milk

1½ cups melted butter

8–10 cups sifted all-purpose flour

Dissolve yeast in the lukewarm water. Add beaten eggs and blend. Add sugar, salt, hot milk, and 1 cup of the melted butter. Gradually blend in flour. Mix well. Then knead on a heavily floured board. Place in a greased bowl and set in a warm place to rise for about 2 hours. When doubled in bulk, knead slightly and form into miniature cloverleaf or pocketbook rolls (see preceding recipe for instructions). Arrange in buttered pans, cover, and let rise until light, about 1 hour. Preheat oven to 425°. Brush tops of rolls with the remaining melted butter. Bake for 15 to 20 minutes or until rolls are golden brown.

YIELD: 4 TO 5 DOZEN ROLLS.

On the Road

Summers in our childhood found us on the train going south, often by ourselves. It was not uncommon for children to be sent alone to stay with relatives—entrusted to the care of Pullman porters, gentlemen of color whose concern and kindness for black travelers were legendary. We boarded the night train in New York City with our mother, who introduced us to the porters, told them our destination, and settled us down. She then rode with us as far as Newark, our home, where our father was waiting, and there they waved us good-bye, knowing that we would be well taken care of—as indeed we were. Traveling at night in sleeping compartments was one way black travelers could avoid the humiliation of sitting in the rear of the cars—a mandatory railroad practice after one reached Washington, D.C.

After our mother learned to drive and could share the responsibility with our father, car trips became more frequent and were incredible fun. We could hardly sleep the night before and would help pack our bags and lunches, which our mother put in shoe boxes with the name of the passenger Scotch-taped to the top so that special requests were not confused. We usually left very early in the morning, but when fully awake we would make up songs, jokes, and games to amuse ourselves on the road. Big fun was waving at passersby, then ducking out of sight in our seats. Our feelings of high excitement were unavoidably tinged with feelings of dread, however. These trips took place during the fifties, and one never knew what dangers or insults would be encountered along the way. Racist policies loomed like unidentified monsters in our childish imaginations and in reality. After the New Jersey Turnpike ended, we would have to be on the alert for the unexpected. So, as we approached that last Howard Johnson's before Delaware, our father would make his inevitable announcement that we had to get out, stretch our legs, and go to the bathroom, whether we wanted to or not. This was a ritualized part of every trip, for, although there would be many restaurants along the route, this was the last one that didn't offer segregated facilities. From this point on, we pulled out our trusty shoe-box lunches.

Any discomfort we experienced during these yearly travels was balanced by a sense of adventure, for after we finished our shoe-box lunches we would have to keep our eyes peeled for black-owned establishments, which usually took us off the main route. If we needed a place to sleep before reaching our destination, we would have to ask random fellow blacks where accommodations could be found. Often total strangers would come to our rescue, offering lodging and feeding us as well. We made many new friends this way, as hospitality and solidarity were by-products of the rigid segregation of the times.

How different traveling in the South is today! But, in spite of all the really remarkable changes, we have continued the habit of stopping with old friends as we travel. They have shared many a fine meal with us, and for this reason we asked our friends on the road to contribute their favorite recipes. This chapter belongs to them.

Shoe-Box Lunch

Fried Chicken (see page 156)
Peanut Butter and Jelly Sandwiches
Deviled Eggs (see page 163)
Carrot and Celery Sticks
Salt and Pepper Packets
Chocolate Layer Cake (see page 273)
Thermos of Lemonade

Everything was neatly wrapped in wax paper, with extra treats, such as fresh fruit and small packs of nuts, raisins, and cheese. When it was gone, we got by with a little help from our friends.

Hot Crab-Meat Salad

It is always a pleasure to visit with our mother's friend Florence Byrd. They taught together in Petersburg, Virginia, where Florence still lives.

1 cup crab meat, flaked

1 cup soft bread crumbs

¼ cup light cream or whole milk

1½ cups mayonnaise

6 eggs, hard-cooked and diced

1 tablespoon minced fresh parsley

½ teaspoon salt

⅛ teaspoon pepper

A few grains of cayenne pepper

½ cup buttered bread crumbs

Preheat oven to 350°. Combine everything except buttered bread crumbs, and place in greased ramekins; sprinkle with buttered crumbs. Bake for about 20 minutes or until crumbs are golden brown.

YIELD: 8 SERVINGS.

Aunt Ruby's Seafood Casserole

Carole arriving at Aunt Norma's in Wilson, North Carolina

Aunt Ruby, our Aunt Norma's protégée when she taught at Bethune–Cookman College, used to live in a little white wooden house at the tip of a small island, called Sullivan's Island, off the coast of Charleston, South Carolina. The waters surrounding her home were filled with a variety of sea creatures. We would fish and crab in the mornings and she would transform our catch into the evening meal. This is one of Aunt Ruby's favorites.

1 pound fresh, uncooked shrimp
1 pound crab meat
1 cup flaked lobster meat
1 can cream of mushroom soup
½ cup milk
2 tablespoons flour

Worcestershire sauce or cooking sherry to taste
Salt and pepper to taste
Dash of ground turmeric
½ pound sharp cheese, grated

Preheat oven to 375°. Peel and devein shrimp, then set aside. Flake crab and lobster meats together with a fork, and place in a lightly greased casserole dish. Empty cream of mushroom soup into a saucepan and heat slowly. Make a paste of the milk and flour and add to mushroom soup, stirring constantly. Season with Worcestershire sauce or cooking sherry, salt, pepper, and turmeric. Add shrimp. Simmer for about 3 minutes, stirring constantly. Pour this mixture into the casserole and stir lightly, lifting gently from the bottom of the dish. Sprinkle grated cheese on top of casserole and bake until cheese melts and browns lightly, about 10 to 15 minutes.

YIELD: 8 TO 10 SERVINGS.

Edna Neal's
Pan-Fried Blowfish

Easy and yet so hard . . . Few people can beat our friend, Mrs. Edna Neal, from Warrenton, North Carolina, in frying fish.

The blowfish is a delicious small, meaty fish that has only one neatly lined set of bones through its center. It is sometimes dubbed "chicken of the sea" because of its flesh's resemblance to the white meat of poultry. Blowfish used to be plentiful and inexpensive but has now grown somewhat scarce on the market. Nevertheless, if you should be so fortunate as to find some, this is a delicious way to prepare it.

Blowfish, allow at least 2 or 3 fish per person

Flour

Salt and pepper

Paprika

Vegetable oil, for frying

1 medium whole clove of garlic

Lemon wedges

Wash fish and pat dry. Coat lightly with flour, seasoned with salt and a spare amount of pepper and paprika. In a heavy skillet heat a ½-inch level of oil until quite hot. Add the whole clove of garlic and swirl in the pan to add flavor to the oil. Then add fish and fry for 3 to 5 minutes per side or until golden brown. Serve hot with lemon wedges.

Mrs. Sheridan's North Carolina Deviled Crabs

Mrs. Sheridan was the short-order cook at the Wilson Drugstore. She loved to cook but didn't like her job. For months she prayed for a new one, and her prayers were answered in the form of a suggestion from the Baptist minister, Reverend Watkins, who asked if she would care for a member of his congregation who was too elderly to look after herself. Soon Mrs. Sheridan had a full-scale home for the elderly, and the senior citizens are truly rejuvenated by her skills in the kitchen.

1 medium onion, minced

1 green bell pepper, seeded and diced

1 stick (½ cup) butter

4 cups saltine cracker crumbs, plus extra

1½ cups milk

4 eggs, well beaten

1 can cream of mushroom soup

2 pounds raw crab meat (save crab shells if possible)

1 tablespoon Worcestershire sauce

1½ tablespoons prepared mustard

Salt and cayenne pepper to taste

Paprika

Lemon wedges

Preheat oven to 350°. Sauté onion and green pepper in butter until onion is almost limp. Remove from heat. In a large bowl soak cracker crumbs in milk until soft. Stir this into the skillet mixture. Add beaten eggs and cream of mushroom soup, blending well. Add crab meat by fluffing it into the mixture with a fork. Season with

Worcestershire sauce, mustard, salt, and cayenne. Stuff empty crab shells or ramekins with mixture. Sprinkle with additional cracker crumbs and paprika. Bake for 20 minutes. Serve with lemon wedges.

YIELD: 10 TO 12 SERVINGS.

VARIATION:

Crab-Meat Loaf—Follow the above recipe but increase the quantity of milk to 3 cups and add 5 eggs instead of 4. Pour into 2 greased loaf pans or a large casserole dish. Bake in a preheated 350° oven for 25 to 30 minutes or until set. Remove from loaf pans and slice.

YIELD: 10 TO 12 SERVINGS.

A beach party at Virginia Beach from Mother's scrapbook

On the Road

Mary McPhale's
Salmon Croquettes

Late in life, Papa Darden decided to remarry. His adult children were very upset, especially C.L. But when his new wife-to-be appeared with her two lovely daughters, they were all won over. Mrs. McPhale, of Wilson, North Carolina, was one of those daughters.

1 large and 1 small can (14¾ ounces and 7½ ounces) salmon

2 small white potatoes, peeled, boiled, and mashed

2 eggs, well beaten

1 stalk celery, chopped fine

1 small onion, chopped fine

¼ cup evaporated milk

Salt and pepper to taste

Vegetable oil, for deep frying

Mix first 7 ingredients well. Form into small croquettes and deep-fry in hot oil, or form into patties and pan-fry until golden brown. Excellent served for breakfast with hominy grits, eggs, and bacon, or for dinner as a main course.

YIELD: APPROXIMATELY 6 SERVINGS.

Shrimp Gumbo

Mrs. Bessie Marsh, of Montclair, New Jersey, by way of Jackson, Tennessee, first introduced us to gumbo, and we've been fans ever since.

2 slices salt pork, diced

1 pound fresh okra, sliced in rounds

Salt and pepper to taste

1 large onion, sliced

1 green bell pepper, seeded and sliced thin

1 cup diced, cooked ham or chicken

5–6 ripe tomatoes

1–2 tablespoons gumbo filé, or to taste (gumbo filé is a seasoning most easily obtained in Louisiana or in shops elsewhere that specialize in seasonings)

1 pound raw fresh shrimp, shelled and deveined, with tails left on

5 slices bacon, fried crisp, then crumbled (optional)

In a large, heavy skillet cook the salt pork until crisp. Season okra with salt and pepper and add to skillet with salt pork. Then add onion and pepper. When okra is tender, add ham or chicken, tomatoes, and gumbo filé. Simmer slowly for approximately 1 hour. Add shrimp and cook about 5 minutes longer or until shrimp turn pink. Adjust seasoning. Serve over steaming hot rice in wide soup bowls. If using bacon, sprinkle over each serving.

YIELD: 6 TO 8 SERVINGS.

North Carolina Turkey Butt Souse

Souse, sometimes called headcheese, is typically made from the head of a hog. The following variation is quite similar and just as tasty.

3 pounds turkey butts (knob at tail of turkey)

1 cup cider vinegar

1 small dried red pepper pod, crumbled

¼ teaspoon dried sage

Salt and pepper to taste

Simmer butts in water to cover until the meat falls off the bone, about 1½ hours. Remove meat, reserving broth. Pick out and discard any bones. Chop meat fine or put through a meat grinder. Return meat to broth and stir in the rest of the ingredients. Set aside and let cool to room temperature. Pour into a large, preferably lidded loaf pan. Let set in the refrigerator until completely firm. Souse is used as a luncheon meat. To serve, it should be sliced and eaten with crackers or corn bread.

YIELD: 12 GENEROUS SERVINGS.

Old Southern Wet Hash

Mrs. Alvin Martin, of Jersey City, New Jersey, by way of Alabama, shared a trip around the world with our mother. She is a Southern cook in the best tradition.

1 cup chopped onion

¼ cup chopped celery

3 medium white potatoes, peeled and diced fine

2 tablespoons margarine

2 tablespoons flour

2 cups beef or chicken stock

2 cups cubed cooked lamb, beef, veal, or chicken

Salt and pepper to taste

Dash of soy sauce (optional)

Sauté onion, celery, and potatoes in margarine until tender but not brown. Add flour to thicken. When flour browns, add stock and meat or chicken. Cook until sauce is thick and potatoes are tender. Season to taste with salt and pepper and a dash of soy sauce, if desired. Aside from being an excellent way to use leftover meats, this hash is good for any meal—over grits for breakfast, over toast for lunch or supper.

YIELD: 4 SERVINGS.

Corn Flake Omelet

We used to bill Cousin Charles James, of Wilson, North Carolina, as "the ladies' pet and the man's threat" because he loved to wear white suits, shoes, ties, etc., and go calling on the womenfolk. He still likes to wear all white, but has been married for many years now. He made up this recipe for a man on the go.

4 eggs

½ cup crumbled corn flakes

2 tablespoons milk

1½ teaspoons ketchup

½ teaspoon celery salt

Salt and pepper to taste

1 tablespoon butter or margarine

If you're in a hurry, you can have your eggs and cereal at the same time. Just beat the first 6 ingredients together and scramble in butter or margarine.

YIELD: 2 SERVINGS.

Gingerbread Waffles

Cousin Charles's wife, Edith, now makes him his Sunday favorite.

2 eggs

¼ cup sugar

½ cup molasses

1 cup sour milk (see Note)

1½ cups all-purpose flour

1 teaspoon ground ginger

¼ teaspoon ground cloves

¼ teaspoon ground cinnamon

¼ teaspoon salt

1 teaspoon baking soda

1 teaspoon baking powder

⅓ cup melted butter

Beat eggs until light. Add sugar, molasses, and sour milk. Sift dry ingredients together. Add to egg mixture and beat together until smooth. Add butter. Cook as you would regular waffles.

YIELD: 6 TO 8 SERVINGS.

NOTE: *To make sour milk, add 1 tablespoon distilled white vinegar to 1 cup milk.*

Filled Coffee Cake

This recipe comes from Gwen Kenney, a warm and vibrant mother of four dear friends whose house in Tuskegee was always a second home to us.

CAKE:
- ¼ cup butter
- ½ cup granulated sugar
- 2 eggs, separated
- 1½ cups all-purpose flour
- 2 teaspoons baking powder
- 1 teaspoon salt
- ½ cup milk
- 1 teaspoon vanilla extract
- Confectioners' sugar

FILLING:
- ½ cup brown sugar
- 1 tablespoon flour
- 1 teaspoon ground cinnamon
- 1 tablespoon melted butter
- ½ cup chopped nut meats

Preheat oven to 350°. For the cake: Cream butter, add sugar, and beat in egg yolks. Sift together flour, baking powder, and salt, and add to yolk mixture, alternating with milk. Add vanilla. Beat egg whites until stiff and fold into batter. For the filling: Combine all ingredients. Pour two thirds of the batter into a buttered 8-inch-square pan. Spread on the filling, and pour the rest of the batter over this. Bake for about 40 minutes or until golden on top and firm in the middle. Cool and sprinkle with powdered sugar. Cut into squares and serve warm with butter.

YIELD: 9 SQUARES.

Brandied Fruit

A love potion. When visiting Opelika, Alabama, we wouldn't miss a visit to Aunt Maude's neighbor, Mrs. Corrine Steele, for a dose of her wry humor and her latest recipes. This one is a magic potion and must be treated with respect. To a large apothecary jar, add the following ingredients in their listed order:

1 cup pineapple tidbits or chunks

1 cup peaches, cut into small pieces

1 cup apricots, cut into small pieces

1 cup halved Maraschino cherries

1 cup sugar

Every 2 weeks you may add 1 cup of each fruit and 1 cup of sugar in the same order. If you are using canned fruit, drain before adding. *Never* add the juice. You *must not add more often than once every 2 weeks*, but you may delay adding ingredients for another day or two without disastrous results. If you do delay, you must, of course, change your calendar for later additions. Keep a calendar marked so as not to forget. You must never allow the contents to go below 3 cups, or fermentation will stop. Whenever you have over 6 cups of fruit, you may wish to divide it into 2 portions with at least 3 cups in each, one of which can be given to a friend as a starter. Bear in mind one condition about sharing this potion with others. The one you give it to must be worthy, because it's a love potion. Always divide *before* adding more fruit and sugar, and *never, never* refrigerate. Keep in a warm place close to the oven. Never put a lid on tightly, as it may explode. Apothecary jars are best because there is room for expansion. Stir mixture occasionally to keep the contents down and the sugar dissolved.

This is delicious served over cake or ice cream or simply eaten by itself. It is ready to eat one month after starting and anytime thereafter, regardless of the adding schedule.

Candied Orange Peel

Sister Sally Gore of Aberdeen, North Carolina, is a minister in the rural part of that state. When we visited her and asked how to make sausage, she said, "Well, you let your hog get to be about five hundred pounds before you kill him . . ." and we immediately became discouraged. It reminded us of Mrs. Elizabeth Sheridan, who told us that she remembered how to make molasses but that we'd need a mule. We had to abandon those recipes, but Reverend Gore was kind enough to give us this old-time favorite that was also a specialty of our Grandma Sampson.

1 cup orange peel (from about 4 oranges)

1 cup granulated sugar

½ cup water

Sugar for coating, granulated or confectioners'

Wash oranges. Remove peel and cut in narrow strips. Put in a pot, cover with water, and boil for 15 minutes or until tender. Drain off water. Then cover with fresh water and again bring to a boil. Pour off water and set aside. Place sugar and ½ cup water in the pot and bring to a boil. Add orange peel and cook until syrup is almost gone, shaking the pan often to avoid scorching. Remove peel with a slotted spoon and place on wax paper to cool. Roll in sugar. Dry and store in a covered jar or canister.

YIELD: ABOUT 1 CUP CANDIED PEEL.

Ginger Beer

This thirst-quenching drink is from our Canadian-Trinidadian friends Albertha Jones and her mother, Alice Anderson.

¼ pound fresh gingerroot

¼ cup lime juice

Peel of 1 lime

¾ pound sugar

1 quart boiling water

Peel the gingerroot and grate it into a large bowl. Place lime juice, peel, and sugar in the bowl and then pour in the boiling water. Cover the bowl and let stand in a warm, draft-free place for 2 days. Then strain through a fine sieve into a bottle. Keep at room temperature for 3 days or longer. Serve chilled, mixed with ginger ale or club soda, or over crushed ice.

YIELD: 2½ PINTS.

Chitlins

Mrs. Elizabeth Simmons, Carole's mother-in-law, originally from North Carolina, now lives in Boston, but she hasn't forgotten how to turn out a chitlin.

10 pounds chitterlings (chitlins/hog intestines)

Salt

1 large onion, sliced or quartered

Vinegar to taste

Hot sauce to taste

Wash chitlins in warm water, rubbing as you would clothes, to remove all grease and residue. When washing water runs clear, they are clean. Place the chitlins in a large pot. Do not add water. The chitlins will produce their own water, aided by the dampness produced from the washing. Add 1 tablespoon salt and the onion (it is the onion that reduces the odor). Simmer slowly for 2 hours, removing water as it builds up, so that mixture remains watery but does not run over. Stir every half hour or so to prevent sticking. After 2 hours, cut chitlins into smaller pieces with a two-pronged fork and a knife. Continue cooking for 1 to 2 more hours or until completely tender. Remove excess liquid. Adjust seasoning with salt, vinegar, and hot sauce to taste. Best served with greens, potato salad, and corn bread.

YIELD: 6 SERVINGS.

Chitlin Salad

Thelma Byers, of Charlotte, North Carolina, and daughter of Annie Darden Barnes, inherited her mother's ability to present a food in many new and exciting ways. Here are some of her chitlin and acorn squash recipes, and her best corn pone.

2 cups cooked chitterlings (chitlins), cut into small pieces

Juice of ½ lemon

½ cup diced celery

½–¾ cup mayonnaise

Salt and pepper to taste

Lettuce

Paprika

Sprinkle the chitlins with lemon juice and let stand for at least 1 hour. Add celery, mayonnaise, salt, and pepper. Serve on beds of lettuce, dusted with paprika.

YIELD: 2 TO 3 SERVINGS.

French Fried Chitlins

10 pounds uncooked chitlins

1 medium onion

¼ cup white vinegar

2 tablespoons salt

BATTER:

¾ cup milk

½ teaspoon baking powder

1 egg, beaten

¼ teaspoon salt

¾ cup flour

Vegetable oil, for deep frying

Clean and cook chitlins in the manner described in the Chitlins recipe on page 305, but do not cut them into small pieces—leave whole instead. Cook for 3 to 4 hours, or until tender. Drain, cool, and cut into finger-length pieces. For the batter: Mix milk and egg together and add dry ingredients. Stir until a smooth consistency is reached. Dip chitlins in batter and fry in very hot, deep oil about 3 to 5 minutes or until brown.

YIELD: 6 SERVINGS.

French Fried Acorn Squash

4 young, tender acorn squash, peeled or unpeeled

2 eggs, beaten

¾ cup plain cracker or bread crumbs

Vegetable oil, for deep frying

Slice squash ¼ to ½ inch thick. Remove seeds and fiber. Soak in salt water for about 20 minutes. Drain and pat dry with paper towels. Dip in beaten eggs, then in cracker or bread crumbs. Fry in deep oil about 5 minutes or until golden brown, and drain on paper towels.

YIELD: 6 TO 8 SERVINGS.

Stuffed Acorn Squash

4 small or 2 medium acorn squash (about 1½ pounds)

½ teaspoon salt

2 eggs

1 tablespoon grated onion

1 cup grated Cheddar cheese

2 tablespoons fine bread crumbs, plus extra for topping

Salt and pepper to taste

Butter

Preheat oven to 350°. Boil whole squash in salted water until almost tender. Remove tops to make cavities for stuffing. Scoop out seeds and stringy insides and discard. Drain any water that collects. Beat eggs until frothy. Add grated onion, cheese, bread crumbs, and salt and pepper. Put bits of butter in cavity of each squash. Fill with stuffing. Place additional butter and bread crumbs on top of each. Place in a foil-lined pan and bake for 30 minutes.

YIELD: 4 SERVINGS.

Thelma's Top-of-the-Stove Eastern North Carolina Corn Pone

1½ cups sifted cornmeal

1 teaspoon baking powder

½ teaspoon salt

1 cup boiling water

1 tablespoon bacon fat or melted lard

Place sifted cornmeal in a bowl. Add baking powder and salt and the water to make a slightly stiff batter. Stir in bacon fat or lard. Grease a medium-size iron skillet and heat on the stove. When the skillet begins to smoke, pour in batter. Cover with a lid and cook over medium heat until mixture is set and under-side is brown. Slide pone onto a plate and return to hot skillet with the uncooked side down. Cover and finish cooking in like manner. Cut in wedges. This bread is very good with collard greens and dipped in pot liquor.

YIELD: 6 TO 8 WEDGES.

Marcus Garvey Bean Salad and Dressing

Hattie Gossett, of Harlem, USA, is an untraditional traditional cook who is not afraid to experiment with black culinary classics. Her Marcus Garvey Bean Salad uses the black, red, and green colors of the Afro-American flag that the nationalist leader designed.

One 15-ounce can snap string beans, washed and drained

One 15-ounce can red kidney beans, washed and drained

One 15-ounce can black beans, rinsed and drained

½ medium green bell pepper, seeded and diced

2 scallions, diced

1 stalk celery, diced

Peanut Oil and Lime Juice Dressing (recipe follows)

Chopped fresh parsley and pimentos, for garnish

Combine the beans and vegetables. Add dressing and mix well. Add garnish.

YIELD: 6 TO 8 SERVINGS.

Peanut Oil and Lime Juice Dressing

In keeping with the spirit of the salad, Hattie uses peanut oil because it was promoted by Afro-American George Washington Carver and because it's a frequently used ingredient in West African cooking.

¼ teaspoon salt

¼ teaspoon pepper

¼ teaspoon garlic powder

3 tablespoons lime juice

¼ cup peanut oil

1 teaspoon prepared mustard

Pinch of dried basil

Pinch of dried parsley

Put salt, pepper, and garlic powder into a mixing jar; add lime juice and shake until seasonings have blended with juice. Add peanut oil, mustard, basil, and parsley. Shake again.

YIELD: ABOUT ½ CUP DRESSING.

Hattie's Marinated Fried Fish

Use any kind of boned whole fish,
   allowing 1 or 2 per person

Salt and pepper

Lemon or lime juice

Soy sauce

Paprika

Vegetable oil for frying

About 2 hours before frying, wash fish and pat dry. Sprinkle with salt and pepper and place a single layer of fish in a shallow pan. Using 2 parts lemon or lime juice to 1 part soy sauce as a marinade, pour in enough liquid to half cover the fish. Be sure to turn it 2 or 3 times while marinating so that it is evenly coated. After 2 hours, remove fish from marinade, sprinkle liberally with paprika, and fry in shallow hot oil until brown on both sides. Serve immediately.

Sister Hattie Gossett's Coleslaw

1 medium head of cabbage

4 carrots

1 cup mayonnaise

6 tablespoons lemon juice

1 teaspoon celery seed

¼ cup sweet pickle relish

Salt and pepper to taste

Remove outer leaves of cabbage and quarter the head. Shred, using the largest holes on the grater. To shred the carrots, use the next smallest size. Place these vegetables in a salad bowl and toss them lightly together. In a small bowl combine the remaining ingredients until smooth and creamy. Blend this into cabbage mixture, using only a small amount at a time. You may not have to use all of it. Simply keep in mind that the mixture should be wet enough to hold everything together without being soupy.

YIELD: 8 SERVINGS.

Cauliflower au Gratin

Charlotte Kyle of North Carolina, Newark, and now New York City keeps moving, but we never lose touch with her or her wonderful cuisine.

1 large cauliflower	*¼ teaspoon pepper*
2 tablespoons butter	*Pinch of grated nutmeg*
⅓ cup flour	*1 cup grated Cheddar cheese*
2 cups scalded milk	*¼ cup bread crumbs*
½ teaspoon salt	

Trim and wash cauliflower. Separate flowerets. Cook in boiling salted water for 15 minutes, or until tender but firm. Drain. In a small, heavy saucepan melt 1 tablespoon of the butter. Add flour. Stir in scalded milk. Add salt, pepper, nutmeg, and cheese. Cook over low flame, stirring constantly, until smooth. Place cauliflower in a shallow oven-proof dish. Cover with cheese sauce. Sprinkle with bread crumbs. Dot with remaining butter. Put under broiler flame until nicely browned.

YIELD: 6 SERVINGS.

North Carolina Chopped Barbecued Pork

From Alvis Hines, Wilson's own Barbecue King. This is the most popular barbecue dish in North Carolina, and, as far as we know, it is indigenous to that state.

1 pork shoulder roast	½ cup ketchup
2 tablespoons vegetable oil	½ teaspoon chili powder
1 teaspoon salt	½ teaspoon ground nutmeg
1 teaspoon celery seed	½ teaspoon sugar
⅛ teaspoon ground cinnamon	1 cup water
⅓ cup cider vinegar, plus extra for seasoning	Hot sauce to taste

Preheat oven to 325°. Brown the roast in the vegetable oil and place in a Dutch oven. Mix next 9 ingredients in a saucepan and bring to a boil. Pour over roast and cover. Bake for 30 minutes to the pound, until done, basting occasionally with drippings. Transfer roast to a chopping board. Remove meat from the bone and chop into fairly fine pieces. Season to taste with additional vinegar and hot sauce. Serve hot with coleslaw and corn bread.

YIELD: 6 TO 8 SERVINGS.

Pigs' Ears and Lentil Stew

Cousin Josiane is an import to our family from Paris. After fifteen years on these shores, her French food has a decided touch of "soul."

6 pigs' ears (or tails)	¼ pound salt pork
½ pound dried lentils	1 bay leaf
2 carrots, sliced	¼ teaspoon dried thyme
2 onions, quartered	Salt to taste
6 cups water	

Wash pigs' ears under running water, cleaning them well and removing any hairs. Place in a Dutch oven or heavy kettle with the lentils, carrots, onions, water, salt pork, and seasonings. Bring to a boil. Then lower heat and cook, covered, very slowly for 3 hours. Adjust seasoning, remove salt pork, and serve in soup bowls.

YIELD: 4 TO 6 SERVINGS.

Cousin Josie's Carrot Salad with Vinaigrette Dressing

DRESSING:

1 teaspoon prepared mustard

2 tablespoons apple cider vinegar

Salt to taste

Pinch of pepper

6 tablespoons olive oil

SALAD:

6 young carrots, finely grated or minced (use blender or food processor if available)

1 small onion, minced

1 stalk celery, grated

1 teaspoon finely chopped parsley

For the dressing: Mix mustard with vinegar. Add salt and pepper. Mix well. Add olive oil, and blend well with a whisk. For the salad: Combine all ingredients and mix well with dressing.

YIELD: 4 TO 6 SERVINGS.

Cousin Josie's
Baba au Rhum

4 eggs

½ cup sugar

1¼ cups sifted all-purpose flour

3 teaspoons baking powder

6 tablespoons melted butter

½ cup lukewarm milk

Rum Syrup (recipe follows)

1 cup heavy cream, whipped

Preheat oven to 325°. In an electric mixer beat eggs with sugar until fluffy. Sift together flour and baking powder and add to egg mixture. Beat at medium speed to combine. Add melted butter and lukewarm milk. Beat at high speed. Pour into a buttered and floured ring mold. Bake for 35 to 40 minutes. Remove from oven, unmold, and pour Rum Syrup slowly over baba while still hot. Serve cold, topped with whipped cream.

YIELD: 8 SERVINGS.

Rum Syrup

½ cup sugar

½ cup water

1 cup dark rum

Cook sugar and water until a thin syrup is formed. Remove from heat and add rum.

YIELD: ENOUGH SYRUP FOR 1 BABA AU RHUM.

Happiness is remembering
A garden tilled and harvested for food
Brought in by Papa's toil-worn hands
Cooked lovingly by Mama for her brood.

Okra Succotash

Our cousin Emma Reno Connor, who is a poet and lives with her husband in St. Albans, New York, recently wrote us that "things certainly don't taste the same as when I lived in Elizabethtown, Kentucky, where the food was grown on lush, blue-green land. I sometimes long for a pot of succotash, just as my Mom, Rutelia, used to make. It was usually served with a salad of lettuce, tomatoes and cucumbers fresh from the garden, corn bread, and was topped off with a dessert of a fresh fruit cobbler. This was my favorite meal."

4 ham hocks	*8 small new potatoes*
2 pounds string beans	*4 cobs of corn*
1 medium onion, sliced, and slices halved	*1 pound okra*
Salt to taste	

Simmer ham hocks in water to cover for about 1 hour. Prepare beans by washing them and breaking or cutting into desired lengths. Add to ham hocks with onion and a little salt. Peel new potatoes and add to one side of the pot. Simmer for 15 minutes. In the meantime, cut corn from the cobs and set aside. Carefully trim pods of okra and leave whole. Then add okra and corn to the pot. Let all cook together until desired tenderness is achieved. Adjust seasonings and serve hot.

YIELD: 4 SERVINGS.

Blackberry Cobbler

Garnett Henderson, of Montclair, New Jersey, our neighbor and friend, remembers her mother making her favorite cobbler dessert. "My mother had no cookbooks or menus as guides, but her food was delicious. I try every so often to make her cobbler and have decided that the following turns out tasty and delicious."

3 cups fresh blackberries

1¼ cups sugar

1 teaspoon lemon juice

1 cup sifted all-purpose flour, plus 2
    tablespoons

¼ cup melted butter, plus extra

1 large egg, beaten

2 teaspoons baking powder

½ teaspoon salt

¼ cup milk

Light cream

Preheat oven to 375°. Mix berries, 1 cup of the sugar, lemon juice, and 2 tablespoons of flour. Spread over the bottom of a well-greased deep pie dish and dot with butter. Combine beaten egg, melted butter, and remaining ¼ cup of sugar. Sift cup of flour together with baking powder and salt. Sift again. Stir a little at a time into egg mixture until well blended. Stir in milk. Spread over berries. Bake for 30 minutes or until batter is puffed and golden. Serve warm with light cream.

YIELD: 6 SERVINGS.

Miss Mary's Banana Pudding

Mrs. Mary Alexander owned a hotel in Birmingham, Alabama. Many weary travelers, particularly gospel and rhythm-and-blues singers, and those touring on the black baseball circuit, pressed on a few extra miles just to reach her well-known kitchen. Everyone called her "Miss Mary."

2 cups milk	1 tablespoon butter
4 eggs, 2 separated	1 teaspoon vanilla extract
½ cup sugar, plus 2 tablespoons	1 box vanilla wafers
2 tablespoons flour	6 bananas, sliced into rounds

Preheat oven to 375°. Pour milk into the top of a double boiler. Beat the 2 whole eggs and the yolks well, then add ½ cup sugar and the flour and blend. Pour the egg mixture into the milk and let simmer for 20 minutes, stirring constantly. Add butter and vanilla, stir, and remove from heat. In a deep oven-proof dish place a layer of vanilla wafers. Cover them with a layer of sliced bananas, and pour over them a portion of the custard. Continue layers 3 times, ending with the custard. Beat egg whites with remaining 2 tablespoons sugar until stiff. Cover pudding with this meringue and bake for 15 minutes or until top is golden brown. Cool and serve chilled.

YIELD: 8 SERVINGS.

Flossie Barnes's South Carolina Corn Pie (Pudding)

On Saturdays we used to go to the Ritz, Wilson's "colored" movie house on Nash Street, with Flossie's children, John Howard, Helen, and Boisie, Jr. We paid 25 cents to see Captain Video and Lash LaRue serials and the fabulous so-called race movies with Lena Horne and Ethel Waters. After the movies, we would go to Flossie's for supper.

4 cups corn, cut from the cob	1–3 teaspoons sugar, to taste
⅓ cup melted butter	Salt to taste
3 eggs	½ cup evaporated milk
1½ cups whole milk	

Preheat oven to 325°. Place corn in a medium-size casserole dish. Stir in melted butter. In a separate bowl beat eggs until light. Add whole milk, sugar, and salt. When well blended, pour over corn. Then pour evaporated milk over the entire mixture. Bake for 30 to 40 minutes until set. Serve hot.

YIELD: 6 SERVINGS.

Tamale Pie

Mrs. Marie Kellar, now of San Francisco, was one of the most renowned cooks in Newark before she decided to move west. All appreciators of great food were truly sad to see her leave.

Motoring 1920s style

FILLING:

1 pound ground lean beef

1 large onion, chopped (about 2 cups)

1 green bell pepper, seeded and chopped

4 cloves garlic, minced

¼ cup vegetable oil

Two 8-ounce cans tomato sauce

3 ounces chili powder

1 tablespoon ground cumin

1 teaspoon sugar

1 teaspoon salt

½ teaspoon black pepper

½ teaspoon cayenne pepper

2 cups water

CORNMEAL CRUST:

5 cups cold water

2 teaspoons salt

2½ cups yellow cornmeal

1 tablespoon chili powder

TOPPING:

1 cup grated Cheddar cheese

1 cup pitted black olives, sliced

For the filling: In a skillet brown meat, onions, green pepper, and garlic in the oil. When well browned, blend in tomato sauce, spices, sugar, salt, and peppers. Add the water and simmer for about 15 minutes. Preheat oven to 350°. For the cornmeal crust: In a saucepan over medium heat, bring water and salt to a boil. Gradually add the cornmeal and chili powder. Stir frequently and cook until thick. Line the bottom and sides of a buttered 2-quart casserole with two thirds of the cornmeal mixture, patting down with fingers. Place the filling in the lined casserole. Put the remaining cornmeal between two sheets of waxed paper and press until it is the size of the pan. Remove top sheet, flip onto top of pie, and trim edges. For the topping, mix grated cheese and black olives, and sprinkle on top of pie. Bake for 20 to 25 minutes, or until cheese is melted and nicely browned.

YIELD: 6 SERVINGS.

Fiesta Rice

2 tablespoons butter

½ cup chopped celery

1 large green bell pepper, seeded and chopped

1 medium onion, chopped

1 clove garlic, minced

4 cups cooked rice (firm, not overcooked)

1½ cups grated sharp cheese

Pimento, for garnish

Preheat oven to 325°. Melt butter in a large skillet. Add celery, green pepper, onion, and garlic. Sauté over low heat until tender. Fold in rice and cheese. Blend well. Spoon into a lightly buttered medium-size casserole dish. Garnish with pimento. Cover and bake for 20 minutes.

YIELD: 6 TO 8 SERVINGS.

Deluxe Fruit Salad
in a Honeydew Bowl

1 honeydew melon

¼ cup milk

12 ounces cream cheese, softened

2 cups chopped walnuts

2 quarts mixed fresh fruit of the season
(such as peaches, plums, apples,
melon balls, blueberries,
strawberries, pineapple, grapes,
cherries, bananas, oranges)

Sugar to taste

Pare skin from the entire melon. Cut off top and scoop out the seeds. Cut off just enough of the bottom so that the melon will stand up. Blend milk and cream cheese to a smooth consistency and spread over outside of the melon. Sprinkle with chopped nuts. Refrigerate until ready for use. In a large bowl slice and mix fruit. Add sugar to taste and chill. When ready to serve, fill honeydew bowl with fruit and place remaining fruit around it on a large platter. To serve, slice a wedge of melon and scoop some fruit around it on each plate.

YIELD: 6 TO 8 SERVINGS.

Cream Cheese Soufflé with Black Cherry Sauce

SOUFFLÉ:

One 8-ounce package cream cheese, softened

1 cup sour cream

1 tablespoon honey

⅛ teaspoon salt

3 eggs, separated

2 tablespoons sugar

SAUCE:

¾ cup orange juice

2 tablespoons sugar

1 tablespoon cornstarch

¼ cup water

One 8-ounce can black cherries and their syrup

3 tablespoons brandy

For the soufflé: Preheat oven to 425°. Whip cream cheese, sour cream, honey, salt, and egg yolks until smooth. Then beat the egg whites until soft peaks are formed. Gradually add sugar to egg whites, beating until stiff peaks form. Then fold into cheese mixture. Pour into a lightly buttered 1½-quart casserole and bake for 45 minutes. While the soufflé cooks, make the sauce: In the top of a double boiler heat orange juice and sugar. Add cornstarch to the water, blend, and stir into orange juice mixture. Cook until thick, then add cherries and their syrup. Reheat, add brandy, and remove from stove. Serve hot or cold over cream cheese soufflé.

YIELD: 6 SERVINGS.

The Sampsons
picnicking at roadside

Glossary of Cooking Terms

Baste: To moisten meat by pouring pan juices or additional liquid over it while roasting or baking.

Blanche: To remove skins of fruits or nuts by dipping in hot water, then cold water.

Cream: To make shortening fluffy and smooth with an electric mixer or by beating with a spoon against the side of the bowl.

Cut: To combine shortening and dry ingredients by slicing through mixture with two knives or pastry blender.

Dice: To cut into very small cubes.

Dredge: To coat with flour.

Fold in: To gently add whipped cream or egg white to other ingredients with an under-and-over motion, usually using a spatula, so that airiness will not be lost.

Fricassee: To stew in liquid over low heat.

Knead: To prepare dough by pressing it away with the palms and heels of hands and doubling it over with the fingertips while rotating it in a circle. (Note: A good place to pick up this skill is by observation in your local pizza parlor.)

Marinate: To soak in a liquid, usually juice, wine, or vinegar, for flavoring purposes.

Parboil: To boil until only partially done.

Pare: To cut off skin.

Puree: To liquefy cooked foods in a blender or through a sieve.

Sauté: To fry to a golden brown in a little fat.

Scald: To heat liquid until bubbly around the edges of the pot but not boiling.

Sour milk: Old milk that has a sour taste. Regular milk can be soured by adding 1 tablespoon of vinegar or lemon juice to a cup of milk.

Sweet milk: Old term for regular milk that set it apart from buttermilk or sour milk.

Equivalents

Brown sugar: 1 pound = about 2¼ cups packed

Butter, shortening: 1 pound = 2 cups 1 stick = ¼ pound = 8 tablespoons = 4 ounces = ½ cup

Cheese, hard: 1 pound = 4 cups grated

Chocolate: 1 square = 1 ounce = 1 tablespoon melted = 4 tablespoons grated

Confectioners' sugar: 1 pound = 3¾ cups

Cornmeal: 1 cup uncooked = 3½ cups cooked

Cream (heavy): 1 cup = 2 cups whipped

Flour, all-purpose: 1 pound = 4 cups sifted

Flour, cake: 1 pound = 4½ cups sifted

Granulated sugar: 1 pound = 2 cups

Lemon or lime: 1 medium = 2–3 tablespoons juice

Lemon rind: 1 medium = 2–3 teaspoons grated

Meat: 1 pound = 2 cups diced

Onion: 1 medium = ½ cup chopped

Orange: 1 medium = ⅓ cup juice

Potatoes: 1 pound = 4 medium = 2½ cups diced = 2 cups mashed

Raisins: 1 pound = 3 cups

Rice, raw: 1¾ cups (½ pound) = 4 cups cooked

    precooked: 1 cup = 2 cups cooked

Tomatoes: 1 pound = 5 medium = 1⅔ cups chopped

Weights and Measures

In the event that some of you wish to prepare portions of recipes and run into odd amounts, we have included this list.

A pinch = less than ⅛ teaspoon

3 teaspoons = 1 tablespoon

2 tablespoons plus 2 teaspoons = ⅙ cup

4 tablespoons = ¼ cup

5 tablespoons plus 1 teaspoon = ⅓ cup

8 tablespoons = ½ cup

12 tablespoons = ¾ cup

⅜ cup = ¼ cup plus 2 tablespoons

⅝ cup = ½ cup plus 2 tablespoons

⅞ cup = ¾ cup plus 2 tablespoons

16 tablespoons = 1 cup = 8 ounces

2 cups = 1 pint = 16 ounces

2 pints = 1 quart

4 quarts = 1 gallon

1 ounce = 2 liquid tablespoons

Index

Ambrosia, 257
Apples
  cookies, 241
  fried, 131
  and sweet potato casserole, 124
  walnut salad, 263
Apricots
  brandied, 303
  muffins, 143–44
  wine, 11–12

Baba au rhum, 316
Bananas
  bread, 146
  doughnuts, 135
  fruit punch, 102
  ice cream, 45–46
  pudding, 319
Beans, 114
  baked, 97
  green string, 251
  salad, 310
Beauty foods, 75–80
Beef
  goulash, 99–100
  grilling, 154
  ground, 223, 321
  and lima bean stew, 69
  pot roast, 201
  stew, 68
Beer
  ginger, 305
  persimmon, 16
Beet relish, 30
Beverages
  banana fruit punch, 102
  chocolate punch, 222
  honey punch, 176
  peach tea, 220
  plant, 108
  strawberry wine punch, 154
  vitamin cocktail, 109
Biscuits
  plain, 141
  sausage, 133

soda, 132
sweet potato, 119
tea, 140
Blackberries
  cobbler, 318
  wine, 13
Blueberries
  ice cream, 49
  muffins, 143
  pie, 282
Brains, scrambled, 95–96
Bread and butter pickles, 27
Breads
  apricot muffins, 143–44
  banana-nut, 146
  blueberry muffins, 143
  bran, 198
  corn, 263–64
  corn pone, 309
  cracklin', 141–42
  cranberry-nut tea cake, 147
  garlic, 154
  health, 109–10
  hush puppies, 142
  peach muffins, 143–44
  pecan muffins, 144
  plain biscuits, 141
  raisin, 145
  sausage biscuits, 133
  soda biscuits, 132
  spoonbread, 186
  sweet potato, 120
  sweet potato biscuits, 119
  tea biscuits, 140
Brownies, 244
Brunch, 130
Buckwheat cakes, 117
Buttermilk, 76
  soup, 231
Butters
  herb, 111
  plum, 34–35

Cakes
  angel pound, 277

brownies, 244
buckwheat, 117
carrot, 276
chocolate-cherry upside-down, 274–75
chocolate chip, 272–73
chocolate layer, 273
coconut, 242
coffee, 302
cold oven, 279
cranberry-nut, 147
devil's food, 211
gingerbread, 63–64
griddle, 133–34
heaven, 278
honey sponge, 175
nutmeg, 280
peach gingerbread upside-down, 64
pineapple upside-down, 103
sheet, 281
shortcake, 137
tipsy, 167–68
watermelon, 219
Candy
  caramel kisses, 59
  chocolate-covered, 60–61
  divinity fudge, 57
  hard, 218
  molasses taffy, 58
  peanut brittle, 56
  pecan brittle, 57
  rose petal, 62
  shoe leather balls, 61–62
  violets, 62
Canning, 20–38
  hot and cold pack, 23–26
  sealing, 22
  tips, 25–26
Caramel
  ice cream, 50
  kisses, 59
Carrots, 114
  cake, 276
  mashed, 251
  salad, 315

Casseroles
   oyster, 88
   seafood, 292
   sweet potato and apple, 124
   vegetable, 114
   white potato and cheese, 72–73
Cauliflower, 114
   au gratin, 312–13
Chicken
   fricassee, 231–32
   fried, 156–57
   fruited honey, 173
   in the pot, 210
   purlo (pilau), 100–1
   roasted, 164
Chitlins, 305–7
Chocolate
   cake, 272–73
   candy, 60–61
   chips, 241, 272–73
   icing, 274
   punch, 222
   upside-down cake, 274–75
Chowchow, 31
Clams, 166
Cobbler, blackberry, 318
Coffee cakes, 302
Coleslaw, 312
Collard greens, 159–60
Compotes, fruit, 167
Conserve, peach-raisin, 35
Cookies
   Christmas, 182–83
   dough for, 240–41
Corn
   on cob, 154
   fried, 101
   pie (pudding), 320
   pone, 309
Cornbread, 263–64
Cough syrup, 176
Crab
   deviled, 294–95
   loaf, 295
   salad, 291
Cranberries
   and pear pie, 286
   sauce, 250
   sherbet, 227
   tea cakes, 147
Croquettes
   salmon, 296

sweet potato, 122
Crunch, rhubarb, 285
Cucumbers, 75
   bread and butter pickles, 27
Cupcakes, pineapple upside-down, 103

Dandelions, 11
Darden, Annie, 115–16
Darden, Artelia, 138–39
Darden, Camillus Lewis, 81–83
Darden, Charles, 83–85
Darden, Charles Henry, 3–6
Darden, Dianah Scarborough, 3–4, 18–21
Darden, James Benjamin, 66–67
Darden, John, 4, 39–43, 115
Darden, Lillian, 74–75
Darden, Lizzie, 128–29
Darden, Mamie Jean Sampson, 213–15
Darden, Maude, 53–55
Darden, Norma Duncan, 91–94
Darden, Russell, 83–85
Darden, Walter (Bud), 148–53
Doughnuts, banana, 135
Dressings
   lime, 310–11
   mayonnaise, 255
   vinaigrette, 315
Duck, 174
Dumplings, 232

Eggnog, 258, 270
   cookies, 241
   pie, 105
Eggplant
   sautéed, 113–14
   stuffed, 98–99
Eggs, 76
   deviled, 162
   omelets, 300
   surprise, 216
Equipment
   canning, 21–22
   preserving, 21–22
   wine-making, 7–8

Figs
   ice cream, 44
   preserves, 34
Fish
   flounder, 235
   fried blowfish, 293
   marinated fried, 311

red snapper, 233–34
   salmon croquettes, 296
Flowers, candied, 62
Foster, Alice, 106–8
Fricassee, 192, 231–32
Fritters, fruit, 136
Frosting. See Icing
Fruitcake
   black, 205
   cookies, 241
   ice cream, 52
   no-bake, 207
   white, 206
Fruits
   apples, 124, 131, 241, 263
   apricots, 11–12, 143–44, 303
   bananas, 45–46, 102, 135, 146, 319
   blackberries, 13, 318
   blueberries, 49, 143, 282
   brandied, 303
   canning, 24–29
   compote, 167
   cranberries, 147, 227, 250, 286
   figs, 34, 44
   grapefruit, 36
   grapes, 15–16, 38, 225
   lemons, 52, 76, 265–66
   limes, 226
   oranges, 33–34, 36, 187, 224–25, 227,
      268, 304
   peaches, 11–12, 24–27, 32–33, 35,
      48–49, 64, 76, 137, 143–44, 220, 282,
      303
   pears, 286
   persimmons, 16
   pineapple, 46, 103, 187, 303
   plums, 17, 34–35, 283
   rhubarb, 285
   salad, 323
   soup, 113
   strawberries, 10, 36, 45, 137, 154,
      238–39
   watermelon, 14–15, 28–29, 75, 219, 226
   wine, 10–17
Fudge, 57
Funeral meals, 271–88

Game
   opossum, 194
   pheasant, 196
   quail, 195
   rabbit, 191–93

squirrel, 192
venison, 193
Gingerbread, 63–64
waffles, 301
Goose, 197
Goulash, 99–100
Grapefruit, 36
Grapes
jelly, 38
sherbet, 225
wine, 15–16
Gravy
cream, 185
fried chicken, 157
giblet, 249
Greens
collard, 159–60
turnip, 159–60
Grilling, 155–56
Grits
baked, 95
soufflé, 132
Gumbo, 90
shrimp, 297

Ham, 70–71
barbecued, 250
Hash, 299
Headcheese, 298
Herbs
butter, 111
parsley salad, 112
Holiday meals, 245–69
Honey, 76
cookies, 241
custard, 174–75
duck, 174
fruited chicken, 173
icing, 176
punch, 176
remedies, 176
sponge cake, 175
Hoppin' John, 261–62
Hush puppies, 142

Ice cream. *See also* Sherbets
banana, 45–46
blueberry, 49
caramel, 50
fig, 44
fruitcake, 52
lemon, 52

peach, 48–49
peanut butter, 51
pineapple, 46
rum raisin, 47
snow, 216
spice, 43–44
strawberry, 45
tutti-frutti, 47–48
Icing
chocolate, 274
dark green, 219–20
honey, 176
seven-minute, 242–43
White Mountain cream, 212
yellow, 281

Jam, strawberry, 36
Jelly
grape, 38
rose petal, 217

Kidneys, 183–84

Lamb, 69–70
Lemon, 76
cookies, 241
ice cream, 52
meringue pie, 265–66
nourishing cream, 80
Lentils, 314–15
Limes, 226
Liver, 185
Lobster, 166
Lollipops, 218

Macaroni
with cheese, 254
and shrimp salad, 161
Marmalade, 36
Mayonnaise, 255
Meats
beef, 68, 69, 99–100, 154, 201, 223, 321–22
ham, 70–71, 250
kidneys, 183–84
lamb, 69–70
liver, 185
pigs' feet, 261
pork, 71, 131, 133, 155–56, 313–14
sausage, 131, 133
spareribs, 158–59
sweetbreads, 184

tongue, 185–86
Meringue cups, 65
Molasses
cookies, 241
taffy, 58
Muffins
apricot, 143–44
blueberry, 143
peach, 143–44
pecan, 144–45

Okra, 317
Omelets, 300
Onions, creamed, 252
Opossum, 194
Oranges
candied peel, 304
marmalade, 36
pie, 268
preserves, 33–34
sherbet, 224–25, 227
tapioca, 187
Oysters
casserole, 88
fried, 89
stew, 87

Pancakes
buckwheat, 117
sweetmilk, 133–34
Peaches, 76
brandied, 32, 303
canning, 24, 25
conserve, 35
ice cream, 48–49
muffins, 143–44
pickled, 26–27
pie, 282
shortcake, 137
tea, 220
upside-down cake, 64
wine, 11–12
Peanut brittle, 56
Peanut butter
cookies, 241
ice cream, 51
Pears, 286
Peas, 236
black-eyed, 261–62
Pecans
brittle, 57
divinity fudge, 57

muffins, 144–45
pie, 64
stuffing, 196
tartlets, 104
waffles, 134
Peppers, sautéed, 113–14
Perfume, 77
Persimmons, 16
Pheasant, 196
Pickles
bread and butter, 27
peaches, 26–27
peppers, 29
sour, 28
watermelon rind, 28–29
Picnics, 153–63
Pies
butterscotch, 267–68
corn, 320
eggnog, 105
lemon meringue, 265–66
mincemeat, 256–57
orange, 268
peach-blueberry, 282
pear-cranberry, 286
pecan, 64
plum, 283
pumpkin, 284
rum, 269
shells, 238–39
strawberry, 238–39
sweet potato, 127
tamale, 321–22
Pigs' ears, 314–15
Pigs' feet, 261
Pineapple
brandied, 303
ice cream, 46
syllabub, 187
upside-down cupcakes, 103
Plant foods, 108–14
Plums
butter, 34–35
pie, 283
wine, 17
Pork
barbecued, 313–14
barbecued spareribs, 158–59
roasted, 71
roast suckling pig, 155–56
Potatoes, 76, 114
casserole, 72–73

hashed brown, 73
salad, 72, 162
Potatoes, sweet
baked, 118
biscuits, 119
bread, 120
casserole, 124
croquettes, 122
custard, 122
french fried, 121
pie, 127
pudding, 126, 253
puffs, 121
salad, 125
stuffed, 118–19
Poultry
chicken, 100–1, 156–57, 164, 173, 210,
231–32
duck, 174
goose, 197
turkey, 229–30, 248, 298
Preserves
fig, 34
orange, 33–34
peach, 32–33
Preserving, 20–38
Puddings
banana, 319
bread, 202
honey custard, 174–75
Indian, 243–44
orange tapioca, 187
pineapple syllabub, 187
sweet potato, 122, 126, 253
syllabub, 168
Pumpkin
cookies, 241
pie, 284

Quail, 195

Rabbit
Brunswick stew, 191
fricasseed, 192
roasted, 192–93
Raisins
bread, 145
conserve, 35
ice cream, 47
stuffing, 233–34
wine, 14
Relishes, 30

Rhubarb, 285
Rice
fiesta, 322
Hoppin' John, 261–62
wine, 14
Rolls
butter, 288
refrigerator, 287
Rose petals
candy, 62
jelly, 217

Sachets, 78
Salads
apple-walnut, 263
bean, 310
carrot, 315
chitlin, 306–7
coleslaw, 312
fruit, 322–23
ginger ale, 221
health, 112
hot crab, 291
hot potato, 72
jubilee, 154
macaroni and shrimp, 161
parsley, 112
potato, 162
sweet potato, 125
tossed green, 255
Sampson, Asa, 208–9
Sampson, Clyde, 188–91
Sampson, Corine Johnson, 179–82
Sampson, Glen, 203–4
Sampson, William, 170–72, 199–200
Sandwiches, 111
Sauces
black cherry, 324
cranberry, 250
horseradish, 185–86
Sausage, 131
biscuits, 133
Seafood
baked stuffed shad, 86
casserole, 292
clams, 166
crab salad, 291
deviled crab, 294–95
flounder, 235
fried blowfish, 293
fried fish, 311
fried oysters, 89

fried salt fish, 89
gumbo, 90
lobster, 166
oyster casserole, 88
oyster stew, 87
salmon, 296
sautéed shad roe, 87
shrimp, 161, 166, 233–34, 297
snapper, 233–34
whitefish, 166
Shad
  baked stuffed, 86
  sautéed roe, 87
Sherbets
  cranberry-orange, 227
  grape, 225
  mint-lime, 226
  orange, 224–25
  watermelon, 226
Shortcakes, 137
Shrimp
  gumbo, 90, 297
  and macaroni salad, 161
  seafood stew, 166
  and stuffed red snapper, 233–34
Soap, 178
Some Mores, 224
Soufflés, 132
  cream cheese, 324
Soups
  cold buttermilk, 231
  fruit, 113
  tomato bisque, 230
  turkey, 229–30
  vegetable-bone marrow, 228–29
Sour pickles, 28
Spareribs, barbecued, 158–59
Spoonbread, 186
Squash, 14
  french fried, 308
  and onions, 237
  sautéed, 113–14
  stuffed, 308–9
Squirrel, 192
Stews
  beef, 68
  beef and lima bean, 69
  Brunswick, 191
  jungle, 223

kidney, 183–84
oyster, 87
pigs' ears and lentil, 314–15
seafood, 166
Strawberries
  ice cream, 45
  jam, 36
  pie, 238–39
  shortcake, 137
  wine, 10
  wine punch, 154
Stuffing
  chestnut and rice, 165
  corn bread, 248
  crab, 235
  pecan, 196
  raisin, 233–34
Sweetbreads, creamed, 184
Syllabub, 168
  pineapple, 187

Taffy, 58
Tarts, 104
Tea, peach, 220
Tomatoes, 75, 114
  bisque, 230
  canned, 30
  chowchow, 31
  fried green, 237
  sautéed, 113–14
  stewed, 262
Tongue, 185–86
Turkey
  butt souse, 298
  roasted, 248
  soup, 229–30
Turnips
  greens, 159–60
  mashed, 251

Vegetables
  baked beans, 97
  beans, 114, 251, 310
  beets, 30
  black-eyed peas, 261–62
  carrots, 114, 251, 276, 315
  casseroles, 114
  cauliflower, 114, 312–13
  collard greens, 159–60

corn, 101, 154, 320
cucumbers, 27, 75
eggplant, 98–99, 113–14
lima beans, 69
okra, 317
onions, 252
peas, 236
peppers, 29, 113–14
potatoes, 72–73, 76, 114, 162
  sautéed, 113–14
  soup, 228–29
squash, 113–14, 237, 308–9
sweet potatoes, 118–27, 253
tomatoes, 30, 31, 75, 113–14, 230, 237, 262
turnip greens, 159–60
turnips, 251
yams, 123, 194
zucchini, 113–14
Venison, 193

Waffles
  gingerbread, 301
  pecan, 134
Watermelon, 75
  cake, 219
  pickled rind, 28–29
  sherbet, 226
  wine, 14–15
Wine
  apricot, 11–12
  blackberry, 13
  dandelion, 10–11
  equipment for making, 7–8
  grape, 15–16
  peach, 11–12
  plum, 17
  rice and raisin, 14
  strawberry, 10
  tips for making, 8–9
  watermelon, 14–15
Winner, Lucy, 245–47
Winner, Mattie, 245–47
Winner, Waltine, 245–47

Yams, candied, 123

Zucchini
  sautéed, 113–14

About the Authors

Norma Jean Darden runs a successful New York City catering business called Spoonbread, Inc. She also operates two restaurants in Manhattan — Miss Mamie's Spoonbread Too in Morningside Heights and Miss Maude's in Harlem. She has also toured the country in her one-woman show, *Spoonbread and Strawberry Wine,* for over a year. The sisters have appeared on TV's FoodNetwork, on *Martha Stewart Living,* and in *O, the Oprah Magazine.* After working as a child therapist for many years, Carole Darden-Lloyd now runs the family real estate business and is a consultant for Spoonbread, Inc. Both Norma Jean and Carole are graduates of Sarah Lawrence College, and both live in New York City.